Food&Wine's
HOLIDAY FAVORITES

Brioche and Oyster Pudding, page 145

Food&Wine's
HOLIDAY FAVORITES

Festive recipes for
Thanksgiving, Christmas, and New Year's

Food&Wine
B O O K S

American Express Publishing Corporation
New York

FOOD & WINE MAGAZINE
Editor in Chief: Dana Cowin
Food Editor: Tina Ujlaki

———

FOOD & WINE BOOKS
Editorial Director: Judith Hill
Assistant Editors: Susan Lantzius and Laura Russell
Copy & Production Editor: Terri Mauro
Wine Editor: Richard Marmet
Art Director: Nina Scerbo
Production Manager: Yvette Williams-Braxton

———

Vice President, Books and Information Services: John Stoops
Marketing Director: Mary V. Cooney
Marketing/Promotion Manager: Roni Stein
Operations Manager: Doreen Camardi
Business Manager: David Geller

———

AMERICAN EXPRESS PUBLISHING CORPORATION
©1996 American Express Publishing Corporation

LIBRARY OF CONGRESS CATALOGING-IN-PUBLICATION DATA
Food & wine's holiday favorites.
p.   cm.
Includes index.
ISBN 0-916103-32-3
1. Holiday cookery.   I. Food & wine (New York, N.Y.)
TX739.F58   1996
641.5'67—dc20   96-24167
                                                          CIP

Published by American Express Publishing Corporation
1120 Avenue of the Americas, New York, New York 10036

Manufactured in the United States of America

CONTENTS

Parsnip Vichyssoise, page 35

INTRODUCTION

During my tenure as Editor in Chief of FOOD & WINE Magazine, I have discovered that when it comes to holiday entertaining, there are two popular, albeit completely different, approaches. The first is what I call "Ritual Rules," wherein the menus are so established that it is considered heresy to change something as simple as the stuffing in the Thanksgiving turkey or to switch the main course at Christmas from roast beef to ham. This approach is not for me—or, probably, you.

The second approach is what I affectionately refer to as the "Tradition Twist." The proponents of this philosophy are happy to hang onto old standard recipes, but welcome new ones, too. This cookbook is for those experimenters among us. It pulls together lots of recipes for traditional foods—roast turkeys, mashed sweet potatoes, cranberry relishes—yet it also offers some surprising solutions. A couple of my favorites are the juicy steamed boned turkey with Asian stuffing from Ken Hom, page 66, and the Icy Fresh-Cranberry Pie, page 232.

I'm sure after spending time with this collection, you'll discover your own new traditions. And who knows—maybe the next generation will end up fighting to keep *these* dishes on the menu.

DANA COWIN
Editor in Chief
FOOD & WINE Magazine

Cranberry Raspberry Sorbet, page 237

ACKNOWLEDGMENTS

The staff of FOOD & WINE Magazine culled at least 200 issues—all the way back to 1978—to find the most frequently requested holiday recipes. And each of those favorites is right here in this book.

As you'll see, a multitude of contributors provided the recipes. We have Julia Child's gorgeous Bûche de Noël, page 211, Jacques Pépin's Bacalao Gloria (named for his wife), page 43, and a host of others. We at FOOD & WINE Books wish to thank all the authors.

The recipes that are not attributed to a writer were contributed by FOOD & WINE staff over the years, or developed in the test kitchen as a joint effort. We thank Food Editor Tina Ujlaki, Associate Test Kitchen Director Marcia Kiesel, Entertaining and Special Projects Director W. Peter Prestcott, and former staff members Warren Picower, Kate Slate, Susan Wyler, John Robert Massie, Catherine Fredman, Tracey Seaman, Mimi Ruth Brodeur, and Jim W. Brown, Jr. The biggest group of recipes from a single contributor is also my personal favorite—the traditional British roasts, dressings, relishes, and puddings from longtime FOOD & WINE Test Kitchen Director Diana Sturgis, our resident Welshwoman. All of these fine cooks have, over the years, shared their own time-honored family recipes with the readers of the magazine.

We are grateful to our own family of contributors, on staff, off staff, and used-to-be staff, and thank them—every one.

JUDITH HILL
Editorial Director
FOOD & WINE Books

chapter 1
HORS D'OEUVRES

Salmon-Caviar Toasts, page 13

SALMON-CAVIAR TOASTS

Simple yet elegant, these hors d'oeuvres make perfect holiday cocktail-party fare. Toast the bread in the afternoon, and the last-minute assembly will take only seconds.

MAKES ABOUT 4 DOZEN TOASTS

½ loaf brioche or good-quality white bread

2½ tablespoons butter, at room temperature

4 ounces salmon caviar

Lemon wedges, for serving

STORING CAVIAR

Caviar will keep for about a week. It should be stored in the coldest part of the refrigerator, usually at the back of the bottom shelf.

---

1. Heat the broiler. Cut the brioche into ⅜-inch-thick slices and remove the crusts. Butter one side of each slice and arrange the slices, buttered-side up, in a single layer on a baking sheet.

2. Broil the bread slices until light golden brown, about 1 minute. Cut each slice into four triangles and let cool.

3. Shortly before serving, spread about 1 teaspoon of the caviar onto the toasted side of each bread triangle. Serve the toasts with lemon wedges.

—LYDIE MARSHALL

MAKE IT AHEAD
The bread can be toasted and cut into triangles up to 2½ hours ahead.

CONFETTI SHRIMP

Though you can serve these stir-fried shrimp hot out of the pan, the flavors improve as the dish sits.

MAKES ABOUT 24 SHRIMP

1 red bell pepper

¼ cup olive oil

1½ pounds large shrimp, shelled

3 tablespoons minced fresh ginger

2 cloves garlic, minced

1½ tablespoons lemon juice

1 tablespoon lime juice

¼ teaspoon salt

½ teaspoon chili oil*, or ¼ teaspoon dried red-pepper flakes

¼ cup chopped fresh chives or scallion tops

*Available at Asian markets

1. Roast the pepper over an open flame or broil, turning with tongs until charred all over, about 10 minutes. When the pepper is cool enough to handle, pull off the skin. Remove the stem, seeds, and ribs. Mince the pepper and set aside.

2. In a large frying pan, heat 2 tablespoons of the olive oil over moderately high heat. Add the shrimp and cook, stirring occasionally, until just done, 2 to 3 minutes. Transfer to a medium bowl. Set aside to cool.

3. Reduce the heat to moderately low, add the ginger and garlic, and cook, stirring, until starting to soften, about 3 minutes. Transfer to a small bowl and whisk in the lemon juice, lime juice, and salt. Whisk in the remaining 2 tablespoons olive oil and the chili oil.

4. Pour the ginger-garlic mixture over the cooled shrimp and stir to coat. Cover and marinate for at least 1 hour. Just before serving, stir in the chives and the minced roasted pepper.

MAKE IT AHEAD
The shrimp can prepared a day ahead of time. After combining the cooled shrimp with the marinade, cover and refrigerate. Bring to room temperature before adding the final ingredients and serving.

PUMPKIN-SEED PUREE

Serve this rich, piquant puree as a dip with fried tortillas, toasted pita triangles, shrimp, or a variety of cut-up vegetables.

MAKES ABOUT 1 1/2 CUPS

1 1/2 cups (about 1/2 pound) hulled pumpkin seeds (pepitas)*

3 tablespoons olive oil

2 cloves garlic, smashed

3/4 cup Chicken Stock, page 57, or canned low-sodium chicken broth, more if needed

1/4 cup lime juice (from about 2 limes)

1 to 2 jalapeño peppers with seeds and ribs removed, minced, or hot-pepper sauce to taste

1 teaspoon salt

1/4 teaspoon fresh-ground black pepper

*Available at health-food stores

1. In a medium frying pan, toast the pumpkin seeds over moderate heat, stirring frequently, until they puff and pop, about 3 minutes. Transfer to a blender or food processor and puree. Leave in the blender.

2. In the frying pan, heat the oil over moderate heat. Add the garlic and cook until fragrant, about 30 seconds. Transfer to the blender. Add the stock, lime juice, jalapeños, salt, and pepper to the blender and puree, stopping occasionally to scrape down the sides. If the mixture is too thick, add a bit more stock, a tablespoon at a time.

—JIM FOBEL

MAKE IT AHEAD
Make the dip a day or two ahead, if you like. If you're serving it with vegetables, they can be prepared the night before and stored in plastic bags in the refrigerator. Choose a colorful assortment, such as red-pepper strips, carrot sticks, and scallions.

PROSCIUTTO-WRAPPED HEARTS OF PALM

You can make these tasty tidbits in just minutes, but be sure to allow a few hours for them to absorb the flavor of the marinade.

SERVES 8

¼ cup white-wine vinegar

½ cup olive oil

3 sprigs thyme, or ½ teaspoon dried

¼ teaspoon fresh-ground black pepper, plus more for serving

2 14-ounce cans hearts of palm, drained and rinsed

½ pound thin-sliced prosciutto

1. In a medium bowl, combine the vinegar, oil, thyme, and pepper.

2. Cut the hearts of palm in half crosswise, using only the tender stalks. If they are thick, halve lengthwise first. Wrap each piece in a slice of prosciutto cut to fit, secure with a toothpick, and put in the marinade. Cover and refrigerate at least 3 hours. Remove from the marinade and serve at room temperature with a grind of black pepper.

MAKE IT AHEAD
Prepare these a day ahead, if you like. Cover and refrigerate. Bring to room temperature before serving.

SAUSAGE-STUFFED MUSHROOMS

Ever-popular stuffed mushrooms can be complicated to make, or as wonderfully easy as these. They taste so delicious your guests will beg for the recipe.

MAKES 16 MUSHROOMS

16 medium mushrooms

1 tablespoon lemon juice

½ pound mild Italian sausage

⅛ teaspoon salt

⅛ teaspoon fresh-ground black pepper

1. Heat the oven to 375°. Remove the mushroom stems and mince them. Toss the caps with the lemon juice. Butter a shallow baking dish.

2. Remove the sausage from its casing; put in a medium bowl. Add the mushroom stems, salt, and pepper. Mix lightly to blend.

3. Fill the cavity of each mushroom cap with the stuffing, mounding it slightly. Put in the prepared dish. Bake until the sausage is no longer pink, about 15 minutes.

MAKE IT AHEAD
Stuff the mushrooms hours ahead and refrigerate. Bring to room temperature before baking or cook an extra minute or two.

MUSHROOM LEEK TURNOVERS

Leeks and mushrooms make a sophisticated filling for luscious little square turnovers.

MAKES 4 DOZEN TURNOVERS

1 ounce dried porcini or other dried mushroom

1 cup boiling water

4 tablespoons butter

3 leeks, white and light-green parts only, washed well and chopped fine

½ pound white mushrooms, chopped

1 tablespoon flour

2 tablespoons Cognac or other brandy

¼ cup heavy cream

½ teaspoon salt

¼ teaspoon fresh-ground black pepper

Pinch dried red-pepper flakes

Pinch dried thyme

¼ cup grated Parmesan cheese

Cream-Cheese Dough, opposite page

1 egg

1. Put the dried porcini mushrooms in a small bowl and pour the boiling water over them. Soak until softened, about 20 minutes. Remove the porcini from the water and strain the liquid through a sieve lined with a paper towel into a frying pan. Rinse the porcini well to remove any grit and chop them.

2. Add the chopped porcini and 1 tablespoon of the butter to the frying pan. Bring to a boil over moderately high heat and boil, stirring occasionally, until the liquid evaporates, about 3 minutes. Transfer the porcini to a bowl.

3. Melt the remaining 3 tablespoons of butter in the frying pan over moderate heat. Add the leeks and cook, stirring occasionally, until soft, about 5 minutes. Add the white mushrooms and cook, stirring frequently, until all their liquid evaporates, about 5 minutes.

4. Add the porcini mushrooms to the pan. Sprinkle with the flour and cook, stirring, for about 1 minute. Stir in the Cognac and cook until it evaporates, about 1 minute. Stir in the heavy cream and remove the pan from the heat.

5. Add the salt, the black pepper, the red-pepper flakes, the thyme, and the Parmesan cheese. Transfer the filling to a bowl. Let cool to room temperature.

6. Remove half of the dough from the refrigerator and let it rest until malleable, about 10 minutes. Butter two baking sheets. Divide the dough in half. On a floured surface, roll out one piece of dough to a 12 by 8-inch rectangle. Cut lengthwise into two 4-inch-wide strips, then crosswise at 2-inch intervals into twelve 2 by 4-inch rectangles.

7. Spoon one heaping teaspoon of filling onto each rectangle. Brush the edges of the pastry with water and then fold the dough over the filling to form squares. Press around the filling to remove any air that may be trapped inside. Crimp with a fork to seal and put on one of the prepared baking sheets.

8. Repeat Steps 6 and 7 with all the remaining dough and filling. Refrigerate the turnovers for at least 30 minutes.

9. Heat the oven to 400°. Butter a baking sheet and arrange the turnovers on it. In a small bowl, whisk the egg with 1 teaspoon of cold water to make a glaze. Brush the glaze over the turnovers. With a small knife, cut a slit in the top of each. Bake until golden brown, about 15 minutes

—DORIE GREENSPAN

MAKE IT AHEAD
The filling can be made up to 3 days ahead. Wrap it tightly and refrigerate. The turnovers can be assembled and frozen, tightly wrapped, for up to 1 month. Unwrap and bake without defrosting, adding 5 minutes to the cooking time.

CREAM-CHEESE DOUGH

1 8-ounce package cream cheese, cut into eight pieces

1/2 pound butter, cut into sixteen pieces

2 cups flour

1. Let the pieces of cream cheese and butter stand at room temperature for 10 minutes.

2. Put the flour in a food processor. Scatter the cream cheese and butter pieces over the flour and pulse briefly, six to eight times. Process until the dough resembles large curds, about 15 seconds, stopping once to scrape the sides of the bowl. Do not let the dough form a ball on the blade. Alternatively, to make the dough by hand or with an electric mixer, first cream together the butter and cream cheese. Blend in the flour to form a smooth dough.

3. Turn the dough out onto a work surface and gather into a ball. Divide the dough in half, wrap tightly in plastic, and refrigerate for at least 2 hours before using.

MAKE IT AHEAD
The dough can be refrigerated for 3 days or frozen for 1 month.

CHICKEN-LIVER AND APPLE CRESCENTS

Apples and hazelnuts fleck this chicken-liver filling, which tastes equally good hot or cold. It can be baked in a pastry wrapper, as suggested here, or chilled and served as an excellent spreadable pâté.

MAKES 40 CRESCENTS

2 tablespoons hazelnuts

1 onion, quartered

1 clove garlic, quartered

2 tablespoons butter

½ tart apple, peeled, cored, and quartered

½ pound chicken livers

1 tablespoon Calvados, applejack, or other apple brandy

½ teaspoon salt

¼ teaspoon fresh-ground black pepper

Pinch ground allspice

Pinch ground cloves

Pinch grated nutmeg

½ teaspoon cinnamon

2 tablespoons heavy cream

Cream-Cheese Dough, page 19

1 egg

1. Put the hazelnuts in a food processor and pulse until chopped fine. Transfer to a small bowl. Put the onion and garlic in the food processor and chop.

2. In a large frying pan, melt 1 tablespoon of the butter over moderately low heat. Add the onion and garlic and cook, stirring occasionally, until translucent, about 5 minutes.

3. Meanwhile, chop the apple in the food processor. Add the apple to the frying pan and cook until softened, 3 to 4 minutes longer. Scrape the mixture back into the food processor.

4. In the same frying pan, melt the remaining 1 tablespoon butter over moderately high heat. Add the livers and cook for 2 minutes. Turn and cook until browned but still pink inside, about 2 minutes longer. Add the Calvados and cook for 30 seconds. Transfer the livers and the pan juices to the food processor. Add the salt, pepper, allspice, cloves, nutmeg, cinnamon, and cream to the food processor. Puree. Add the hazelnuts and pulse several times just until combined. Let cool to room temperature.

5. Remove half of the Cream-Cheese Dough from the refrigerator and let stand until malleable, about 10 minutes. Butter two baking sheets. Divide the dough in half. On a floured surface, roll out one piece of the dough about ⅛ inch thick. Using a 3- or 3¼-inch round cutter, cut the dough into circles. Collect the scraps, chill them briefly, reroll them, and continue cutting. You should have about ten circles in all.

6. Put one heaping teaspoon of filling in the center of each round. Brush half of

the edge of each round with a little water and then fold the dough over the filling to make a crescent. Press around the filling to remove any air that may be trapped inside. Pinch the edges to seal them, crimp with a fork, and put the crescents on one of the prepared baking sheets.

7. Repeat Steps 5 and 6 with all the remaining dough and filling. Refrigerate for at least 30 minutes.

8. Heat the oven to 400°. Butter a baking sheet and arrange the crescents on it. In a small bowl, beat the egg with 1 teaspoon of water to make a glaze. Brush the glaze over the crescents. With a small knife, cut a slit in the top of each crescent. Bake until golden brown, about 15 minutes.

—DORIE GREENSPAN

MAKE IT AHEAD
See instructions for Mushroom Leek Turnovers, page 19.

SALT AND PEPPER PRETZELS

Shaping pretzels is easy: Curve each rope of dough into a horseshoe shape with the ends pointing toward you, twist the ends of dough backward, and press the ends onto the curve, using a dab of water if necessary to make the dough stick (see photo, page 24).

MAKES ABOUT 20 PRETZELS

1 package dry yeast (about 2¼ teaspoons)

Pinch sugar

1½ cups lukewarm water

1 clove garlic, minced

1½ tablespoons olive oil

4 cups flour, more if needed

½ teaspoon dried thyme

½ teaspoon fresh-ground black pepper

2 tablespoons plus 1 teaspoon table salt

3 quarts water

2 tablespoons coarse salt

2 tablespoons sesame seeds

1. In a medium bowl, combine the yeast, sugar, and 6 tablespoons of the water. Set aside until the mixture foams, about 10 minutes. Add the remaining water, garlic, and oil. Mix well.

2. In a large bowl, stir together the flour, thyme, pepper, and the 1 teaspoon table salt. Add the yeast mixture and stir until the dough can be gathered into a ball.

3. Turn the dough out onto a floured surface and knead until smooth and elastic, about 10 minutes. If the dough is still sticky, knead in a little additional flour. Form the dough into a ball and put it into a lightly oiled bowl. Cover with plastic wrap. Set aside in a warm place until the dough has doubled in bulk, about 30 minutes.

4. On a floured surface, knead the dough for 15 minutes. Roll the dough into a 12 by 6-inch rectangle and cut it into about twenty strips. Roll each strip into a smooth 16-inch-long rope. Form into pretzel shapes (see instructions above). Arrange the pretzels on two parchment-paper-lined baking sheets. Set aside to rise for 10 minutes.

5. Heat the oven to 425°. In a large pot, combine the remaining 2 tablespoons table salt and the water. Bring to a boil. Drop about six of the pretzels into the boiling water. Cook until they rise to the surface. With a slotted spoon, return the pretzels to the baking sheets. Sprinkle each pretzel with a pinch each of coarse salt and sesame seeds. Repeat with the remaining pretzels.

6. Spray the bottom and sides of the oven with water to create steam, and bake the pretzels until they are evenly browned, about 30 minutes.

—NANCY CHRISTY AND LAURE CANTOR KIMPTON

PARMESAN CHRISTMAS TREES

If you don't have tree-shaped cookie cutters, use whatever design you like—or just remove the crust from each slice of bread and cut the slices into squares, triangles, or rectangles.

MAKES 2 DOZEN TOASTS

¾ cup grated Parmesan cheese

½ cup mayonnaise

2 tablespoons grated onion

¼ teaspoon fresh-ground black pepper

24 slices good-quality white bread

1. Heat the oven to 400°. In a small bowl, combine the Parmesan, mayonnaise, onion, and pepper.

2. Lay the bread on a work surface and cut each slice with a tree-shaped cutter. Spread about 2 teaspoons of the cheese mixture evenly onto each bread tree. Arrange the trees on a large baking sheet and bake until golden and bubbly, 5 to 7 minutes. Serve immediately.

KITCHEN TIP

Save any bread scraps for crumbs or stuffing. If you don't need them right away, freeze them.

ROMANO LEAF WAFERS

Cheese-flavored batter is spread into a stencil to make leaf-shaped wafers. Metal leaf stencils are available in kitchenware stores in large and small sizes; we recommend a large one for this wafer. Of course, you can make the wafers in other shapes, too.

MAKES ABOUT 2 DOZEN WAFERS

2 tablespoons sesame seeds

2½ tablespoons butter, at room temperature

1 teaspoon sugar

2 egg whites, lightly beaten

½ cup grated Romano cheese

¼ teaspoon salt

½ teaspoon fresh-ground black pepper

½ cup flour

1. Heat the oven to 325°. Line a large baking sheet with parchment paper.

2. Put the sesame seeds in a small frying pan and toast them over moderate heat, stirring frequently, until light brown, about 3 minutes. Set aside.

3. In a medium bowl, cream the butter with the sugar. Gradually beat in the egg whites and continue beating for 1 minute. Add the cheese, salt, and pepper. Fold in the flour.

4. Place the stencil on the parchment paper. Using a long, narrow metal spatula, spread 2 teaspoons of the batter evenly and smoothly over the stencil and scrape off any excess. Carefully lift the stencil straight up, leaving the leaf on the paper. Wipe the underside of the stencil. Repeat with the remaining batter. Sprinkle with sesame seeds.

5. Bake the wafers in the middle of the oven until firm, 8 to 10 minutes. Using a wide metal spatula, flip the wafers and bake until light golden, about 2 minutes more. Cool on a rack.

—NANCY CHRISTY AND LAURE CANTOR KIMPTON

Mediterranean Animal Crackers

Grab your duck, turkey, and elephant cookie cutters to bring these festive snacks to life. They're pictured on page 24.

MAKES ABOUT 100 CRACKERS

¼ cup sesame seeds

1½ cups all-purpose flour

1¼ cups whole-wheat flour

Salt

1 teaspoon fresh-ground black pepper

2 cloves garlic, crushed

¾ teaspoon dried thyme

1 cup water

Cooking oil, for frying

1. Put the sesame seeds in a small frying pan. Toast over moderate heat, stirring frequently, until light brown, about 3 minutes. Transfer to a large bowl and whisk in both flours, 1½ teaspoons salt, and the pepper.

2. In a small bowl, combine the garlic, thyme, and water. Using a wooden spoon, stir the water mixture into the sesame-seed mixture until combined.

3. Turn the dough out onto a floured surface. Sprinkle it with flour and divide it in half. Roll each piece into a 20-inch round about ⅟16 inch thick. (Lift the dough occasionally and sprinkle flour underneath to prevent it from sticking.)

4. Stamp out the crackers using 3- to 5-inch animal-shaped cookie cutters. Roll out any scraps of dough and stamp out additional crackers.

5. Pour about 1½ inches of oil into a large, deep frying pan and heat to 425° on a deep-fat-frying thermometer.

6. Fry the crackers a few at a time, turning once, until crisp, lightly browned, and puffy, 1 to 2 minutes. Using a slotted spoon, remove the crackers from the frying pan and place them on paper towels to drain. Dab off any excess oil. Sprinkle lightly with salt. Let cool.

—Nancy Christy and Laure Cantor Kimpton

BLUE-CORN PIZZELLE

Similar in concept to a waffle iron, the old-fashioned pizzelle iron sits directly on the burner to cook the batter. These pizzelle are pictured on page 24.

MAKES ABOUT 16 PIZZELLE

- 2 fresh or canned green chiles, minced
- 3 eggs
- 3 tablespoons sugar
- ¼ pound butter, melted, plus more for the pizzelle iron
- ½ cup masa harina*
- 2 teaspoons baking powder
- ¾ teaspoon salt
- ¼ teaspoon cayenne
- ½ teaspoon fresh-ground black pepper
- ¼ teaspoon chopped fresh thyme, or ⅛ teaspoon dried
- ¼ cup plus 3 tablespoons blue cornmeal* or white or yellow cornmeal

*Available at Latin American markets

1. Pat the chiles dry and, if using canned chiles, squeeze them between paper towels to remove any excess liquid.

2. Heat the pizzelle iron on both sides. In a large bowl, using a hand-held electric mixer, beat the eggs with the sugar until thick and pale yellow in color, about 3 minutes. Beat in the melted butter.

3. In another bowl, mix together the masa harina, baking powder, salt, cayenne, and black pepper. Sift the mixture over the beaten eggs, add the chiles and the thyme, and mix lightly. Fold in the blue cornmeal.

4. Grease the pizzelle iron with a small amount of butter just once—before making the first cracker. Spoon 1 tablespoon of the batter in the middle of the heated iron and gently press down the other half of the iron. Using a knife, scrape off any excess batter and place the iron over the burner for 1 minute. Flip the iron and cook on the second side until browned, about 30 seconds. Transfer the pizzelle to a rack to cool. Repeat with the remaining batter.

—NANCY CHRISTY AND LAURE CANTOR KIMPTON

MAKE IT AHEAD
The pizzelle can be prepared a few hours ahead, but should be crisped in a 350° oven for 1 to 2 minutes before serving.

chapter *2*

SOUPS &
OTHER FIRST COURSES

Cauliflower Oyster Stew, page 31

CAULIFLOWER OYSTER STEW

Luscious, rich, and quick to make—served in small portions, this twist on oyster stew makes an ideal first course.

WINE RECOMMENDATION

Try a light, lively white such as Muscadet de Sèvre-et-Maine, a classic French shellfish wine. The acidic briskness of the wine pairs well with the cauliflower and counterpoints the dish's richness.

SERVES 6

1 head cauliflower (about 2 pounds), cut into pieces

2½ cups milk

1 cup heavy cream

½ teaspoon turmeric

Salt and fresh-ground black pepper

2 dozen fresh-shucked oysters

¼ cup oyster liquor (see "Cleaning Oyster Liquor," right)

1 tablespoon chopped fresh chervil or parsley

1 tablespoon chopped fresh chives

1. Put 1 inch of water in a large saucepan. Add the cauliflower, cover the pan, and steam over high heat until tender, about 10 minutes.

2. Transfer the cauliflower to a food processor or blender and puree with ½ cup of the milk. Put the puree back into the saucepan. Whisk in the remaining 2 cups milk and the cream. Cook over moderate heat, whisking, until very hot, about 3 minutes. Don't let the mixture boil. Season with ¼ teaspoon of the turmeric, ½ teaspoon salt, and ¼ teaspoon pepper.

3. Add the oysters and the liquor and cook, stirring frequently, until just heated through, about 3 minutes. Don't let the mixture boil, or the oysters will become tough. Taste and add more salt and pepper if needed. Serve the stew sprinkled with the chervil, chives, and the remaining ¼ teaspoon turmeric.

—SUSAN HERRMANN LOOMIS

CLEANING OYSTER LIQUOR

To get the grit out, first lift the oysters from their liquor and set them aside. Then pour the liquor through a paper-towel-lined sieve into a measuring cup.

OYSTER AND SPINACH SOUP

Like oysters Rockefeller in a bowl, this luxurious soup will start your holiday dinner off right.

WINE RECOMMENDATION
Sauvignon blanc, an aggressive, tart, and full-bodied white wine, will work perfectly with both the vegetables and the shellfish. Try a bottle from New Zealand or South Africa.

SERVES 12

4½ dozen shucked oysters, liquor reserved

2 to 2½ cups bottled clam juice

1½ tablespoons butter

1½ tablespoons olive oil

2 leeks, white and light-green parts only, split lengthwise, cut into thin slices, and washed well (about 2 cups)

3 cloves garlic, minced

3 cups water

1½ pounds spinach, stems removed and leaves washed

3 cups heavy cream

Salt and fresh-ground black pepper

1. Remove the oysters from their liquor and put them in a bowl. Cut the large ones in half. Pour the liquor through a sieve lined with a paper towel into a 1-quart measuring cup. Add enough clam juice to measure 3 cups.

2. In a large saucepan, melt the butter with the oil over moderately low heat. Add the leeks and cook, stirring occasionally, until softened, about 5 minutes. Add the garlic and cook, stirring, for 30 seconds. Stir in the 3 cups shellfish liquid and the water and bring to a boil.

3. Add the spinach, boil for 1 minute, and then add the cream, 1 teaspoon salt, and 1½ teaspoons pepper. Bring to a simmer, add the oysters, and continue simmering until just heated through, about 3 minutes. Season with additional salt and pepper to taste.

—JACQUES PEPIN

MAKE IT AHEAD
The soup can be prepared through Step 2 up to 8 hours in advance and refrigerated until shortly before serving time. Bring the soup to a boil before proceeding with the recipe.

BUTTERNUT-SQUASH AND LEEK SOUP

Both squash and leeks boast full, harvest-time flavor. Even the yellow-orange color of this soup says autumn.

WINE RECOMMENDATION
The strong but mellow flavors of this soup are ideal with a rich, full-bodied white wine with plenty of flavor of its own. Try a pinot gris from France's Alsace region.

SERVES 8

4½ pounds butternut squash, halved lengthwise, seeds removed

5 tablespoons butter

4 leeks, white and light-green parts only, split lengthwise, chopped, and washed well (about 4 cups)

7 sprigs fresh thyme, or 1 teaspoon dried

5 cups Chicken Stock, page 57, or canned low-sodium chicken broth

Salt and fresh-ground black pepper

½ cup sour cream

3 tablespoons chopped fresh chives

8 slices bacon, fried and crumbled

1. Heat the oven to 400°. Put the squash, cut-side down, on a baking sheet. Bake until tender, about 40 minutes. Let cool slightly and then scoop out the flesh.

2. Meanwhile, in a large pot, melt the butter over moderately low heat. Add the leeks and thyme and cook, stirring occasionally, until soft and beginning to brown, about 15 minutes. Discard the thyme sprigs.

3. Add the squash and the stock to the pot and simmer for 20 minutes. Puree the soup in a food processor or blender. Pour the soup back into the pot and season with 1 teaspoon salt and ½ teaspoon pepper. If the soup is too thick, add as much water as needed. Taste and add more salt and pepper if needed. Top each serving with a dollop of sour cream and sprinkle with chives and crumbled bacon.

MAKE IT AHEAD
The soup can be prepared several days ahead and refrigerated. Simply reheat when ready to serve.

Parsnip Vichyssoise

Inspired by the classic vichyssoise, this rich soup has parsnips, potatoes, leeks, and garlic. The flavors are brightened by a splash of lemon juice.

WINE RECOMMENDATION
Look for an acidic white wine to play off the sweetness of the parsnips and to contrast with the soup's creamy texture. A good choice would be a young chenin blanc from the Loire Valley in France. Make sure to buy a bottle labeled *sec* (dry).

SERVES 12

- 2 large leeks, white part only, split lengthwise, cut into thin slices, and washed well (about 2 cups)
- 2½ pounds parsnips, peeled and cut into 2-inch chunks
- ¾ pound boiling potatoes, peeled and cut into 2-inch chunks
- 8 cloves garlic, lightly crushed
- 1 large onion, cut into thin slices
- 2 tablespoons light-brown sugar
- 1 teaspoon ground cardamom
- 6 cups Chicken Stock, page 57, or canned low-sodium chicken broth
- ¼ pound butter, cut into small pieces
- ¼ cup lemon juice
- 3 cups milk
- 2 cups heavy cream
  Salt and fresh-ground black pepper
- ¼ cup chopped chives or scallion tops

1. Heat the oven to 350°. In a large, shallow roasting pan, combine the leeks, parsnips, potatoes, garlic, and onion. Sprinkle with the brown sugar and cardamom and stir to combine. Pour 2 cups of the stock over the vegetables and dot with the butter. Cover tightly with aluminum foil and bake, stirring occasionally, until the vegetables are very tender, about 1½ hours.

2. Transfer the vegetables and their liquid to a large pot. Add the remaining 4 cups stock and the lemon juice. Bring to a boil over high heat. Reduce the heat and simmer, covered, for 20 minutes.

3. In a food processor or blender, puree the soup until very smooth. Return the puree to the pot. Add the milk and cream and warm through over moderately low heat, stirring occasionally. Season the soup with salt and pepper to taste and serve topped with chives.

—Sheila Lukins

MAKE IT AHEAD
The soup can be made several days in advance. Reheat it gently on the stove.

JERUSALEM-ARTICHOKE SOUP

Curiously enough, Jerusalem artichokes are neither artichokes nor are they from Jerusalem. The tuber is native to North America and a member of the sunflower family.

WINE RECOMMENDATION
A brisk but simple white will complement the tangy lemon and enliven the root vegetables in this soup. Try a bottle of pinot grigio from the northeastern part of Italy.

SERVES 8

6   tablespoons butter

2   onions, chopped

2   carrots, chopped

2   leeks, white part only, split lengthwise, chopped, and washed well

6   sprigs flat-leaf parsley

1   teaspoon dried thyme

5   cups Chicken Stock, page 57, or canned low-sodium chicken broth

    Juice of 2 lemons

3   pounds Jerusalem artichokes
    Salt and fresh-ground black pepper

6 to 8 tablespoons heavy cream

1. In a large pot, melt the butter over moderate heat. Add the onions, carrots, leeks, parsley, and thyme. Cover, reduce the heat to moderately low, and cook, stirring occasionally, until the vegetables are tender and beginning to brown, about 15 minutes.

2. Add the stock and bring to a boil. Reduce the heat and simmer, partially covered, for 25 minutes. Strain the stock and press the vegetables firmly to get all their juice. Return the stock to the pan.

3. Meanwhile, fill a large bowl halfway with cold water and add the lemon juice. Peel the Jerusalem artichokes and put them in the acidulated water to prevent darkening.

4. When the stock is ready, drain the Jerusalem artichokes and cut them into 1-inch chunks. Add them to the stock, season with 1¼ teaspoons salt and ½ teaspoon pepper, and bring to a boil. Reduce the heat and simmer, partially covered, stirring occasionally, until the Jerusalem artichokes are very tender, about 45 minutes.

5. Puree the soup in a food processor or blender. Return the puree to the pot and reheat it gently, stirring often. Thin to the desired consistency with the cream, and season with additional salt and pepper to taste.

—MICHAEL McLAUGHLIN

MUSHROOM CONSOMME

Consommé comforts like no other soup. Its perfect simplicity and deep flavor contribute to the continued popularity of this special brew.

WINE RECOMMENDATION The deep, earthy flavors of this consommé are delightful paired with a lush, mellow red wine. Try an oak-aged merlot from California or Australia.

SERVES 8

2 pounds white mushrooms, chopped

1½ ounces dried porcini or other dried mushroom

1½ pounds onions, unpeeled, cut into eighths

5 carrots, cut into 1-inch pieces

1 14-ounce can tomatoes (about 1¾ cups), drained and chopped

12 parsley stems

3 cloves garlic, unpeeled, lightly crushed

3 cups Chicken Stock, page 57, or canned low-sodium chicken broth, all fat removed

¼ teaspoon dried thyme

Fresh-ground black pepper

2 quarts cold water

Salt

Enoki mushrooms, or white mushrooms cut into very thin slices, for garnish

1. In a large pot, combine the chopped white mushrooms, the dried mushrooms, onions, carrots, tomatoes, parsley, garlic, stock, thyme, and ¼ teaspoon pepper. Add the water and bring to a boil over moderate heat. Reduce the heat, cover, and simmer, skimming occasionally, for 1 hour.

2. Strain the consommé. Press the vegetables firmly to get all the liquid. Return the strained consommé to the pot and boil over high heat until reduced to about 2 quarts. Season with salt and additional pepper to taste and serve topped with the enoki mushrooms.

—ANNE DISRUDE

MAKE IT AHEAD Make the consommé a week before serving and refrigerate, or even farther ahead and freeze.

FENNEL TART WITH ROSEMARY

Briny black olives set off the mellow fennel filling, and a whole-wheat crust with rosemary adds a pleasing, earthy quality.

The strong flavor and acidity of a sauvignon blanc work well alongside fennel. To echo the Mediterranean feel of this dish, look for a bottle from the Friuli or Veneto region of Italy.

SERVES 10 TO 12

- 1 cup all-purpose flour
- ½ cup whole-wheat flour
- 3 tablespoons chopped fresh rosemary, or 3 teaspoons dried rosemary, crumbled
  Salt
- 4 tablespoons cold vegetable shortening, cut into pieces
- 6½ tablespoons cold butter, 4½ tablespoons cut into pieces
- ¼ cup cold water
- 7 small fennel bulbs with tops (about 3 pounds)
- 1 large onion, halved lengthwise
- 4 tablespoons olive oil
  Fresh-ground black pepper
- 1½ teaspoons chopped fresh parsley, for garnish
- 12 black olives, such as Kalamata or Gaeta, pitted and halved

1. Heat the oven to 350°. Put the all-purpose flour, whole-wheat flour, 1½ tablespoons of the fresh rosemary or 1½ teaspoons of the dried, and ¼ teaspoon salt in a food processor. Add the shortening and the 4½ tablespoons cut-up butter. Pulse until the mixture resembles coarse meal.

2. With the machine running, gradually add the cold water and process just until the dough comes together. Shape the dough into a disk. Wrap tightly and refrigerate for at least 30 minutes.

3. On a floured work surface, roll the dough into an 11-inch round. Drape the round over a 9-inch tart pan and press the dough into the pan and against the sides. Trim the pastry even with the rim. Prick the bottom of the shell every inch or so with a fork. Freeze until firm, about 5 minutes. Press a double thickness of aluminum foil against the dough. Bake for 10 minutes. Remove the foil. Bake until the rim of the pastry is golden brown, about 25 minutes longer. Let cool to room temperature.

4. Meanwhile, trim the tops of the fennel bulbs and chop enough of the greens to make ¼ cup. Halve the bulbs, cut out the central cores, and cut the fennel into ¼-inch slices; transfer the slices to a large bowl. Cut the onion halves into ¼-inch slices and add to the fennel slices. Stir in 3 tablespoons each of the oil and the fennel greens, the remaining 1½ tablespoons fresh

rosemary or 1½ teaspoons dried, 1½ teaspoons salt, and ½ teaspoon pepper.

5. In a large saucepan, melt the remaining 2 tablespoons butter over moderate heat. Stir in the fennel-and-onion mixture. Cover and cook, stirring occasionally, until the vegetables are very soft and jamlike, about 40 minutes. Uncover, increase the heat to moderately high, and cook until the mixture is golden brown, about 5 minutes longer. Season with additional salt and pepper to taste and let the filling cool.

6. Spread the fennel filling in the tart shell. Drizzle the remaining 1 tablespoon oil over the tart and sprinkle with the parsley and the remaining 1 tablespoon fennel greens. Arrange the olive halves on the tart. Serve the tart at room temperature.

—SHEILA LUKINS

MAKE IT AHEAD
The tart dough can be refrigerated for 2 days. The filling can also be prepared 2 days ahead. Keep it refrigerated and let it return to room temperature before filling the tart shell. Since the tart is served at room temperature, it can be made several hours before serving.

MUSHROOMS WITH DILLED SOUR CREAM ON TOAST

Served here as a first course, this dish is similar to one that would be served as part of a Russian *zakuska* (small bites) table.

WINE RECOMMENDATION
A wine has to have plenty of personality to deal with the dill in this dish. Sauvignon blanc, with its acidity, body, and strong flavor, is an ideal choice. Try one from New Zealand.

SERVES 6

- 12   tablespoons butter
- 6   slices white or whole-wheat bread, crusts removed
- 1   pound small mushrooms
-     Juice of ½ lemon
- 1½   cups sour cream
- ½   cup minced fresh dill, or 2 teaspoons dried dill
- 1   tablespoon onion juice (squeezed from grated onion)
-     Salt and fresh-ground black pepper
-     Pinch cayenne
-     Paprika, for garnish

1. Heat the oven to 400°. Melt 8 tablespoons of the butter. Brush the trimmed slices of bread on both sides with melted butter. Put the bread slices on a baking sheet and toast them in the oven, turning once, until they are crisp, about 5 minutes per side.

2. Heat the broiler. Remove the stems from the mushrooms and discard. Toss the caps with the lemon juice.

3. In a medium frying pan, melt the remaining 4 tablespoons butter over moderate heat. Add the mushroom caps and cook for 1 minute, without letting them brown or soften.

4. In a medium bowl, mix the sour cream, dill, and onion juice. Add salt, black pepper, and cayenne to taste.

5. Spoon the mushrooms over the toast and cover with the dilled cream. Dust with paprika and broil until bubbly, about 1 minute.

—PEARL BYRD FOSTER

POTTED SHRIMP

Scoop the potted shrimp onto lettuce leaves and, if you like, serve mayonnaise flavored with a little extra lemon juice, pepper, and mustard alongside. The shrimp can also be spread on melba toast or crackers and served as a cocktail accompaniment.

WINE RECOMMENDATION
A rich (but not overly oaky) California chardonnay, with its butter and citrus flavors, will do nicely with the rich taste and texture of the shrimp paté.

SERVES 8

1¼ pounds medium shrimp, in the shell
⅔ cup dry white wine
1 clove garlic, bruised
1 bay leaf
4 drops hot-pepper sauce
2 tablespoons minced onion
2 tablespoons minced scallion
2 teaspoons chopped fresh parsley
½ teaspoon celery seed
½ teaspoon fresh-ground black pepper
½ teaspoon salt
⅛ teaspoon dried thyme
1 tablespoon lemon juice
1 egg, beaten to mix
½ cup fresh bread crumbs
4 tablespoons butter, melted

1. Cook the unpeeled shrimp in boiling salted water for 1 minute. Then, when the shrimp are cool enough to handle, peel and devein them.

2. Heat the oven to 350° and butter a 1½-quart baking dish. Coarsely chop the shrimp in a food processor or with a knife.

3. In a small saucepan, combine the wine, garlic, bay leaf, and hot-pepper sauce. Bring to a simmer and cook for 5 minutes. Let the mixture cool and then discard the garlic and bay leaf.

4. In a large bowl, combine the shrimp, onion, scallion, parsley, celery seed, pepper, salt, thyme, and lemon juice. Stir in the wine mixture, egg, and bread crumbs. Add the melted butter and mix to combine.

5. Spoon the shrimp mixture into the prepared baking dish. Bake until set, about 30 minutes. Refrigerate for at least 1 hour.

—LEE BAILEY

MAKE IT AHEAD
This recipe can be prepared several days ahead. Remove from the refrigerator about half an hour before serving. The shrimp should be served cold but not icy.

BACALAO GLORIA

In the Spanish tradition, *bacalao* (salt cod) is cooked with potatoes and served as a Christmas dish. This lightened version has less oil and more vegetables than the traditional and is served over toast. There are different kinds of salt cod, some saltier than others. The saltier the fish, the longer it must soak.

WINE RECOMMENDATION
The hearty flavors in this dish will be delightful with a refreshing white with some body. Try a dry California chenin blanc.

SERVES 12

1 pound boneless salt cod

¼ cup plus 2 tablespoons olive oil

2 onions, cut into thin slices

4 cloves garlic, cut into thin slices

1 large baking potato, peeled and cut into ½-inch dice

12 slices whole-wheat bread, crusts removed

1 35-ounce can tomatoes, drained and chopped (about 1 quart)

1 yellow bell pepper, peeled with a vegetable peeler and cut into ½-inch strips

½ teaspoon fresh-ground black pepper

⅛ teaspoon cayenne

18 oil-cured olives, pitted and sliced

¾ cup cilantro leaves, for garnish

1. Rinse the cod under cold running water to remove the salt from the surface. Put it in a bowl with 10 cups cold water. Let soak 24 to 48 hours, changing the water twice daily, until just mildly salty. Drain and rinse.

2. Put the cod in a large saucepan with enough cold water to cover. Bring to a boil over high heat. Drain the fish and rinse under cold water to cool; pat dry. Flake the cod, discarding any pieces of sinew or skin.

3. In a large frying pan, heat ¼ cup of the oil. Add the onions and cook over moderate heat, stirring, for 2 minutes. Add the garlic and cook until fragrant, about 30 seconds. Add the potato and cod and cook, stirring, for 1 minute. Reduce the heat to low, cover, and cook, stirring occasionally, until the potato is soft, about 20 minutes.

4. Heat the oven to 400°. Put the bread on a baking sheet and toast in the oven, turning once, until crisp, about 5 minutes per side.

5. Add the tomatoes, bell pepper, the remaining 2 tablespoons oil, the black pepper, and the cayenne to the frying pan. Bring to a boil over moderate heat. Cover, reduce the heat, and simmer for 5 minutes. Stir in the olives.

6. Put the toast on individual plates and top with a large spoonful of the *bacalao* and a sprinkling of cilantro leaves.

—JACQUES PEPIN

CHESAPEAKE SCALLOPED OYSTERS

Crackers sprinkled over the top of the dish provide a nice crisp complement to the creamy oysters. Though best when just shucked, oysters can be stored in their liquid in the refrigerator for up to three days.

WINE RECOMMENDATION
The creamy scalloped oysters pair perfectly with the bracing acidity of a classic French shellfish wine, Muscadet de Sèvre-et-Maine. Try to find a bottle labeled *sur lie* (on the lees).

MAKE IT AHEAD
The dish must be put together just before baking or the crumb topping will get soggy. To save time, though, several steps can be completed ahead. You can drain the oysters, season the cream, and toast the bread crumbs earlier in the day and store each one separately. Last-minute assembly will be quick and painless.

SERVES 8

- 1 cup crushed saltine crackers
- 2 dozen shucked oysters, drained
- ½ cup heavy cream
- ½ teaspoon salt
- ¼ teaspoon cayenne
- ½ cup fresh bread crumbs, toasted
- 4 tablespoons butter, cut into pieces

1. Heat the oven to 400°. Sprinkle ¾ cup of the crushed saltines into a large, shallow baking dish. Top with the oysters in a single layer. Season the heavy cream with the salt and the cayenne and drizzle it over the oysters.

2. In a small bowl, toss the remaining ¼ cup crushed crackers with the toasted bread crumbs. Sprinkle them over the dish. Dot with the butter and bake in the middle of the oven until the topping is light golden brown, about 20 minutes.

—CAMILLE GLENN

BROILED CRUMBED OYSTERS AND SHALLOTS

Oysters are broiled on the half-shell with a savory coating of buttered bread crumbs and shallots. A splash of Pernod is optional, but brings a distinctive flavor to the dish.

WINE RECOMMENDATION
A very acidic white wine with personality is a good match for this dish. Try the classic French oyster wine, Chablis, or a bottle of Sancerre or another sauvignon-blanc-based wine from France's Loire Valley.

SERVES 8

- 5 tablespoons butter
- 3 shallots, chopped
- ¾ cup dry bread crumbs
- ¼ cup lemon juice
- ½ teaspoon Pernod (optional)
- ¼ cup chopped fresh parsley
- ¼ cup grated Parmesan cheese
- 2 dozen oysters, shucked, cupped bottom shells reserved and scrubbed well

  Rock salt (optional; see "Kitchen Tip," right)

1. Heat the broiler. In a medium frying pan, melt the butter over moderate heat. Add the shallots and sauté, stirring occasionally, until golden, about 5 minutes. Add the bread crumbs and sauté until they have absorbed all of the butter, about 1 minute. Remove the pan from the heat. Mix in the lemon juice, Pernod, parsley, and Parmesan.

2. Arrange the oysters, in their shells, in a large, shallow baking pan filled with rock salt. Top the oysters with the crumb mixture.

3. Broil the oysters until bubbly and light brown, about 3 minutes. Serve at once.

—JEAN ANDERSON

KITCHEN TIP

Partially filling a baking pan with rock salt makes it easy to steady oysters on the half-shell so that they won't tip as they broil. Crumbled aluminum foil is less traditional but also does the trick.

chapter 3
TURKEY

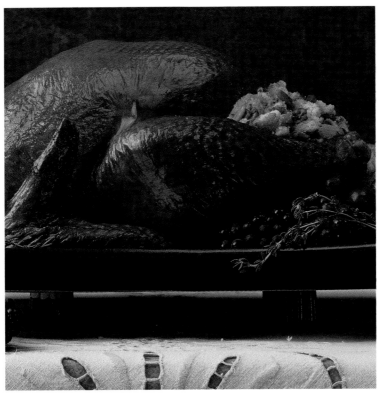

Traditional Roast Stuffed Turkey with Pan Gravy, page 49

Traditional Roast Stuffed Turkey with Pan Gravy

Try wrapping a few slices of bacon around each drumstick. Not only will this keep the meat particularly moist, but the smokiness of the bacon imparts delicious flavor, too.

This traditional turkey can be paired with either white wine or red. If you choose a red wine, try something light and fruity such as a Beaujolais or a California zinfandel; if a white, try a pinot blanc from Alsace in France.

SERVES 10 TO 12

1 14- to 16-pound turkey with neck and giblets, at room temperature

Salt and fresh-ground black pepper

Pecan Corn-Bread Stuffing, page 110

¼ pound plus 2 tablespoons butter

2 tablespoons flour

3 cups Turkey Stock, next page, or canned low-sodium chicken broth

1. Heat the oven to 450°. Reserve the turkey neck and giblets for the stock. Season the bird inside and out with salt and pepper.

2. Put the turkey breast-side down on a work surface. Loosely fill the neck cavity of the turkey with some of the stuffing. Pull the neck skin over the cavity. Fasten the skin to the back of the turkey with metal skewers or wooden toothpicks. Turn the turkey breast-side up.

3. Loosely fill the main cavity of the bird with stuffing and close the cavity with skewers or toothpicks. Twist the wings behind the bird and tie the legs together.

4. In a medium saucepan, melt the ¼ pound of butter. Soak a 2-foot-long double layer of cheesecloth or a clean kitchen towel in the melted butter. Put the turkey, breast-side up, on a rack in a roasting pan and cover the breast with the butter-soaked cloth. Let the remaining 2 tablespoons butter soften.

5. Put the turkey in the oven. Immediately reduce the heat to 325°. Roast the bird, basting frequently with the pan juices after the first 30 minutes, until an instant-read thermometer stuck into the inner thigh registers 155°, about 3½ hours. Remove the cheesecloth from the breast. Continue roasting the turkey, basting, until the thigh temperature reaches 180°, about 1 hour longer. The juices will run clear when the thigh is pierced with a fork. Transfer the turkey to a carving board and leave to rest in a warm spot for about 15 minutes.

6. Meanwhile, mash together the 2 tablespoons softened butter and the flour to

make a smooth paste. Pour the pan juices into a bowl and skim off the fat. Return the pan juices to the roasting pan and set the pan over moderate heat. Add the Turkey Stock. Bring to a boil, scraping the bottom of the pan to dislodge any brown bits. Gradually whisk in the butter paste and boil, whisking, until thickened. Reduce the heat and simmer for 5 minutes. Season with salt and pepper.

7. Remove the string from the bird. Spoon the stuffing into a bowl and carve the turkey. Serve the turkey with the stuffing and gravy.

—Lee Bailey

Turkey Stock

MAKES 3 CUPS

Turkey neck and giblets
1 onion, chopped
1 rib celery, chopped
1 carrot, chopped
3 parsley sprigs
1 quart water

1. In a medium saucepan, combine the neck and giblets, the onion, celery, carrot, parsley, and water.

2. Bring to a boil and reduce the heat to low. Simmer, skimming occasionally, for 1½ hours. Strain the stock.

Extra Stuffing

If you have more stuffing than you need to fill the bird, wrap the extra in buttered aluminum foil and bake in the oven with the turkey during the last 30 minutes of cooking.

Quick-Roasted Turkey with Lemon Corn-Bread Stuffing

Quick-roasting helps keep the turkey moist and cuts down on cooking time; we were able to cook a sixteen-pound bird to perfection in only three hours.

WINE RECOMMENDATION

Look for a crisp, refreshing white wine to pair with the lemon in the stuffing. Try a Côtes de Gascogne from France or an alvariño from Spain, both of which are light and have loads of fresh-fruit flavor.

SERVES 10 TO 12

- 1 14- to 16-pound turkey with neck and giblets, at room temperature

   Salt and fresh-ground black pepper

   Lemon Corn-Bread Stuffing, page 106, still warm

- 1 tablespoon olive oil

- ¼ cup flour

- 2 cups Turkey Stock, page 50, or canned low-sodium chicken broth

- ¾ cup dry white wine, Turkey Stock, or canned low-sodium chicken broth

1. Heat the oven to 475°. Reserve the turkey neck and giblets for the stock. Season the turkey inside and out with salt and pepper. Put it breast-side down on a work surface. Loosely fill the neck cavity with 1 cup of the stuffing. Pull the neck skin over the cavity and fasten to the back of the turkey with metal skewers or wooden toothpicks. Turn the turkey breast-side up. Loosely fill the main cavity with the remaining stuffing.

Close the cavity with skewers or toothpicks. Twist the wings behind the bird and tie the legs together. Rub the turkey with the oil.

2. Put the turkey, breast-side up, on a rack in a roasting pan and roast in the lower third of the oven for 45 minutes. The turkey will begin to brown very quickly. Lower the oven temperature to 400° and loosely cover the turkey with aluminum foil. Continue to roast, basting frequently with the pan juices, until an instant-read thermometer stuck into the inner thigh registers 180°, about 2¼ hours longer. The juices will run clear when the thigh is pierced with a fork. Transfer the turkey to a carving board and leave to rest in a warm spot for at least 15 minutes.

3. Pour the pan juices into a bowl. Skim off the fat. Return the juices to the roasting pan and set it over moderate heat. Add the flour and cook, stirring, until bubbling, about 3 minutes. Add the 2 cups Turkey Stock and the wine. Bring to a boil, scraping the bottom of the pan to dislodge any brown bits. Boil until thickened, about 2 minutes. Season with salt and pepper.

4. Remove the string from the bird. Spoon the stuffing into a bowl and carve the turkey. Serve with the stuffing and gravy.

Roast Turkey
with Three-Bread Stuffing

With a hint of paprika in the gravy and cubes of pumpernickel, rye, and sour-dough bread in the stuffing, Tina Ujlaki, the Food Editor at FOOD & WINE Magazine, incorporates her Hungarian heritage into this holiday bird.

WINE RECOMMENDATION
A light wine will enliven this dish. Try a dry sparkling wine from California or a slightly chilled red wine such as a Beaujolais Nouveau.

SERVES 10 TO 12

1 14- to 16-pound turkey with neck and giblets, at room temperature
  Salt and fresh-ground black pepper
  Three-Bread Stuffing, page 118
¼ pound plus 2 tablespoons butter
½ teaspoon paprika
2 tablespoons flour
3 cups Turkey Stock, page 50, or canned low-sodium chicken broth

1. Heat the oven to 450°. Reserve the turkey neck and giblets for the stock. Season the turkey inside and out with salt and pepper. Turn the turkey breast-side down on a work surface and loosely fill the neck cavity with about 2 cups of the stuffing. Pull the neck skin over the cavity. Fasten the skin to the back of the turkey with metal skewers or wooden toothpicks. Turn the turkey breast-side up. Loosely fill the main cavity of the bird with about 5 cups of the Three-Bread Stuffing. Close the cavity with skewers or toothpicks. Twist the wings behind the bird. Tie the legs of the turkey together. Wrap the remainder of the stuffing separately in buttered aluminum foil and bake it in the oven with the turkey during the last 30 minutes of cooking.

2. In a medium saucepan, melt the ¼ pound butter. Soak a 2-foot-long double layer of cheesecloth or a clean kitchen towel in the melted butter. Let the remaining 2 tablespoons butter soften.

3. Put the turkey, breast-side up, on a rack in a roasting pan and cover the breast with the butter-soaked cloth.

4. Put the turkey in the oven and immediately reduce the heat to 325°. Roast the bird, basting frequently with any pan juices, until an instant-read thermometer stuck into the inner thigh registers 135°, about 3½ hours. Remove the butter-soaked cloth and add the paprika to the pan. Continue roasting the turkey, basting, until the inner thigh temperature reaches 180°, about 1 hour longer. The juices will run clear when the thigh of the turkey is pierced with a fork.

5. Transfer the turkey to a carving board and leave to rest in a warm spot for about 15 minutes.

6. Meanwhile, mash together the 2 tablespoons softened butter and the flour. Pour the pan juices into a bowl and skim off the fat. Set the roasting pan over high heat and when it starts to sizzle and smoke, add the stock. Bring to a boil, scraping the bottom of the pan to dislodge any brown bits. Reduce the heat, add the pan juices, and simmer for 5 minutes. Gradually whisk the butter paste into the gravy and bring to a boil, whisking until smooth. Season with salt and pepper.

7. Remove the string from the bird. Spoon the stuffing into a bowl and carve the turkey. Serve with the stuffing and gravy.

THE SECOND TIME AROUND

Even a few hours after a huge Thanksgiving dinner, there's nothing better than a leftover-turkey sandwich. But if you're looking for something a little more creative to serve over the days that follow, here are some suggestions.

■ **Club sandwiches:** Try sliced turkey, bacon, jack cheese, tomato, lettuce, mayonnaise, and sliced avocado.

■ **Southwest turkey chili:** Follow your favorite chili recipe, leaving out the ground beef and adding cubed turkey at the very end.

■ **Turkey hash:** Sauté diced onions, potatoes, and peppers until golden brown. Add cubed turkey and season with salt, pepper, and chopped fresh parsley.

■ **Turkey noodle soup:** Make stock from the leftover carcass, simmer some carrots or other root vegetables and noodles in the stock until tender, and stir in cubes of turkey.

■ **Turkey-and-watercress sandwiches:** Spread cranberry sauce on one slice of seven-grain bread, grainy mustard on the other, and put turkey and watercress in between.

■ **Turkey tossed salad:** Toss romaine lettuce, diced turkey, toasted pecans, and crumbled blue cheese with vinaigrette.

■ **Turkey-salad sandwiches:** Toss turkey with roasted red peppers and herb mayonnaise; serve on croissants.

THANKSGIVING TURKEY WITH TWO STUFFINGS

For an especially festive meal, this turkey is stuffed with two different dressings—one cooks in the neck cavity and the other in the main cavity. Of course, you can always simplify matters and make just one.

WINE RECOMMENDATION
The latest vintage of Beaujolais Nouveau or its California cousins, which are based on such crowd-pleasing varieties as gamay or grenache, will be ideal with this classic bird.

SERVES 8 TO 10

1   10- to 12-pound turkey, at room temperature, neck reserved

½   lemon

Chestnut Dressing, page 123

Corn-Bread Sausage Stuffing, page 107

Salt and fresh-ground black pepper

¼   pound plus 1½ tablespoons butter, softened

½   pound mushrooms, sliced

3   tablespoons flour

3   cups Chicken Stock, page 57, or canned low-sodium chicken broth

1   tablespoon chopped fresh parsley

1. Heat the oven to 425°. Rub the inside of the turkey with the lemon half.

2. Put the turkey breast-side down on a work surface. Loosely fill the neck cavity with some of the Chestnut Dressing. Pull the neck skin over the cavity and fasten the skin to the back of the turkey with metal skewers or wooden toothpicks. Turn the turkey breast-side up.

3. Loosely fill the main cavity of the turkey with about 8 cups of the Corn-Bread Sausage Stuffing and close the cavity with skewers or toothpicks. Twist the wings behind the bird and tie the legs together. Wrap the remainder of the dressings separately in buttered aluminum foil and bake them in the oven with the turkey during the last 30 minutes of cooking.

4. Season the turkey with salt and pepper. Coat the skin with 4 tablespoons of the butter. Set the turkey on its side in a large roasting pan.

5. Roast the bird until the top side is brown, about 30 minutes. Turn the turkey and roast until the other side is brown, about 30 minutes longer

6. Meanwhile, in a medium saucepan, melt 4 tablespoons of the butter. Dampen a 2-foot-long double layer of cheesecloth or a clean kitchen towel and soak it in the melted butter.

7. When both sides of the turkey are brown, set it breast-side up and cover the bird with the butter-soaked cloth. Add the reserved turkey neck to the roasting pan.

8. Reduce the oven temperature to 325°. Continue roasting the turkey for 1½ hours, basting twice. Remove the buttered cloth and roast the turkey, basting every 15 minutes, until an instant-read thermometer stuck into the inner thigh registers 180°, about 60 to 70 minutes longer. The juices will run clear when the thigh is pierced with a fork.

9. Meanwhile, in a large frying pan, melt the remaining 1½ tablespoons butter over moderately high heat. Add the sliced mushrooms and cook, stirring occasionally, until the mushrooms soften and all the liquid evaporates, about 5 minutes.

10. When the turkey is done, transfer it to a carving board and leave to rest in a warm spot for about 15 minutes.

11. Discard the neck. Pour the pan juices into a bowl and skim off the fat. Put the flour into the roasting pan and cook over moderate heat, stirring, until bubbling, about 3 minutes. Add the pan juices and the Chicken Stock to the roasting pan and bring the mixture to a boil, scraping the bottom of the roasting pan to dislodge any brown bits. Boil until the gravy thickens, about 2 minutes. Add the cooked mushrooms, the chopped fresh parsley, ½ teaspoon salt, and ½ teaspoon pepper.

12. Remove the string from the bird. Spoon the stuffings into separate bowls and carve the turkey. Serve with the stuffings and gravy.

—CAMILLE GLENN

KITCHEN TIP

To make both stuffing and carving the turkey (or any bird for that matter) easier, have your butcher remove the wishbone. To remove it yourself, loosen the skin over the wishbone area with your hands. Cut out the bone with a small knife and pat the skin back in place. If you like, save the wishbone for stock.

STUFFED VENETIAN TURKEY

The inspiration for this recipe comes from a traditional Venetian dish in which turkey is spit-roasted and basted with fresh pomegranate juice and port. The turkey is stuffed with a rich combination of pureed chestnuts, ground pork and veal, prunes, and port. Thin slices of pancetta flavor and protect the bird while it roasts, and the pomegranate juice adds a deep mahogany color.

WINE RECOMMENDATION
The stuffing, with its meatiness and the sweetness from the fruit, will go nicely with a subtly sweet, fruity red wine such as a reasonably priced California pinot noir.

SERVES 8 TO 10

1   10- to 12-pound turkey with neck and giblets, at room temperature

   Salt and fresh-ground black pepper

   Venetian Stuffing, page 124

7   tablespoons butter

4 to 6 thin slices of pancetta

1½   cups unsweetened pomegranate juice*

3   quarts Chicken Stock, opposite page, or canned low-sodium chicken broth

1   cup white or tawny port

   Fresh pomegranate seeds, for garnish (optional)

*Available at health-food stores

1. Reserve the turkey neck and giblets. Season the bird inside and out with salt and pepper. Put it, breast-side down, on a work surface. Loosely fill the neck cavity with some of the stuffing. Pull the neck skin over the cavity and fasten it to the back of the turkey with metal skewers or wooden toothpicks. Turn the turkey breast-side up.

2. Loosely fill the main cavity of the bird with stuffing and close the cavity with skewers or toothpicks. Twist the wings behind the bird and tie the legs together.

3. Heat the oven to 400°. Coat the skin of the turkey with 3 tablespoons of the butter. Cover the turkey breast with the thin slices of pancetta and secure the pancetta slices to the turkey with small metal skewers or wooden toothpicks.

4. Roast the turkey in the preheated oven. After 1½ hours, baste the turkey generously with pomegranate juice. Roast the turkey, basting every 30 minutes with pomegranate juice and the pan juices, until the turkey is deep golden brown and an instant-read thermometer stuck into the inner thigh registers 180°, about 2 hours longer. The juices will run clear when the thigh is pierced with a fork.

5. Meanwhile, put the stock in a large pot with the reserved neck and giblets. Boil until the liquid is reduced to 3 cups. Strain the stock. Add the port.

6. When the turkey is done, transfer it to a carving board. Peel off the pancetta and leave the turkey to rest in a warm spot for about 15 minutes.

7. Meanwhile, cut the remaining 4 tablespoons butter into pieces. Pour the pan juices into a bowl and skim off the fat. Return the pan juices to the roasting pan and set the pan over moderate heat. Add the stock mixture. Bring to a boil, scraping the bottom of the pan to dislodge any brown bits. Boil until the sauce is reduced to 3 cups again, about 15 minutes. Strain into a small saucepan. Bring to a boil and whisk in the butter, a few pieces at a time.

8. Remove the string from the bird. Carve the turkey and serve with the sauce. Garnish each serving with pomegranate seeds, if you like.

—SILVIO PINTO

CHICKEN STOCK

MAKES 1 1/2 QUARTS

4 pounds chicken carcasses, backs, wings, and/or necks, plus gizzards (optional)

2 onions, quartered

2 carrots, quartered

2 ribs celery, quartered

8 parsley stems

5 peppercorns

2 quarts water

1. Put all the ingredients in a large pot. Bring to a boil and skim the foam that rises to the surface. Reduce the heat and simmer, partially covered, for 2 hours.

2. Strain. Press the bones and vegetables firmly to get all the liquid. Skim the fat from the surface if using immediately. If not, refrigerate for up to a week or freeze. Scrape off the fat before using.

ARMADILLO TURKEY

You use only the skin of a pineapple for this unusual turkey—the rest can be reserved for another use, such as a winter fruit salad or the Pineapple Crumbcake on page 222. We suggest buying pineapple juice in a carton or bottle to avoid the unpleasant metallic taste of the canned variety.

WINE RECOMMENDATION
Pineapple and wine—now there's an interesting combination! Match the sweetness and acidity of the pineapple with a red wine such as Beaujolais-Villages, which is all fruit and lightness with a touch of acidity.

SERVES 10 TO 12

1 lime, cut in half

1 14- to 16-pound turkey, at room temperature

1 small onion, quartered
 Fresh-ground black pepper

1½ cups unsweetened pineapple juice

1 large pineapple (about 2 pounds)

3 tablespoons butter
 Salt

1. Heat the oven to 325°. Squeeze the juice from the lime into the cavity of the turkey and leave the lime halves inside. Put the onion quarters in the cavity. Sprinkle pepper all over the turkey, inside and out. Twist the wings behind the bird and tie the legs together.

2. Put the turkey, breast-side up, on a rack in a stainless-steel roasting pan. Pour ½ cup of the pineapple juice over the turkey and roast in the lower third of the oven for 30 minutes. Pour another ½ cup of the pineapple juice on top and roast for another 30 minutes.

3. Meanwhile, using a large stainless-steel knife and cutting from top to bottom, remove the skin from the pineapple in four equal pieces, leaving ¼ inch of pineapple on the skin.

4. Pour the remaining ½ cup pineapple juice over the turkey and cover the turkey breast with the four pieces of pineapple skin. Secure the pieces of pineapple skin with small skewers. Continue to roast the turkey, basting the legs and pineapple skin every 30 minutes, until the turkey is deep golden brown and an instant-read thermometer stuck into the inner thigh registers 180°, about 2½ hours longer. The juices will run clear when the thigh is pierced with a fork.

5. Remove the turkey and prop it up with the legs slightly higher than the breast to let the juices run back into the breast meat. Leave to rest in a warm spot for about 30 minutes.

6. Meanwhile, pour the pan juices into a bowl and skim off the fat. Return the pan

juices to the roasting pan and set the pan over moderate heat. Bring to a boil, scraping the bottom of the pan to dislodge any brown bits. Boil for 1 minute. Remove from the heat and let cool slightly. Whisk in the butter. Season with salt and pepper to taste.

7. Remove the string from the bird. Present the turkey on a platter. Remove the pineapple skins before carving at the table. Serve the turkey with the gravy.

—SUSAN HERRMANN LOOMIS

FIVE TIPS FOR A PERFECT TURKEY

■ Check your thermometer a few days before you plan to roast the turkey. If you put it in a pot of boiling water and it registers 212° (the boiling point), you're all set. If it doesn't, buy a new thermometer.

■ Set the turkey on a rack in a large roasting pan to promote maximum air and heat circulation and to ensure that the bird cooks evenly.

■ Protect the turkey breast from overcooking by roasting the bird on the lowest rack in the oven. Once the breast skin is browned, loosely cover it with aluminum foil to prevent it from becoming too dark.

■ Keep a careful eye on the thermometer during the last half-hour of cooking, since the turkey's temperature may rise rapidly toward the end.

■ Check for doneness in the thickest, meatiest parts of the turkey. Using your thermometer, test the widest section of the breast near the wing joint; the temperature should be 165°. Test the legs at the thickest part of the thigh; the temperature should be 180°. Also check the juices. If they have a pinkish tinge, continue roasting; if they're clear, the turkey's done. Try to use the thermometer as infrequently as possible so that no more precious juices than necessary escape.

ROAST TURKEY WITH CELERY AND LEMON STUFFING

A buttered cloth covers the turkey while it roasts to ensure a golden brown bird, and a light dusting of flour towards the end of cooking produces an appealingly crisp skin.

WINE RECOMMENDATION

The bright citrus flavor of a California chardonnay or a Mâcon (also made from chardonnay) from France will work well with the lemon here. Make sure to ask for a non-oaky bottling.

SERVES 6 TO 8

1   8- to 10-pound turkey, at room temperature

Salt and fresh-ground black pepper

Celery and Lemon Stuffing, page 117

¼   pound butter

Flour, for dusting

1.   Heat the oven to 350°. Season the turkey inside and out with salt and pepper.

2.   Loosely fill the main cavity of the bird with the stuffing. Close the cavity with metal skewers or wooden toothpicks. If there is enough stuffing, loosely fill the neck cavity as well. Pull the neck skin over the cavity and fasten the skin to the back of the turkey with skewers or toothpicks. Twist the wings behind the bird and tie the legs together.

3.   In a medium saucepan, melt the butter. Soak a 2-foot-long double layer of cheesecloth or a clean kitchen towel in the melted butter. Put the turkey, breast-side up, on a rack in a roasting pan and cover the breast and legs with the butter-soaked cloth.

4.   Roast for 3 hours, basting frequently with the pan juices after the first 30 minutes. Remove the buttered cloth. Lightly dust the turkey with flour. Continue to roast until an instant-read thermometer stuck into the inner thigh registers 180°, about 30 minutes longer. The juices will run clear when the thigh is pierced with a fork.

5.   Transfer the turkey to a carving board and leave to rest in a warm spot for about 15 minutes. Remove the string from the bird. Spoon the stuffing into a bowl and carve the turkey. Serve with the stuffing.

FRESH VS. FROZEN TURKEYS

Frozen turkeys are more readily available than fresh ones and are generally quite satisfactory. However, if you can get a fresh turkey, do. The moistness and full flavor of the bird will surprise you.

ROAST TURKEY WITH MADEIRA GRAVY

The Madeira adds just a hint of sweetness to this richly flavored gravy. The turkey and gravy pair up perfectly with Country-Ham and Wild-Mushroom Dressing, page 126.

SERVES 8 TO 10

1	10- to 12-pound turkey with neck and giblets, at room temperature
	Salt and fresh-ground black pepper
12	tablespoons butter
1/4	cup plus 1 tablespoon cooking oil
5½	cups Chicken Stock, page 57, or canned low-sodium chicken broth
2	onions, chopped
2	leeks, white and light-green parts only, chopped
3	carrots, chopped
1	teaspoon dried thyme
1	bay leaf
	Stems from 1 bunch of parsley
1	cup Madeira
1/4	cup flour

1. Heat the oven to 325°. Cut off the first joint of each turkey wing and reserve them, along with the turkey neck and giblets, for the gravy. Season the turkey inside and out with salt and pepper. Twist the wings behind the turkey and tie the legs together.

2. Put the turkey, breast-side up, on a rack in a roasting pan. Dampen a 2-foot-long double layer of cheesecloth or a clean kitchen towel and cover the bird with the cloth. Roast the turkey for 30 minutes.

3. Meanwhile, in a small saucepan, heat 6 tablespoons of the butter with ¼ cup of the oil and ½ cup of the stock until the butter melts. After the turkey has roasted for 30 minutes, baste it liberally through the cloth with half of the butter mixture. Baste again with the remaining butter mixture after another 30 minutes. After another 15 minutes, baste the turkey with the accumulated juices from the roasting pan and repeat every 15 minutes until the turkey is done and an instant-read thermometer stuck into the inner thigh registers 180°, about 2 hours and 15 minutes longer. The juices will run clear when the thigh is pierced with a fork.

4. While the turkey roasts, make the gravy. In a medium saucepan, heat 2 tablespoons of the butter with the remaining 1 tablespoon oil over moderate heat until foaming. Add the reserved neck, giblets,

and wing tips and cook, stirring frequently, until very brown, about 20 minutes.

5. Add the onions, leeks, carrots, thyme, bay leaf, and parsley stems. Cover, reduce the heat, and cook, stirring occasionally, until the vegetables are soft and light brown, about 20 minutes longer.

6. Add the Madeira and the remaining 5 cups stock. Bring to a boil, scraping the bottom of the pan to dislodge any brown bits. Reduce the heat and simmer, partially covered, skimming occasionally, for 30 minutes. Strain. You should have 5 cups of gravy. Let the remaining 4 tablespoons butter soften.

7. Wipe out the pan and return the gravy to the pan. Bring back to a boil. Boil, uncovered, until reduced to 3 cups, about 30 minutes. In a small bowl, mash the 4 tablespoons softened butter with the flour to form a smooth paste. Reduce the heat to low and whisk the butter paste into the gravy, 1 tablespoon at a time. Increase the heat to moderate and simmer, whisking, for 5 minutes. Season with salt and pepper to taste.

8. When the turkey is done, transfer it to a carving board and leave to rest in a warm spot for about 15 minutes. Remove the string from the turkey. Carve the bird and serve with the gravy.

—MICHAEL MCLAUGHLIN

ROAST WILD TURKEY WITH BLUE-CORN-BREAD AND CHORIZO STUFFING

You'll probably need to order a wild turkey in advance from your butcher. It will have less meat than a farm-raised bird, but more flavor. Of course, you can make this recipe with a regular supermarket turkey, too.

WINE RECOMMENDATION
A pitcher of beer would be perfect with this dish from a palate perspective, but might not fit into the atmosphere of a holiday celebration. Try a fruity, slightly chilled red wine such as a grenache or gamay from California.

SERVES 8 TO 10

1   10- to 12-pound turkey with neck and giblets, at room temperature
    Salt and fresh-ground black pepper
    Blue-Corn-Bread and Chorizo Stuffing, page 108

¼   pound plus 2 tablespoons butter

2   tablespoons flour

3   cups Turkey Stock, page 50, or canned low-sodium chicken broth

1. Heat the oven to 450°. Reserve the turkey neck and giblets for the stock. Season the turkey inside and out with salt and pepper.

2. Put the turkey breast-side down on a work surface. Loosely fill the neck cavity with some of the stuffing. Pull the neck skin over the cavity and fasten the skin to the back of the turkey with metal skewers or wooden toothpicks. Turn the turkey breast-side up.

3. Loosely fill the main cavity of the bird with stuffing and close the cavity with skewers or toothpicks. Twist the wings behind the bird and tie the legs together.

4. In a medium saucepan, melt the ¼ pound of butter. Soak a 2-foot-long double layer of cheesecloth or a clean kitchen towel in the melted butter. Put the turkey, breast-side up, on a rack in a roasting pan and cover the breast with the butter-soaked cloth. Let the remaining 2 tablespoons butter soften.

5. Put the turkey in the oven. Immediately reduce the heat to 325°. Roast the bird, basting every 30 minutes with the pan juices, until an instant-read thermometer stuck into the inner thigh registers 135°, about 2 hours. Remove the buttered cloth from the turkey breast. Continue roasting the turkey, basting every 20 minutes, until an instant-read thermometer stuck into the inner thigh registers 180°, about 1 hour longer. The juices will run clear when the thigh of the turkey is pierced with a fork. Transfer the turkey to a carving board and

leave it to rest in a warm spot for about 15 minutes.

6. Meanwhile, mash together the 2 tablespoons softened butter and the flour to make a smooth paste. Pour the pan juices into a bowl and skim off the fat. Return the pan juices to the roasting pan and set the pan over moderate heat. Add the stock to the pan. Bring to a boil, scraping the bottom of the pan to dislodge any brown bits. Gradually whisk in the butter paste and boil, whisking, until thickened. Reduce the heat and simmer for 5 minutes. Season with salt and pepper.

7. Remove the string from the bird. Carve the turkey and serve with the stuffing and gravy.

—STEPHAN PYLES

KEEPING LEFTOVERS

■ **Turkey:** Bundle portions of turkey in aluminum foil or in freezer bags. Date, label, and freeze for up to four months. Thaw before using.

■ **Stuffing:** The USDA recommends "unstuffing" the bird as soon as it's done. At meal's end, wrap the stuffing in aluminum foil. Date, label, and freeze for up to one month.

■ **Gravy:** Pour leftover gravy in half-pint freezer containers, leaving a half-inch of headroom, and snap on the lids. Date, label, and freeze the gravy for up to one month.

■ **Carcass:** Refrigerate or freeze the carcass and use it to make stock. Turkey stock can be frozen up to six months.

—JEAN ANDERSON

KEN HOM'S BONED STUFFED TURKEY

Cooking instructor Ken Hom marinates a boned bird overnight, fills it with an Asian stuffing, and then steams the turkey for especially moist meat that's wonderfully easy to carve. Ask your butcher to do the boning for you, but to give you the carcass for the turkey stock.

WINE RECOMMENDATION
Try a classic wine pairing for Oriental foods such as a gewürztraminer from Alsace in France or a dry chenin blanc from the Loire Valley in France.

SERVES 8 TO 10

1   10- to 12-pound turkey, boned but in one piece, neck, giblets, and carcass reserved

    Salt and fresh-ground black pepper

3   tablespoons Asian sesame oil

½   cup lemon juice (from about 2 lemons)

    Oriental Stuffing, page 119

2   quarts Chicken Stock, page 57, made with reserved turkey neck, giblets, and carcass in addition to the chicken bones

1. Season the turkey on both sides with 2 teaspoons salt, 1 teaspoon pepper, the sesame oil, and the lemon juice. Put the turkey in a large bowl, cover, and refrigerate overnight.

2. Remove the turkey from the marinade and pat dry with paper towels. Using a needle and thread, sew the turkey closed from the tail almost to the neck, leaving an opening 4 to 5 inches long for stuffing. Fill the turkey with the stuffing and sew up the opening. Tie the filled turkey with kitchen string at 2-inch intervals.

3. Put the turkey, seam-side down, on a heat-proof platter. Set the platter on a rack in a large roasting pan. Add enough water to the pan to come just below the rack. Cover the roasting pan tightly with aluminum foil and set the pan on the stove. Bring the water to a boil over high heat. Reduce the heat to moderate and steam the the turkey until an instant-read thermometer stuck into the center of the stuffing registers 160°, about 1½ hours. The juices will run clear. Add more water to the pan during steaming if necessary. Remove the turkey from the platter, reserving any juices that have collected on the platter. Discard the water in the pan.

4. Heat the oven to 450°. Put the turkey on the rack in the roasting pan and roast until golden brown, 15 to 20 minutes. Transfer to a carving board and leave to rest in a warm spot for about 15 minutes.

5. Meanwhile, put the stock and the reserved turkey juices into a medium saucepan. Boil over high heat until reduced to 3 cups, about 15 minutes. Strain the sauce

and skim off any fat. Season with salt and pepper to taste.

6. Remove the thread and strings from the turkey. Carve and serve with the sauce.

—KEN HOM

SAFETY TIPS

■ Rinse the turkey inside and out and pat dry before roasting.

■ Wash your hands, utensils, and all work surfaces with hot sudsy water after handling raw turkey.

■ Don't thaw a frozen, prestuffed turkey before roasting.

■ Refrigerate leftover turkey within two hours after serving.

—JEAN ANDERSON

chapter 4
OTHER BIRDS

Roasted Goose with Chicken-Liver Stuffing, page 71

ROASTED GOOSE WITH CHICKEN-LIVER STUFFING

A goose has an enormous amount of fat just inside the cavity, and it's important to pull that out before roasting. Don't discard it, though; render and use it to make confit, sautéed wild mushrooms, roasted potatoes, or the stuffing for this recipe. In the freezer, goose fat will keep for months. The goose is pictured here with Candied Quinces, page 161.

WINE RECOMMENDATION
This rich dish should be paired with a dense, rough-hewn wine. Try a gutsy red from the northern Rhône Valley of France, such as a Gigondas or a more moderately priced Crozes-Hermitage.

SERVES 6

1   10-pound goose with gizzard and liver, excess fat removed

3   cloves garlic, minced

1   tablespoon dried thyme

Coarse salt

Rich Chicken-Liver Stuffing, page 125

3½ cups Chicken Stock, page 57, or canned low-sodium chicken broth

4   tablespoons butter, cut into pieces

Fresh-ground black pepper

1. Remove the wishbone from the goose, if you like (see "Kitchen Tip," page 55). Reserve the gizzard and liver for the stuffing.

2. The day before you roast the goose, combine the garlic, thyme, and 1 tablespoon salt. Rub this mixture all over the breast, thighs, and legs of the goose. Wrap and refrigerate. Remove the bird from the refrigerator 1 to 2 hours before roasting.

3. Heat the oven to 425°. Prick the skin of the goose all over. Loosely fill the cavity with the stuffing. Close the cavity with metal skewers or wooden toothpicks. Twist the wings behind the bird and tie the legs together. Put the goose, breast-side down, in a roasting pan just large enough to hold the bird. Pour 1 cup of the stock in the pan.

4. Roast the goose for 15 minutes. Baste with the pan juices. Reduce the oven temperature to 350° and continue to roast, basting every 10 minutes, for 1 hour longer. Remove the goose from the oven. Carefully loosen it from the pan and remove. Pour all the fat into a large bowl. Return the goose to the pan, breast-side up. Add another ½ cup stock to the pan. Continue roasting for 30 minutes, basting with the pan juices every 10 minutes. Again, remove the fat.

5. Add another ½ cup of the stock to the pan and roast until the goose is golden brown and tender, about 30 minutes longer. An

instant-read thermometer stuck in the inner thigh should register 180°. Transfer the goose to a carving board and leave to rest in a warm spot for about 15 minutes. Pour the fat into the large bowl, adding it to the fat already collected. At the bottom of the fat in the bowl, you'll have the juice from the roast. Spoon off all the fat.

6. Pour the pan juices into the roasting pan and set the pan over high heat. Add the remaining 1½ cups stock to the pan and bring to a boil over high heat, scraping the bottom of the pan to dislodge any brown bits. Boil until the liquid is reduced to 1 cup. Strain into a saucepan and whisk in the butter, a few pieces at a time. Season with salt and pepper to taste. Remove the string from the goose. Carve the bird and serve with the stuffing and gravy.

—LYDIE MARSHALL

MAKE IT AHEAD
The goose can be marinated up to 2 days in advance. Wrap it in aluminum foil and refrigerate. One to two hours before roasting, let the goose come to room temperature.

INSTANT GOOSE STOCK

If you like, add the goose neck and giblets to Chicken Stock, page 57, along with the chicken backs and wings. Or, add them to canned chicken broth along with one carrot, one rib celery, and one onion, all quartered, and several parsley stems. Simmer for about one hour and then strain. You can also cut the wing tips and first wing joint off the uncooked birds and add them along with the neck to the stock or broth.

ROAST GOOSE WITH SAUSAGE, FRUIT, AND NUT STUFFING

The tangerines and cranberries in the stuffing are a tangy and refreshing contrast to the goose and sausage.

WINE RECOMMENDATION Match the mild sweetness of the sausage, fruit, and nuts to a red such as a California pinot noir with its sweet, round fruit.

SERVES 6

- 1 10-pound goose, at room temperature, excess fat removed
- Sausage, Fruit, and Nut Stuffing, page 111
- 1 lemon, cut in half
- ½ cup Madeira
- 1¾ cups Chicken Stock, page 57, or canned low-sodium chicken broth
- Salt and fresh-ground black pepper
- 2 tablespoons butter

1. Heat the oven to 425°. Remove the wishbone from the goose, if you like (see "Kitchen Tip," page 55). Loosely fill the main cavity of the bird with stuffing. Seal the cavity with metal skewers or wooden toothpicks. Twist the wings behind the bird and tie the legs together.

2. Rub the goose all over with the lemon halves. Put the goose, breast-side up, on a rack in a roasting pan. Prick the skin with a fork at ½-inch intervals. Roast for 15 minutes and then reduce the oven temperature to 350°. Roast, basting the goose with 2 tablespoons of hot water every 20 minutes, until an instant-read thermometer stuck in the inner thigh registers 160°. As the fat accumulates, remove it with a bulb baster or large spoon.

3. Increase the oven temperature to 425° and roast the goose until the skin is crisp and an instant-read thermometer stuck in the inner thigh registers 180°, about 15 minutes longer. Transfer the goose to a carving board and leave to rest in a warm spot for about 15 minutes.

4. Meanwhile, pour the pan juices into a large bowl and skim off the fat. Return the pan juices to the roasting pan and set the pan over moderate heat. Add the Madeira and stock and bring to a boil, scraping the bottom of the pan to dislodge any brown bits. Boil until the liquid is reduced to 1½ cups, about 4 minutes. Season with salt and pepper to taste. Whisk in the butter, 1 tablespoon at a time. Remove the string from the goose. Carve the bird and serve with the stuffing and sauce.

—MELANIE BARNARD

ROASTED GOOSE WITH CHESTNUT AND APPLE STUFFING

Succulent and golden brown, this holiday goose is stuffed with the simple combination of apples, raisins, prunes, and chestnuts. If you have other nuts or dried fruits on hand, feel free to try them along with or in place of the ones here.

WINE RECOMMENDATION
The combination of the tart and sweet flavors in the stuffing and the richness of the goose will work well with a red wine that blends sweetness and acidity. Try a pinot noir from Oregon.

SERVES 6

30   chestnuts

6   apples, peeled, cored, and cut into sixths (about 1½ quarts)

½   cup raisins

1   cup pitted prunes (optional)

1   10-pound goose with neck and giblets, at room temperature, excess fat removed

Salt and fresh-ground black pepper

⅔   cup water, more if needed

1. Bring a saucepan of water to a boil. Cut an "X" through the shell on the flat side of each chestnut. Add the chestnuts to the water and simmer until just tender and the shell and inner brown skin of a nut can be easily removed with a paring knife. Drain. As soon as the chestnuts are cool enough to handle, peel, skin, and cut into quarters. Put the chestnuts in a large bowl. Add the apples, raisins, and prunes, and toss.

2. Heat the oven to 400°. Remove the wishbone from the goose for easier carving, if you like (see "Kitchen Tip," page 55). Loosely fill the main cavity of the goose with stuffing. Seal the cavity with metal skewers or wooden toothpicks. Twist the wings behind the bird and tie the legs together. Put the goose, breast-side up, on a rack in a roasting pan. Rub the goose all over with salt. Add the neck and the giblets to the pan.

3. Roast the goose for 1 hour. Prick the skin with a fork at ½-inch intervals to release the fat. As the fat accumulates, remove it from the pan with a bulb baster or a large spoon. Reduce the oven temperature to 350° and roast the goose until it is golden and tender, about 1 hour longer. An instant-read thermometer stuck in the inner thigh should register 180°. If the goose is not done, lower the heat to 325° and continue to roast until the goose tests done. Transfer the goose to a carving board and leave to rest in a warm spot for about 15 minutes.

4. Meanwhile, pour the pan juices into a bowl and spoon off all the fat. Return the pan juices to the roasting pan and set the

pan over moderate heat. Add the water and bring to a boil, scraping the bottom of the pan to dislodge any brown bits. Season the sauce with salt and pepper to taste. Remove the string from the goose. Carve the bird and serve with the stuffing and gravy.

—JOAN NATHAN

TO CARVE A GOOSE

Cut the skin of the goose between one of the legs and the body and push down on the leg to expose the thigh joint; cut through the joint. Slice the meat from the bones. Repeat on the other side. With a long thin carving knife, cut the breast meat into thin slices.

ROAST EAST HAMPTON GOLDEN GOOSE

The long, slow cooking recommended here is your best bet for a tender goose.
Be sure to reserve the goose liver to add to the stuffing.

WINE RECOMMENDATION
The flavors of the stuffing pair nicely with a fruity red. Try a pinot-noir-based wine from the Côte Chalonnaise in France, such as a Givry or Montagny.

SERVES 8

1   12- to 14-pound goose with giblets, at room temperature, excess fat removed and reserved

1   lemon, cut in half

Salt and fresh-ground black pepper

Apricot Walnut Stuffing, page 115

¼   pound butter, melted

¾   cup Chicken Stock, page 57, or canned low-sodium chicken broth

2   tablespoons arrowroot or cornstarch

2   tablespoons cold water, Chicken Stock, or canned low-sodium chicken broth

1.   Heat the oven to 550°. Reserve the goose liver for the stuffing. Rub the skin and cavity of the goose with the cut lemon. Season inside and out with salt and pepper. Prick the skin around the legs and wings with a fork.

2.   Loosely fill the cavity of the goose with stuffing. Close the cavity with metal skewers or wooden toothpicks. Twist the wings behind the bird and tie the legs together. Brush with the melted butter.

3.   Put the goose, breast-side down, on a rack in a roasting pan. Roast for 30 minutes. Reduce the oven temperature to 300° and continue to roast, basting frequently with the pan juices and pricking the skin often with a fork to release the fat.

4.   After 2 hours, turn the goose breast-side up. Cover the breast with slices of the reserved fat, pressing the pieces together into a sheet to cover the breast. Roast until the joints move readily and the meat feels soft, about 1 hour longer. The juices will run clear when the thigh is pricked with a fork.

5.   Remove the crusty pieces of fat from the breast and increase the oven temperature to 450°. Roast the goose until the skin is golden and crisp. Transfer the goose to a serving platter and leave in a warm spot for about 15 minutes.

6.   Pour the pan juices into a large bowl. Remove all but 3 tablespoons fat. Return the pan juices to the roasting pan and set the pan over moderate heat. Add the port reserved from the stuffing, or 1 cup port if you're using a different stuffing, and the stock and bring to a boil, scraping the bottom of the pan to dislodge any brown bits.

7.   In a small bowl, stir together the arrowroot and the cold water. Whisk the

arrowroot mixture into the sauce and boil, whisking constantly, until thickened. Season the sauce with salt and pepper to taste. Remove the string from the goose. Carve the bird and serve with the stuffing and gravy.

—PEARL BYRD FOSTER

WHERE'S THE PORT?

You'll need one cup of port to complete this recipe, but you won't find it in the ingredient list. That's because, if you make the Apricot Walnut Stuffing as suggested, you already have the port you need—it's the soaking liquid for the apricots and raisins. Using it here rather than throwing it out not only avoids waste, but adds extra flavor to the gravy.

CHUTNEY-GLAZED ROAST CHICKENS WITH PECAN STUFFING

These sumptuous chickens are ideal for Thanksgiving. (Be sure to order large chickens in advance.) You may want to double the amount of stuffing—it's impossible to resist—and bake the extra separately.

WINE RECOMMENDATION
Look for a full-bodied, powerfully flavored white wine with plenty of acidity to pair with this imposing dish. A great (and unusual) choice would be a gewürztraminer from France, a classic accompaniment to Indian foods.

SERVES 8

2 4½-pound chickens with neck and giblets, at room temperature

1 lemon, cut in half

Salt and fresh-ground black pepper

¼ pound cold butter

Pecan Stuffing, page 114

2 cups Chicken Stock, page 57, or canned low-sodium chicken broth, more if needed

2 9-ounce jars Major Grey's Chutney, or other mango chutney

¼ cup flour

2 tablespoons chopped fresh parsley

1. Heat the oven to 450°. Remove the excess fat from the chickens and set it aside. Reserve the livers for the stuffing, and the neck and remaining giblets for the gravy. Rub the chickens inside and out with the cut lemon, and season inside and out with salt and pepper. Cut the butter into sixteen thin pats. Put the butter on a plate and refrigerate.

2. Loosely fill the cavities of the chickens with stuffing. Close the cavities with metal skewers or wooden toothpicks. Beginning with the loose flap of skin at the neck end of each chicken and using your fingers, loosen the skin from the breasts. Lay eight of the cold pats of butter under the skin of each chicken breast. Press the reserved pieces of chicken fat flat and lay over each breast. Carefully remove the skin from each chicken neck, slitting it open lengthwise. Lay the neck skin flat over the fat on the breasts; this will baste the chickens as they roast. Twist the wings behind the birds and tie the legs together.

3. Put the chickens, breast-side up, in a large roasting pan (preferably one with a cover). Scatter the necks and giblets around the birds. Pour the stock into the pan and cover tightly with aluminum foil. Add the cover if you have one. Roast in the lower third of the oven for 20 minutes.

4. Reduce the oven temperature to 325° and roast the birds for 45 minutes. Remove

the cover and the foil and check the chickens. They should be tender and almost done. The juices will still be somewhat pink when the thigh is pricked with a fork. If the stock has evaporated, add enough to cover the bottom of the pan. Raise the heat to 450° and roast, uncovered, until the chickens are slightly browned, about 10 minutes longer.

5. While the chickens are roasting, puree the chutney in a blender or food processor until smooth. Transfer the chickens to an ovenproof platter and brush the chutney over them. Return the birds to the oven and roast until the skin is golden brown, about 5 minutes. Transfer the chickens to a carving board and leave to rest in a warm spot for about 15 minutes.

6. Strain the pan juices into a bowl. Skim off the fat, return the fat to the roasting pan, and set the pan over moderate heat. Whisk in the flour. Cook, whisking, until the flour is bubbling. Add the pan juices and bring to a boil, scraping the bottom of the pan to dislodge any brown bits. Reduce the heat and simmer the gravy until thickened, about 3 minutes. Season with salt and pepper to taste. Add the parsley. Remove the string from the chickens. Serve the birds with the stuffing and gravy.

—Pearl Byrd Foster

ROAST CAPON WITH DATE-NUT DRESSING AND CHESTNUT SAUCE

Notice that the capons are cooked here breast-side down for much of the time. The juices run into the breasts, which makes for a very juicy capon. The birds need basting only when they are turned over near the end. The same cooking technique can be used for small turkeys. The capon is pictured with Gratin of Pumpkin, page 135.

WINE RECOMMENDATION
Try this dish with a rustic but fruity red wine such as a Corbières from the South of France or a zinfandel from California.

SERVES 12

1½   pounds chestnuts

3   cups plus 3 tablespoons water

1¾   teaspoons salt

6   large carrots, cut into 1-inch pieces

2   large onions, cut into eighths

2   7-pound capons with neck and giblets, at room temperature, excess fat removed and reserved

¾   cup red wine

2   cups Chicken Stock, page 57, or canned low-sodium chicken broth

1   tablespoon arrowroot or potato starch

¼   teaspoon pepper

Date and Nut Dressing, page 116

1. Heat the oven to 450°. Cut an "X" through the shell on the flat side of each chestnut. Put the chestnuts on an un-greased baking sheet. Bake in the oven until the shell at each "X" lifts away from the chestnut, about 15 minutes. As soon as they are cool enough to handle, peel the chestnuts. Reduce the oven temperature to 400°. Put the chestnuts, the 3 cups of water, and ½ teaspoon of the salt in a large saucepan. Bring to a boil over high heat. Reduce the heat and simmer until the chestnuts are tender, about 30 minutes. Break into pieces when cool.

2. In a large roasting pan, combine the carrots, the onions, and the reserved fat, neck, and giblets from the capons. Season the birds inside with ½ teaspoon of the salt. Twist the wings behind the birds and tie the legs together. Set the capons, breast-side up, on top of the bed of vegetables and trimmings in the roasting pan.

3. Sprinkle the outside of the capons with ½ teaspoon of the salt. Roast the birds for 20 minutes. Turn the capons over, breast-side down, and roast them for 40 minutes. Turn the capons breast-side up again and continue roasting, basting once, until they are browned. An instant-read thermometer stuck into the inner thigh of the capons should register 180°. Transfer the capons to

a carving board and leave them to rest in a warm spot for about 15 minutes. Pour the pan juices into a large bowl and skim off the fat. You should have about 1/2 cup pan juices.

4. Set the roasting pan with the vegetables and trimmings over high heat. When they begin to sizzle, add the wine, stock, and pan juices. Bring to a boil, scraping the bottom of the pan to dislodge any brown bits. Boil until the liquid is reduced to about 1 cup, about 5 minutes. Strain into a medium saucepan. Press the vegetables firmly to get all the liquid.

5. In a small bowl, combine the arrowroot with the remaining 3 tablespoons water and stir until dissolved. Whisk into the liquid from the roasting pan. Bring just to a boil over moderately high heat. Simmer until slightly thickened. Reduce the heat to low and add the chestnuts. Simmer for 5 minutes. Add any accumulated juices from the capons. Season with the remaining 1/4 teaspoon salt and the pepper. Remove the string from the capons. Carve the birds and serve them with the dressing and sauce.

—JACQUES PEPIN

PEELING CHESTNUTS

When it comes to peeling, cool chestnuts put up a stronger fight than warm ones. You might want to bake the nuts in batches so that you're sure to get them while they're hot. For this recipe, you needn't worry about wresting them from their shells whole, since they're broken up in the sauce anyway.

DUCK WITH SWEET-AND-SOUR SAUCE

We suggest shiitakes because they're available in most supermarkets, but you can substitute virtually any wild mushroom—or even white mushrooms.

WINE RECOMMENDATION
The complex flavors here are best suited to a white with plenty of acidity and some sweetness (to complement the cider), plus lots of body. Try a gewürztraminer or pinot gris, both from Alsace in France.

SERVES 2

1 4½- to 5-pound duck, at room temperature, excess fat removed
  Salt and fresh-ground black pepper
1 onion, quartered
2 ribs celery, chopped
1 bay leaf
½ pound sliced bacon, cut crosswise into 1-inch pieces
½ pound shiitake mushrooms, stems removed, caps chopped coarse
2 cups apple cider
1 tablespoon flour
2 tablespoons Cognac or other brandy
2 tablespoons red-wine vinegar
½ teaspoon dried thyme

1. Heat the oven to 400°. Season the duck inside and out with ½ teaspoon salt and ½ teaspoon pepper. Twist the wings behind and tie the legs together. Prick all over at 1-inch intervals and put, breast-side down, in a roasting pan just large enough to hold it. Arrange the onion, celery, and bay leaf around.

2. Roast the duck for 15 minutes. Turn breast-side up; prick again. Roast, turning every 15 minutes, until browned and the juices run clear when the thigh is pricked with a fork, 45 to 55 minutes longer.

3. Meanwhile, in a large frying pan, cook the bacon until crisp. Transfer to paper towels to drain. Pour off all but 2 tablespoons of the fat from the pan. Add the mushrooms and cook, stirring, until the liquid evaporates, about 10 minutes. Add ½ cup of the cider. Bring to a boil. Cook until reduced to ¼ cup, about 4 minutes. Whisk in the flour. Remove from the heat and set aside.

4. When the duck is cooked, remove it from the pan and let it rest in a warm spot for about 15 minutes. With poultry shears, cut the duck lengthwise in half.

5. Discard the fat and vegetables from the roasting pan. Pour the remaining 1½ cups cider into the pan. Bring to a boil over moderately high heat, scraping the bottom of the pan. Pour into the frying pan. Add the cognac, vinegar, and thyme. Bring to a boil over moderate heat. Cook, stirring frequently, until slightly thickened, about 10 minutes. Stir in the bacon. Season with salt and pepper to taste. Remove the string from the duck. Serve the bird with the sauce.

—LINDA MERINOFF

ROAST DUCK
WITH PORT-SOAKED PRUNES

The deep black-purple prunes and golden-brown caramelized onions add an autumnal feel to this dish. Serve it with roasted potatoes and sautéed Swiss chard.

WINE RECOMMENDATION

Pinot noir is a natural with roast duck, and the prunes make the varietal an even more compelling choice. Try a bottle from Oregon or look for a red Burgundy (made from pinot noir) from the Côte de Beaune in France.

SERVES 4

- 4 cloves garlic, minced
- 1¼ teaspoons cinnamon
- 1 tablespoon plus 1 teaspoon lemon juice
- 2 4½- to 5-pound ducks, at room temperature, excess fat removed
- ¾ teaspoon salt
- ¾ teaspoon fresh-ground black pepper
- 24 pitted prunes (about ½ pound)
- 2¼ cups port
- 1 pint pearl onions
- 2 tablespoons butter
- 1 teaspoon sugar
- 1 cup Chicken Stock, page 57, or canned low-sodium chicken broth
- 3 tablespoons orange juice
- 1 teaspoon grated orange zest

1. Heat the oven to 500°. In a small bowl, combine the garlic, 1 teaspoon of the cinnamon, and the lemon juice. Crush the mixture with the back of a spoon to make a rough paste. Rub the insides of the ducks with the paste and season the outsides of the birds with ¼ teaspoon of the salt and ¼ teaspoon of the pepper.

2. Twist the wings behind each bird and tie the legs together. Put the ducks, breast-side up, on a rack in a large roasting pan and roast until the skin is browned and the juices run clear when the thigh is pierced with a fork, about 1 hour. Remove and let rest in a warm spot for about 15 minutes.

3. Meanwhile, in a small stainless-steel saucepan, combine the prunes with 1 cup of the port. Bring to a simmer over moderately high heat. Remove from the heat, cover, and let the prunes soak for at least 30 minutes.

4. Make a cross in the root end of each of the pearl onions. In a medium saucepan of boiling, salted water, cook the onions until tender, 5 to 7 minutes. Drain the onions and, when they are cool enough to handle, peel them.

5. In a small frying pan, melt the butter over high heat. Add the onions and sprinkle with the sugar. Cook, shaking the pan

constantly, until the onions are cara-melized, about 3 minutes. Set aside.

6. In a medium stainless-steel saucepan, combine the remaining 1¼ cups port and the stock. Bring to a boil over high heat. Boil until the liquid is reduced to 1 cup, about 10 minutes.

7. Add the orange juice, orange zest, the remaining ¼ teaspoon cinnamon, the prunes with their liquid, and the onions. Season with the remaining ½ teaspoon salt and ½ teaspoon pepper. Cook until hot, about 3 minutes.

8. Remove the strings from the ducks. Cut the breast meat from the birds and slice each breast in half. Remove the legs and separate the drumsticks and thighs. Spoon the prunes, onions, and sauce on top.

—JOYCE GOLDSTEIN

ROAST CRANBERRY-GLAZED DUCKS WITH CRANBERRY GRAVY

Cranberries cook just until they pop; half are pureed and reduced to a shiny glaze and the rest are added to the savory gravy. Just a hint of honey sweetens the tart fruit.

WINE RECOMMENDATION
With their tanginess, cranberries do well with a fruity, acidic red wine, and duck is always delicious with a pinot noir. Try a bottle from Oregon or California.

SERVES 4

2   4½- to 5-pound ducks with neck and giblets, at room temperature, excess fat removed
    Salt and fresh-ground black pepper

2   small sprigs fresh rosemary, or ½ teaspoon dried, crumbled

1   rib celery, diced

1   onion, diced

1   tart apple, such as Granny Smith, peeled, cored, and diced

2   cups water

6   tablespoons light honey

1½ cups fresh or frozen cranberries

1½ cups Savory Duck Stock, opposite page

2   teaspoons red currant jelly

2   teaspoons lemon juice

1½ tablespoons butter, at room temperature

1.   Heat the oven to 450°. Reserve the neck and giblets for the stock. Season the ducks inside and out with 1 teaspoon salt, ¼ teaspoon pepper, and the dried rosemary, if using. If using fresh rosemary, stick a sprig into the cavity of each duck.

2.   In a medium bowl, toss together the celery, onion, and apple. Put the mixture in the cavities of the ducks. Twist the wings behind each bird and tie the legs together.

3.   With a fork, prick each duck well all over and set, breast-side down, on a rack in a large shallow roasting pan. Roast the ducks for 20 minutes. Lower the oven temperature to 350°. Prick the ducks again, turn onto one side, and roast for another 20 minutes. With a bulb baster or large spoon, remove the fat from the roasting pan as it accumulates. Once again, prick the ducks well, turn breast-side up, and roast, pricking lightly about every 20 minutes and removing the fat as it collects, until the juices run clear when the thigh is pricked with a fork, about 1 hour.

4.   Meanwhile, in a heavy, medium saucepan, bring 1½ cups of the water and the honey to a boil over moderate heat. Add the cranberries and boil until the skins pop, about 5 minutes.

5. With a slotted spoon, remove half of the cranberries and set them aside. In a blender or food processor, puree the remaining cranberry mixture. Return the puree to the saucepan. Boil until reduced to about 1½ cups. (The mixture should be glistening and about the consistency of corn syrup.) Remove the glaze from the heat and cover to keep warm.

6. When the ducks are done, remove them from the oven but leave the oven on. Pour the pan juices into a bowl and skim off the fat.

7. With a pastry brush, generously paint each duck with some of the cranberry glaze. Return to the oven and roast for 10 minutes. Remove the ducks from the oven and brush generously with the glaze. Set the remaining glaze aside. Transfer the ducks to a large carving board and leave to rest in a warm spot for about 15 minutes.

8. Set the roasting pan over moderate heat, add the remaining ½ cup water and bring to a boil, scraping the bottom of the pan to dislodge any brown bits. Strain into the saucepan of cranberry glaze and add the stock. Bring to a boil over high heat, whisking frequently. Boil until reduced by one-third, 15 to 20 minutes. Whisk in the currant jelly, lemon juice, and butter. Stir in the reserved cranberries. Season with salt and pepper to taste. Remove the strings from the ducks. Carve the birds and serve with the sauce.

—JEAN ANDERSON

SAVORY DUCK STOCK

MAKES ABOUT 3 CUPS

Necks from 2 ducks, plus gizzards (optional)

1½ cups Beef Stock, page 101, or canned low-sodium chicken broth

1½ cups Chicken Stock, page 57, or canned low-sodium chicken broth

1½ cups water

1 large carrot, quartered

1 large rib celery, quartered

1 large onion, quartered

8 parsley stems

1 sprig sage, or ¼ teaspoon dried

1 sprig thyme, or ¼ teaspoon dried

1 1-inch strip orange zest

8 peppercorns

1. Put all the ingredients in a large pot. Bring to a boil and skim the foam that rises to the surface. Reduce the heat and simmer, partially covered, for 2 hours.

2. Strain. Press the bones and vegetables firmly to get all the liquid. Measure out 1½ cups of stock for the Cranberry Gravy; freeze the rest.

chapter 5
ROASTED MEATS

Pork Loin with Wild-Mushroom Sage Stuffing, page 91

PORK LOIN WITH WILD-MUSHROOM SAGE STUFFING

Since pork is much leaner these days, it should be cooked for a shorter time than old-fashioned pork, or it will be dry. Remember, too, that the internal temperature will rise five to ten degrees as the meat sits after it's removed from the oven. The loin is pictured here with Fragrant Barley, page 149.

WINE RECOMMENDATION
A rustic Italian red wine will work well with the sage and mushrooms here. Try a Chianti Classico or splurge on a Barbaresco.

SERVES 10

- 4 tablespoons olive oil
- 4 large shallots, chopped
- 9 large cloves garlic, eight chopped and one cut in half
- 2 teaspoons dried thyme
- 2 pounds wild mushrooms, such as shiitakes and chanterelles, stems removed, caps cut into $\frac{1}{2}$-inch pieces
- $\frac{1}{2}$ cup coarse-chopped fresh sage, plus 2 tablespoons fine-chopped sage
- 3 tablespoons butter
  Salt and fresh-ground black pepper
- 1 to $1\frac{1}{2}$ tablespoons grated lemon zest
- 2 $2\frac{1}{2}$-pound boneless center-cut pork loins, with a pocket for stuffing cut in one end and going almost to the other end of each loin
- $\frac{1}{2}$ cup Calvados, applejack, or other apple brandy
- $1\frac{1}{2}$ cups Chicken Stock, page 57, or canned low-sodium chicken broth
- 1 teaspoon red-currant jelly

1. In a large nonstick frying pan, heat 2 tablespoons of the oil over moderately low heat. Add the shallots, the chopped garlic, and $1\frac{1}{4}$ teaspoons of the thyme. Cook, stirring, until the shallots are slightly softened, about 3 minutes. Increase the heat to moderately high and stir in the mushrooms. Cover and cook until the mushrooms soften, about 5 minutes longer.

2. Add the $\frac{1}{2}$ cup coarse-chopped sage, 2 tablespoons of the butter, $1\frac{1}{2}$ teaspoons pepper, and the lemon zest. Cook, stirring, until the mushrooms give off some of their liquid, about 5 minutes. Season with salt and additional pepper to taste. Transfer the stuffing to a large bowl and let cool to room temperature.

3. Heat the oven to 350°. Rub the surface of the pork loins with the cut garlic clove. Reserve the garlic clove. Fill the pocket in each pork loin with half of the stuffing, pushing the stuffing through with the handle of a wooden spoon if necessary. Tie each loin in four places.

4. In a large, heavy frying pan, melt the remaining 1 tablespoon butter with the

remaining 2 tablespoons oil over moderately high heat. Add the reserved garlic-clove halves and cook for 1 minute. Discard the garlic. Add one of the stuffed pork loins to the pan and cook, turning, until well browned all over, about 8 minutes. Transfer the loin to a large roasting pan. Repeat with the second loin.

5. Increase the heat to high. Add the Calvados to the frying pan and boil until slightly thickened, about 3 minutes. Stir in the stock, jelly, the fine-chopped sage, the remaining ¾ teaspoon thyme, and ½ teaspoon pepper. Pour this liquid over the meat.

6. Roast the loins until an instant-read thermometer stuck into one of the loins registers 150°, about 50 minutes. Transfer the loins to a carving board and leave to rest in a warm spot for about 15 minutes.

7. Pour the pan juices into a bowl and skim off the fat. Carve the loins into ½-inch slices and pass the sauce separately.

—SHEILA LUKINS

MAKE IT AHEAD You can make the stuffing a couple of days ahead, and prepare the pork loins through Step 3 several hours before roasting.

BAKED FRESH HAM WITH COFFEE GLAZE AND TURNIPS

Instant coffee fortifies fresh-brewed in this unique glaze without diluting it with too much liquid. At the restaurant Gordon in Chicago, the ham and turnips are served atop steamed turnip greens, kale, or spinach.

WINE RECOMMENDATION
What wine goes with coffee? Or pineapple juice? Or turnips and chile peppers? Use this dish as an excuse for discovering how incredibly versatile a kabinett riesling from Germany can be.

SERVES 12

1   7½- to 8-pound small bone-in shank end of fresh ham

2   quarts strong brewed coffee

1   quart pineapple juice

1   cup dry white wine

½   cup cooking oil

2   Spanish onions, chopped

1   head garlic, peeled and chopped

4   plum tomatoes, chopped

3   small dried red chile peppers, with seeds, chopped

¼   cup wine vinegar

2   teaspoons ground cumin

¼   cup instant espresso powder or ¾ cup instant coffee granules

1   cup Chicken Stock, page 57, or canned low-sodium chicken broth

1   tablespoon coarse salt

1   tablespoon fresh-ground black pepper

4   tablespoons butter

3   pounds turnips, peeled and cut into thin slices

1. With a sharp knife, trim away the heavy skin and fat from the ham. Put the ham in a large stainless-steel pot. Add the brewed coffee, the pineapple juice, and the wine. Cover and marinate in the refrigerator for 2 days, turning the ham two or three times each day. Remove the ham from the refrigerator about 2 hours before baking.

2. Heat the oven to 300°. In a large, heavy frying pan, heat the oil over moderately low heat. Add the onions and garlic and cook, stirring occasionally, until soft but not brown, about 10 minutes.

3. Stir in the tomatoes and chiles and sauté for 2 minutes longer. Add the vinegar, cumin, instant espresso powder, and stock. Boil until the mixture is reduced to about ½ cup, about 5 minutes. Remove from the heat and stir in 1 cup of the ham marinade. Put the mixture in a food processor or blender and puree until smooth.

4. Remove the ham from the remaining marinade and discard the marinade. Season

the ham with the salt and pepper and put it, meatier-side down, on a rack in a large roasting pan. Brush the ham with some of the puree, lightly covering the top and the sides. Reserve the remaining puree.

5. Bake the ham for 3½ hours, basting with the reserved puree every 30 minutes and turning once. Transfer the ham to a carving board and leave to rest in a warm spot for about 15 minutes.

6. Meanwhile, in a large, heavy frying pan, melt the butter over moderately high heat. Add the turnips and sauté, turning frequently, until golden and tender, 10 to 12 minutes. Carve the ham into slices. Arrange the carved ham and the turnip slices on a large platter and serve.

—GORDON, CHICAGO

MAKE IT AHEAD
The ham marinates for 2 days, so right there you have a head start. On the second day of marinating, you can make the glaze. That way, most of the work is done ahead, and all you have to do on the day you serve is bake the ham. You'll need to remove the ham from the marinade about 6 hours before you plan to serve it, let it sit at room temperature for 2 hours, and then bake for 3½ hours.

ROAST FRESH HAM WITH RIESLING, DILL, AND MUSTARD SAUCE

The ham bakes on a bed of leeks and dill, which infuses the meat with flavor during the long roasting. We finish the creamy sauce with chopped fresh dill, but you might choose a different herb for both the leeks and the sauce, such as sage or marjoram.

WINE RECOMMENDATION
Riesling—particularly an Alsatian from France—is an obvious wine pairing, due to its full flavor and acidity. Because of the dill, a sauvignon-blanc-based Sancerre from France (which has a different taste but the same qualities) might be even better.

SERVES 12

- 7 leeks, white and light-green parts only, washed well
- 2 tablespoons dried dill
- 1 7- to 8-pound bone-in shank end of fresh ham
- 3 cups riesling or other white wine
- 2 teaspoons salt
- 2 cups heavy cream
- 2½ tablespoons Dijon mustard
- ¼ cup finely chopped fresh dill

1. Heat the oven to 325°. Spread the leeks in a roasting pan, arranging them in an area no larger than the ham. (If exposed, they will burn.) Sprinkle with the dried dill. Put the ham on top, flat-side down. Roast for 1 hour. Turn the ham over and roast another hour. Turn again and roast one more hour.

2. Transfer the ham to a carving board. With a sharp knife, trim away the skin, leaving the layer of fat on the meat. Loosen the leeks with a spatula if they have stuck to the pan. Return the ham to the pan, flat-side down. Baste with 1 cup of the wine. Sprinkle with 1 teaspoon of the salt. Roast for 30 minutes.

3. Remove the ham from the oven. Increase the temperature to 350°. Score the ham fat with crisscross lines to form a diamond pattern. Be careful not to cut into the meat. Baste with the pan juices. Pour another cup of wine over the ham. Sprinkle with the remaining teaspoon salt. Return to the oven.

4. Continue to roast, basting every 10 minutes with pan juices, until an instant-read thermometer stuck into the thickest part registers 170°. Transfer to a carving board. Let rest in a warm spot about 15 minutes.

5. In a stainless-steel frying pan, boil the remaining 1 cup wine and the cream until they are reduced to 1½ cups, about 8 minutes. Whisk in the mustard and the fresh dill. Carve the ham and serve the sauce alongside.

CRUSTY BAKED HAM

An apple-cider-marinated ham is coated with Dijon mustard and rolled in bread crumbs, which crisp during baking. The marinade is cooked down and flavored with mustard and vinegar for an easy sweet-and-sour sauce.

WINE RECOMMENDATION
The strong, full flavor and refreshing acidity of riesling are ideal with ham in general and with the sweet apple flavors of this ham in particular. Try a bottle from the Alsace region in France.

SERVES 10

- 1   5-pound boneless smoked ham
- 1   quart apple cider
- 1/2   cup Calvados, applejack, or other apple brandy
- 4   tablespoons Dijon mustard
- 2   cups fresh bread crumbs
- 1/2   cup light-brown sugar
- 2   teaspoons apple-cider vinegar

1. Put the ham in a deep stainless-steel pot or casserole a bit wider than the ham. Pour in the cider and Calvados. Cover and refrigerate for 8 hours or overnight, turning the ham occasionally. Remove the ham from the refrigerator about 2 hours before baking to allow it to come to room temperature.

2. Heat the oven to 350°. Remove the ham from the marinade and pat dry with paper towels. Reserve the marinade. Coat the ham with 3 tablespoons of the mustard. On a long sheet of waxed paper, mix together the bread crumbs and the brown sugar. Roll the mustard-covered ham in this crumb mixture to coat.

3. Put the ham in a roasting pan and bake until golden brown and heated through, about 1 hour. Transfer to a carving board and leave to rest in a warm spot for about 15 minutes before slicing.

4. Meanwhile, in a small saucepan, bring the marinade to a boil over high heat. Continue boiling until the liquid is reduced to 1/2 cup, about 15 minutes. Whisk in the remaining 1 tablespoon mustard and the vinegar. Serve a small amount of the sauce with each serving of ham.

BAKED HAM WITH MUSTARD AND APPLE-JELLY GLAZE

Smoked hams are generally fully cooked. Bake this one for about ten minutes a pound just to heat the ham thoroughly and to set the glaze.

WINE RECOMMENDATION
The combination of ham and the tart sweetness of the glaze are delightful with the combination of sweet fruit and acidity that a kabinett riesling from Germany can deliver. Try a bottle from the Mosel-Saar-Ruwer region.

SERVES 20

1   10-ounce jar apple jelly

¼   cup Dijon mustard

1   14-pound partially boned smoked ham

1. In a small stainless-steel saucepan, combine the apple jelly and the Dijon mustard. Bring to a boil over moderate heat, stirring constantly. Cook until the mixture is slightly reduced, about 2 minutes. Set aside half of this glaze to serve with the ham as a condiment.

2. Heat the oven to 325°. With a sharp knife, trim away any excess fat from the ham, leaving a thin layer. For decoration, score the fat with long shallow cuts at ¼-inch intervals. Set the ham, fat-side up, on a rack in a large roasting pan and bake for 1½ hours. (If you don't have a rack, put the ham directly in the roasting pan and add 1½ cups of water.)

3. Remove the ham from the oven and brush all over with the glaze. Bake for 15 minutes and brush the ham again with the glaze. Continue to bake the ham until it is heated through to the bone and the glaze is set, about 30 minutes longer.

4. Transfer the ham to a carving board and leave to rest in a warm spot for about 15 minutes. Slice the ham and pass the reserved glaze separately.

MAKE IT AHEAD
The glaze can be made a day ahead. Let it cool. Cover and refrigerate.

CIDER-GLAZED HAM WITH SWEET-AND-SOUR GRAPE SAUCE

Baking in apple cider gives this ham real apple flavor, and the addition of unsweetened applesauce to the gravy mirrors the flavor of the meat.

WINE RECOMMENDATION
A gewürztraminer will be great with the sweet and sour flavors here. Try a version from Alsace in France, which offers more acidity than West Coast bottlings.

SERVES 18

- 1   12-pound bone-in smoked ham
- 2   large cloves garlic, cut into thin slivers
- 4   cups apple cider or apple juice
- ½   cup golden raisins
- ½   cup dry sherry
- 3   cups seedless green grapes
- 2   teaspoons Dijon mustard
- 3   tablespoons brown sugar
- 2   tablespoons sherry vinegar or other wine vinegar
- ½   cup unsweetened applesauce
- 1   teaspoon arrowroot
- ½   cup Chicken Stock, page 57, or canned low-sodium chicken broth

1. Heat the oven to 325°. Put the ham, fat-side up, on a rack in a roasting pan. Score the fat with crisscross lines to form a diamond pattern. With the tip of a small knife, make a slit about ½ inch deep in the center of each diamond. Insert a garlic sliver in each. Bake in the lower third of the oven for 45 minutes.

2. Pour 2 cups of the cider over the ham; bake 15 minutes. Baste with some of the pan juices and bake another 15 minutes. Pour the remaining 2 cups cider over the ham and continue baking, basting every 10 minutes, until heated through to the bone, about 45 minutes more. Transfer to a carving board. Leave to rest in a warm spot for about 15 minutes.

3. Meanwhile, in a medium saucepan, combine the raisins and the sherry. Bring to a boil over moderate heat. Reduce the heat and simmer until almost evaporated.

4. In a food processor, puree 2 cups of the grapes. They will be quite watery. Add the puree to the raisins. Add the mustard, brown sugar, vinegar, and applesauce. Bring to a boil over moderate heat, stirring occasionally.

5. In a small bowl, stir together the arrowroot and the stock. Stir into the simmering sauce. Cook over moderate heat, stirring constantly, until thickened, about 2 minutes. Using your fingers or a small knife, peel or halve the remaining 1 cup grapes. Add them to the sauce. Serve the ham hot or at room temperature. Serve the sauce warm or hot over the ham.

ORANGE AND BOURBON GLAZED COUNTRY HAM

Because country ham is so salty, we suggest soaking it for about two days before cooking. Though the soaking and baking time is quite long, very little attention is required.

WINE RECOMMENDATION The variety of flavors in this dish (saltiness, sweetness, bitterness, and all those cloves) makes your best choice a fruity and exuberant red wine. Open a bottle of slightly chilled Beaujolais-Villages from France.

SERVES 25 TO 30

1 14-pound bone-in country-style cured ham
1 quart apple cider or apple juice
30 whole cloves
3 bay leaves
1 quart water
1 cup bourbon
1 cup bitter-orange marmalade
¼ cup Dijon mustard

1. Wash the ham under tepid running water, using a brush to scrub away any surface mold or dust. Place the ham in a large pot and cover with cold water. Set aside in a cool place (do not refrigerate); let soak, changing the water at least twice, for about 48 hours.

2. Remove the ham from the pot. Discard the soaking water. Put the ham in a large stockpot. Add the cider, twelve of the cloves, the bay leaves, and the water. Set over moderate heat and bring to a boil. Cover, reduce the heat to moderately low, and simmer until the shank bone is loose enough to move in its socket, 3 to 4 hours, or about 15 minutes per pound. Remove the ham and drain. When the ham is cool enough to handle, use a large, sharp knife to remove the skin and enough fat so that only a ½-inch layer remains. Score the fat with crisscross lines to form a diamond pattern.

3. Heat the oven to 400°. In a small saucepan, combine the bourbon, marmalade, and mustard. Bring to a boil over moderate heat, stirring occasionally, about 5 minutes.

4. Stick a clove in each intersection of the diamond pattern. Using a small brush, coat the ham evenly with the glaze. Put the ham in a large roasting pan. Bake in the lower third of the oven until nicely browned, 20 to 30 minutes.

5. Transfer the ham to a carving board and leave to rest in a warm spot for about 15 minutes. Carve into thin slices and serve warm or at room temperature.

—NANCY HARMON JENKINS

ROAST BEEF WITH PAN GRAVY

The miniature Yorkshire puddings here make a terrific traditional addition to roast beef. Be sure to reserve the rendered fat from the roast to use in the pudding recipe.

WINE RECOMMENDATION
The simpler the dish, the more reason to serve a complex wine. Break out your best bottle of Bordeaux or a prized California cabernet sauvignon or merlot for this one.

SERVES 8

1	4- to 4½-pound eye of round, including a thin layer of fat, rolled and tied
	Fresh-ground black pepper
¼	pound beef suet
3	tablespoons flour
2	tablespoons Madeira or port (optional)
2	cups Beef Stock, opposite page, or canned low-sodium beef broth
	Salt
	Individual Yorkshire Puddings, opposite page

1. Heat the oven to 350°. Heat a heavy roasting pan over moderate heat until very hot. Season the meat with ½ teaspoon pepper and put it, fat-side down, in the hot pan. Increase the heat to high and cook the roast, turning without piercing the meat, until browned all over, about 8 minutes.

2. Add the piece of suet to the pan, turn the roast fat-side up, and put the pan in the center of the oven. Roast for 20 minutes.

Remove the pan from the oven. Tilt the pan, draw off the rendered fat with a bulb baster, and reserve. Return the pan to the oven and roast until the meat is done, about 40 minutes longer for rare (120°).

3. Transfer the roast to a carving board; leave to rest in a warm spot for about 15 minutes. Discard the piece of suet in the roasting pan. Pour off the rendered fat in the pan, adding it to the fat already collected.

4. Put the roasting pan over moderately low heat. Add 3 tablespoons of the reserved rendered beef fat to the pan. (Reserve the remaining rendered fat for use in the Individual Yorkshire Puddings.) Sprinkle in the flour and cook, stirring constantly, over moderately low heat, until lightly browned, 2 to 3 minutes.

5. Whisk in the Madeira, if using, and the stock. Bring to a boil. Reduce the heat and simmer, stirring occasionally, until the gravy thickens, about 3 minutes. Add any accumulated meat juices. Season the sauce with salt and pepper to taste, and strain. Carve the roast into thin slices and serve with the gravy and the Yorkshire puddings.

Individual Yorkshire Puddings

The batter in this recipe can be baked in a nine-inch square pan rather than in muffin cups. Bake 35 to 40 minutes.

MAKES 12 INDIVIDUAL PUDDINGS

- ¾ cup flour
- ½ teaspoon salt
- 2 large eggs, beaten to mix
- ¾ cup plus 2 tablespoons milk
- ¼ cup rendered beef fat, reserved from the roast, or melted butter

1. Put the flour and salt in a medium bowl. Add the eggs and pour in half the milk. Beat well with a wooden spoon until fairly smooth.

2. Add the remaining milk and beat for 2 minutes. The batter need not be perfectly smooth. Cover and set aside for 30 minutes to 1 hour.

3. Heat the oven to 400°. Spoon 1 teaspoon of the rendered beef fat into each of twelve 3-inch muffin cups. Put the muffin tin in the oven and heat until the fat begins to smoke, about 3 minutes.

4. Stir the batter, then ladle about ¼ cup into each muffin cup to fill halfway. Promptly return to the top third of the oven and bake until the puddings are puffed, golden brown, and crisp, 20 to 25 minutes. Serve warm.

Beef Stock

MAKES 1 QUART

- 2 pounds beef bones, cut into pieces
- 1 onion, quartered
- 2 carrots, quartered
- 2 ribs celery, quartered
- 2½ quarts water
- 1 14-ounce can tomatoes, drained
- 8 parsley stems
- ¾ teaspoon dried thyme
- 1 bay leaf
- 4 peppercorns

1. Heat the oven to 450°. Put the bones in a large roasting pan. Brown in the oven for 40 minutes, stirring once or twice. Add the onion, carrots, and celery. Continue cooking until well browned, about 20 minutes longer.

2. Put the bones and vegetables in a large pot. Pour off the fat in the roasting pan. Add 1 cup of the water. Bring to a boil, scraping the bottom of the pan to dislodge any brown bits. Add to the pot with the rest of the water and the remaining ingredients. Bring to a boil and skim the foam that rises to the surface. Reduce the heat and simmer the stock, partially covered, for 4 hours.

3. Strain. Skim the fat if using at once. If not, refrigerate for up to a week or freeze. Scrape off the fat before using.

chapter 6
STUFFINGS

Ten-Thousand-Lakes Wild-Rice, Mushroom, and Carrot Dressing, page 121

SOUTHWEST CORN DRESSING

Spicy and full of flavor, this distinctive dressing has a surprise ingredient: sharp cheddar cheese.

MAKES ABOUT 15 CUPS

6	slices bacon, cut crosswise into thin strips
1	large onion, chopped
1	red bell pepper, chopped
4	tablespoons butter, melted
4	cups fresh (cut from about 6 ears) or frozen corn kernels
½	cup pine nuts
	Old-Fashioned Corn Bread, page 127, crumbled
6	ounces sharp cheddar cheese, grated (about 2 cups)
1	4-ounce can green chiles, drained and chopped
⅓	cup chopped cilantro
1½	tablespoons poultry seasoning
1½	teaspoons dried sage
1½	teaspoons chili powder
1	teaspoon dried oregano
¾	teaspoon ground cumin
¾	teaspoon salt
¼	teaspoon fresh-ground black pepper
1½	cups Chicken Stock, page 57, or canned low-sodium chicken broth

1. Heat the oven to 350°. Butter a deep 4-quart baking dish and a large square of aluminum foil. In a medium frying pan, cook the strips of bacon until they are crisp.

With a slotted spoon, transfer the bacon to a very large bowl.

2. Add the onion and bell pepper to the pan and cook over moderate heat, stirring frequently, until the onion is soft and golden, about 10 minutes. Using a slotted spoon, transfer the onion mixture to the large bowl. Add 2 tablespoons of the melted butter to the pan and reduce the heat to low. Add the corn and cook, stirring often, until tender, about 5 minutes. Add the corn to the bowl.

3. In a small frying pan, toast the pine nuts over moderately low heat, stirring frequently, until golden brown, about 4 minutes. Alternatively, toast them in a 350° oven for about 6 minutes. Add to the bowl.

4. Add the crumbled corn bread, cheddar cheese, chiles, cilantro, poultry seasoning, sage, chili powder, oregano, cumin, salt, and black pepper to the bowl and toss. Stir in the remaining 2 tablespoons melted butter and 1 cup of the stock.

5. Spoon the dressing into the prepared baking dish and drizzle the remaining ½ cup stock evenly over all. Cover with the buttered foil and bake in the middle of the oven until hot, 40 to 45 minutes.

—JEAN ANDERSON

LEMON CORN-BREAD STUFFING

Filling a Thanksgiving turkey with homemade corn bread is a tried-and-true tradition. The lemon juice and zest here give the stuffing an unusually refreshing flavor that carries over to the whole bird.

MAKES ABOUT 10 CUPS

Old-Fashioned Corn Bread, page 127

¼ cup olive oil

¼ pound butter

2 onions, chopped

6 ribs celery, chopped

2 large cloves garlic, minced

1 cup chopped fresh parsley

1 tablespoon grated lemon zest

½ cup lemon juice (from about 2 lemons)

1 tablespoon salt

1 teaspoon fresh-ground black pepper

4 eggs, beaten to mix

½ cup Chicken or Turkey Stock, page 57 or 50, or canned low-sodium chicken broth

1. Heat the oven to 350°. Cut the corn bread into cubes. Put the cubes on a baking sheet and bake until golden brown and crisp, about 40 minutes.

2. In a large frying pan, heat the oil and butter over moderately low heat. Add the onions and celery and cook, stirring occasionally, until the onions are translucent, about 5 minutes. Add the garlic and cook for 2 minutes more. Stir in the corn-bread croutons and cook, stirring, until heated through, about 3 minutes. Remove the pan from the heat and stir in the parsley, lemon zest, lemon juice, salt, and pepper.

3. In a medium bowl, whisk the eggs with the stock until blended. Add to the stuffing and toss.

CORN-BREAD SAUSAGE STUFFING

Sausage, corn bread, and sage are classic holiday-stuffing ingredients. Here's a variation on that combination that adds lots of onions and includes only a modicum of sage.

MAKES ABOUT 12 CUPS

1	pound pork sausage
	Old-Fashioned Corn Bread, page 127, crumbled
4	onions, chopped
4	ribs celery, chopped
1¼	teaspoons dried thyme
½	teaspoon dried sage
½	teaspoon baking powder
1¾	teaspoons salt
1¼	teaspoons fresh-ground black pepper
2	eggs, beaten to mix
½	cup Chicken Stock, page 57, canned low-sodium chicken broth, or water

1. Form the sausage into patties. Heat a heavy frying pan over moderate heat. Add the sausage patties and cook, turning, until light brown, about 5 minutes. Remove the sausage with a slotted spoon and let cool. Break the sausage into small pieces and put into a large bowl along with the crumbled corn bread.

2. In a medium saucepan, combine the onions, celery, and enough cold water to cover. Bring to a boil over high heat and cook the vegetables for 3 minutes. Drain well and add to the corn bread and sausage.

3. Sprinkle the thyme, sage, baking powder, salt, and pepper over the stuffing. Add the eggs and the stock and toss to combine.

—CAMILLE GLENN

Blue-Corn-Bread and Chorizo Stuffing

Here Southwestern flavors—blue corn, chorizo, chiles, and chayote—dominate an unusual stuffing.

MAKES ABOUT 6 CUPS

5	tablespoons butter
1	pound chorizo sausage, casing removed and sausage chopped
1	small onion, chopped
¼	cup diced celery
¼	cup diced carrot
3	serrano chiles or 2 jalapeños, seeds and ribs removed, minced
6	cloves garlic, minced
¼	cup peeled and diced chayote (optional)
¼	cup bourbon
1	teaspoon chopped fresh thyme, or ¼ teaspoon dried
1	teaspoon chopped fresh sage, or ¼ teaspoon dried
2	teaspoons chopped cilantro
	Serrano-Chile Blue-Corn Bread, opposite page, crumbled
1	teaspoon salt
¼	cup Turkey Stock, page 50, or canned low-sodium chicken broth
	Fresh-ground black pepper

1. In a large frying pan, melt 1 tablespoon of the butter over moderately high heat. Add the chorizo and cook, stirring occasionally, until lightly browned, about 5 minutes. Remove the chorizo and wipe out the frying pan.

2. In the same pan, melt the remaining 4 tablespoons butter over moderate heat. Add the onion, celery, carrot, chiles, garlic, and chayote. Cook, stirring frequently, until the vegetables soften, about 8 minutes. Add the bourbon and cook until the liquid reduces to approximately 2 tablespoons, about 5 minutes.

3. Remove from the heat and stir in the thyme, sage, cilantro, chorizo, crumbled corn bread, and salt. Add the stock and toss. Season with pepper to taste.

—Stephan Pyles

MAKE IT AHEAD
The time to stuff your bird is right before it goes into the oven. Stuffing it in advance is risky because that gives bacteria time to reproduce. You can, however, prepare the bird and the stuffing in advance and refrigerate them separately. Stuff the bird while the oven is heating.

SERRANO-CHILE BLUE-CORN BREAD

**MAKES ABOUT 5 CUPS
CRUMBLED BREAD**

2 teaspoons cooking oil

3 serrano chiles or 2 jalapeños, seeds and ribs removed, minced

1 red bell pepper, cut into ¼-inch dice

1 green bell pepper, cut into ¼-inch dice

3 cloves garlic, minced

1 cup flour

1¼ cups blue cornmeal*

2 tablespoons sugar

1 tablespoon baking powder

1 teaspoon salt

6 tablespoons butter, melted and cooled

6 tablespoons vegetable shortening, melted and cooled

1 cup buttermilk, at room temperature
Pinch baking soda

2 large eggs, at room temperature, beaten to mix

3 tablespoons chopped cilantro

*Available at Latin American markets

1. Heat the oven to 375°. Butter an 8 by 12-inch baking pan. In a small frying pan, heat the oil over moderate heat. Add the chiles, bell peppers, and garlic. Cook, stirring occasionally, until softened, about 5 minutes. Let cool.

2. In a large bowl, whisk together the flour, cornmeal, sugar, baking powder, and salt. In a medium bowl, stir together the butter and shortening. In another medium bowl, mix the buttermilk with the baking soda and then stir in the eggs. Pour both the shortening and the egg mixtures into the flour mixture and stir until just blended. Fold in the cooked vegetables and the cilantro.

3. Pour the corn-bread batter into the prepared pan. Bake until the top is golden and a toothpick stuck in the center comes out clean, about 50 minutes. Let cool on a rack. If using for stuffing, crumble onto a baking sheet and let stand overnight. Or dry the crumbled bread in a 350° oven for 10 minutes.

PECAN CORN-BREAD STUFFING

Give your guests a taste of Southern hospitality with a stuffing that starts with the Creole trilogy of celery, green pepper, and onion, and goes on to include the Dixie staples corn bread, pecans, and cayenne pepper.

MAKES ABOUT 8 CUPS

8	tablespoons butter
3	ribs celery, chopped
1	green bell pepper, chopped
1	onion, chopped
1	bunch scallions including green tops, chopped
¾	cup Turkey Stock, page 50, or canned low-sodium chicken broth
½	recipe Old-Fashioned Corn Bread, page 127, crumbled
1½	cups cubed white toast
2	hard-cooked eggs, grated coarse
2	eggs, beaten to mix
1	cup chopped pecans
¼	cup chopped fresh parsley
2	teaspoons salt
1	teaspoon fresh-ground black pepper
¼	teaspoon cayenne
¼	teaspoon dried thyme

1. In a large frying pan, melt 4 tablespoons of the butter over moderately low heat. Add the celery, bell pepper, onion, and scallions. Cook, stirring occasionally, until soft, about 8 minutes.

2. In a small saucepan, combine the remaining 4 tablespoons butter with the Turkey Stock. Heat the mixture just until the butter melts.

3. In a large bowl, toss together the corn bread and the white bread. Stir in the vegetable mixture, the hard-cooked and raw eggs, the stock mixture, the pecans, parsley, salt, black pepper, cayenne, and thyme.

—LEE BAILEY

SAUSAGE, FRUIT, AND NUT STUFFING

A change of pace from the usual holiday stuffing, this fruit-studded version brings a hint of sweetness to the table. It's delicious with goose as well as turkey.

MAKES ABOUT 12 CUPS

1 pound pork sausage

¼ pound butter

2 large onions, chopped

2 ribs celery, chopped

6 ounces mushrooms, sliced

½ cup chopped fresh parsley

1 cup chopped pecans

¾ teaspoon dried marjoram

¾ teaspoon dried rosemary, crumbled

¾ teaspoon dried thyme

   Salt

4 cups crumbled Old-Fashioned Corn Bread, page 127

2½ cups crumbled day-old white bread

5 tangerines, peeled, sectioned, and halved crosswise

½ pound fresh or frozen cranberries

½ pound fresh or frozen lingonberries

   Fresh-ground black pepper

1. In a large frying pan, cook the sausage over moderately high heat, stirring with a fork to break up the meat, until browned, about 5 minutes. Remove with a slotted spoon. Reduce the heat to moderately low.

2. Melt the butter in the pan over moderately low heat. Add the onions and celery and cook, stirring occasionally, until the onions are soft, about 8 minutes.

3. Add the mushrooms, parsley, pecans, marjoram, rosemary, thyme, and 1½ teaspoons salt to the pan. Cook, stirring, until the mushrooms start to brown, about 3 minutes.

4. In a large bowl, combine the sausage, corn bread, and white bread. Add the mushroom mixture, the tangerines, cranberries, and lingonberries, and toss. Season with salt and pepper to taste.

—MELANIE BARNARD

CHESAPEAKE OYSTER DRESSING

Fresh-shucked oysters smell faintly of the sea. Their brininess adds a delicious and distinctive flavor to this dressing.

MAKES ABOUT 12 CUPS

- 3 dozen shucked oysters, in their liquor
- ½ recipe Old-Fashioned Corn Bread, page 127, crumbled
- 4 cups coarsely crumbled saltines
- 4 ribs celery, chopped
- 1 onion, chopped
- ¼ cup chopped fresh parsley
- 1 tablespoon chopped fresh dill
- 2 teaspoons poultry seasoning
- ½ teaspoon grated lemon zest
  Salt and fresh-ground black pepper
- 6 ounces butter, melted
- 1 tablespoon lemon juice

1. Heat the oven to 350°. Butter a deep 3-quart baking dish and a large square of aluminum foil.

2. Remove the oysters from their liquor. Pour the liquor through a sieve lined with a paper towel into a measuring cup. Add enough water to measure 1 cup. Chop the oysters.

3. In a large bowl, toss the oysters with the corn bread, saltines, celery, onion, parsley, dill, poultry seasoning, lemon zest, ½ teaspoon salt, and 1 teaspoon pepper. Stir in the melted butter, lemon juice, and ½ cup of the oyster liquor. Season with additional salt and pepper to taste.

4. Spoon the dressing into the prepared baking dish and drizzle the remaining oyster liquor evenly on top. Cover with the buttered foil and bake in the middle of the oven until hot, about 40 minutes.

—JEAN ANDERSON

PECAN STUFFING

Luxurious with lots of pecan halves, this Southern stuffing is wonderful with turkey, chicken, or capon.

MAKES ABOUT 8 CUPS

½ pound butter

2 chicken livers

6 shallots or 2 small onions, minced (about 1½ cups)

8 ribs celery, chopped with the leaves (about 2 cups)

2 cloves garlic, minced

Salt and fresh-ground black pepper

Pinch cayenne

1 teaspoon dried rosemary, crumbled

2 tablespoons chopped fresh parsley

2 cups pecan halves

6 cups cubed good-quality white bread

1. In a small saucepan, melt ¼ pound of the butter over low heat. Set aside.

2. In a large frying pan, melt the remaining ¼ pound butter. Cook the chicken livers over moderately high heat until they are firm, about 2 minutes. Remove the chicken livers from the pan with a slotted spoon and chop them.

3. Reduce the heat to moderate. Add the minced shallots to the pan and cook, stirring, until soft, about 5 minutes. Add the celery and the garlic. Cook until the vegetables begin to soften, about 5 minutes longer.

4. Transfer the vegetable mixture to a large bowl. Add 2½ teaspoons salt, 1 teaspoon black pepper, the cayenne, rosemary, and parsley. Stir in the pecans, then toss with the cubed bread and the chopped chicken livers.

5. Add the melted butter. Season with additional salt and pepper to taste.

—PEARL BYRD FOSTER

Apricot Walnut Stuffing

Fruit-and-nut stuffings taste especially good with goose, but don't miss out on this one if you're serving a different bird. It's also good with turkey, duck, chicken, or capon.

MAKES ABOUT 6 CUPS

½ pound dried apricots or pitted prunes

½ cup raisins

1 cup port

1 lemon, cut into thin slices

4 tablespoons butter, melted

1 goose liver or liver from whatever bird you're stuffing

1 onion, chopped

1 tart apple, such as Granny Smith, cored and chopped

1 cup chopped walnuts

½ teaspoon ground mace

2 tablespoons lemon juice

½ cup minced celery, including leaves

2 cups cubed good-quality white or whole-wheat bread

Salt and fresh-ground black pepper

1. Soak the apricots and raisins in the port overnight.

2. In a large stainless-steel saucepan, combine the apricots, raisins, port, and lemon slices. Simmer until almost tender, about 5 minutes. Drain. (Reserve the liquid if you are making the Roast East Hampton Golden Goose, page 76.) Chop the drained fruit and transfer to a large bowl.

3. In a medium frying pan, heat 1 tablespoon of the butter and cook the liver until firm, about 2 minutes. Chop the liver and add it to the fruit.

4. Add 1 tablespoon of butter to the pan. Add the onion and cook over moderately low heat, stirring occasionally, until translucent, about 5 minutes. Transfer to the bowl along with the apple, walnuts, and mace. Toss with the remaining 2 tablespoons butter, the lemon juice, celery, and bread cubes. Season the stuffing with salt and pepper to taste.

—Pearl Byrd Foster

DATE AND NUT DRESSING

Pistachios add crunchiness and a nice touch of color to this dressing, while dates lend a sweetness and mellowness.

MAKES ABOUT 11 CUPS

- 8 cups cubed French bread
- 3 tablespoons olive oil
- 1 large onion, chopped
- 6 cloves garlic, minced
- 6 ribs celery, cut into ¼-inch dice
- 10 scallions including green tops, chopped
- ¾ cup water
- 1½ teaspoons dried sage
- 1½ teaspoons ground cumin
- ½ teaspoon fresh-ground black pepper
- ¼ teaspoon cayenne
- 1½ cups pitted dates, chopped
- 1 teaspoon salt
- ¾ cup fat rendered from the roasting bird, or melted butter
- 1 cup unsalted pistachios, shelled

1. Heat the oven to 400°. Spread the bread cubes on a baking sheet and bake until browned, about 10 minutes. Set aside.

2. In a large saucepan, heat the oil over moderately low heat. Add the onion and garlic and cook, stirring occasionally, until the onion is translucent, about 5 minutes. Add the celery, scallions, and water. Bring to a boil, cover, and cook for 5 minutes. Stir in the sage, cumin, black pepper, cayenne, dates, and salt. Cover and set aside.

3. Reheat the oven to 400°. Thirty minutes before serving, reheat the date mixture in the large saucepan over high heat. Remove from the heat and toss with the rendered fat, pistachios, and toasted bread cubes. Transfer the dressing to a large, shallow baking dish and put it in the preheated oven. Turn the oven off and leave the dressing until warm, 10 to 15 minutes.

—JACQUES PEPIN

MAKE IT AHEAD
The dressing can be prepared through Step 2 a day ahead. Don't combine all the ingredients until shortly before serving, or the dressing will get soggy.

CELERY AND LEMON STUFFING

Zingy with lemon and simple as can be, this stuffing is a delight any time of year.

MAKES ABOUT 5 CUPS

¼ pound butter

1 large onion, chopped

2 ribs celery, chopped

4 cups fresh bread crumbs

⅓ cup lemon juice (from about 2 lemons)

1 tablespoon grated lemon zest

2 eggs, beaten to mix

   Salt and fresh-ground black pepper

1. In a large saucepan, melt the butter over moderately low heat. Add the onion and celery and cook, covered, stirring occasionally, until the vegetables are soft, about 10 minutes.

2. Add the bread crumbs, lemon juice, lemon zest, and eggs, and toss. Season with salt and pepper.

> ## STUFFING TIPS
>
> ■ Stuff the turkey just before roasting. The stuffing should be at room temperature, not hot.
>
> ■ Stuffing should be loosely packed in the neck and main cavities of the turkey to allow room for it to expand and cook through. If it is packed too tightly, the stuffing will be dense.
>
> ■ Roast the turkey until the center of the stuffing reaches 165°.
>
> ■ Scoop the leftover stuffing from the turkey and refrigerate separately.

THREE-BREAD STUFFING

A trio of breads brings a complex earthy taste to this spicy stuffing, and their colors produce a calico effect.

MAKES ABOUT 12 CUPS

4 cups cubed rye bread

4 cups cubed pumpernickel bread

5 cups cubed sourdough bread

¼ pound butter

1 large onion, chopped

2 ribs celery, chopped

1 teaspoon paprika

1 pound spicy sausage, such as Hungarian, hot Italian, or chorizo

2 cups water

1 tart apple, such as Granny Smith, peeled, cored, and chopped

3 tablespoons good-quality green olives, pitted and chopped

1 jalapeño pepper, seeds and ribs removed, minced (optional)

¼ cup chopped fresh parsley

1 tablespoon chopped fresh thyme, or 1 teaspoon dried

½ teaspoon salt

½ teaspoon fresh-ground black pepper

2 eggs, beaten to mix

1. Spread the bread cubes out on a large baking sheet. Let them dry overnight. Alternatively, dry in a 350° oven for 10 minutes.

2. In a large frying pan, melt the butter over low heat. Add the onion and celery and cook, stirring occasionally, until softened, about 8 minutes. Sprinkle with the paprika and cook 2 minutes longer.

3. Put the sausage in a medium saucepan and cover with the water. Bring to a simmer over moderately high heat, reduce the heat, and poach until cooked through, about 10 minutes. Remove the sausage and reserve 1 cup of the poaching liquid. Chop the sausage.

4. In a large bowl, combine the dried bread cubes with the onion-and-celery mixture, the sausage, apple, olives, jalapeño, parsley, thyme, salt, pepper, the reserved 1 cup sausage-poaching liquid, and the eggs. Mix until well blended.

ORIENTAL STUFFING

You have to soak the glutinous rice for this stuffing overnight, but you can complete the rest of the preparation in minutes.

MAKES ABOUT 5 CUPS

1½   cups glutinous rice*

3   cups water

1   tablespoon peanut oil

4   shallots, minced

2   scallions including green tops, minced

¼   cup Chinese rice wine or dry sherry

¼   pound Chinese pork sausage*, cut into ¼-inch dice

¼   pound Chinese duck-liver sausage* or an additional ¼ pound Chinese pork sausage, cut into ¼-inch dice

1½   cups Chicken Stock, page 57, or canned low-sodium chicken broth

½   teaspoon salt

⅛   teaspoon fresh-ground black pepper

¾   pound fresh water chestnuts*, or ¼ pound jicama, peeled and chopped

½   red bell pepper, chopped

¾   teaspoon dried tarragon

½   teaspoon dried thyme

2   tablespoons Chinese chives*, fresh chives, or scallion tops, chopped

*Available at Asian markets

1. Put the glutinous rice in a large bowl. Add the water and let the rice soak overnight. Drain well.

2. In a large frying pan, heat the oil over moderate heat. Add the shallots and scallions and cook, stirring occasionally, until the shallots are soft, about 5 minutes. Add the wine and cook until the liquid evaporates, about 4 minutes. Add the pork and liver sausages and cook for 1 minute. Add the rice, stock, salt, and pepper. Cook, uncovered, stirring occasionally to prevent sticking, until all the stock is absorbed, about 8 minutes.

3. Add the water chestnuts, bell pepper, tarragon, thyme, and chives, and cook, stirring frequently, for 3 minutes.

—KEN HOM

TEN-THOUSAND-LAKES WILD-RICE, MUSHROOM, AND CARROT DRESSING

A truly American dish, this wild-rice dressing is sure to elicit thoughts of pilgrims and Indians sharing the first Thanksgiving dinner.

MAKES ABOUT 8 CUPS

2	cups wild rice
1½	teaspoons salt
7	cups water, more if needed
2	cups cubed good-quality white bread
¼	cup cooking oil
1	large onion, chopped
6	scallions including green tops, sliced
3	ribs celery, diced
2	carrots, chopped
1	teaspoon dried marjoram
½	teaspoon dried rosemary, crumbled
½	teaspoon dried thyme
½	teaspoon fresh-ground black pepper
1	pound mushrooms, sliced
2	tablespoons butter
3	tablespoons flour
1⅔	cup Chicken Stock, page 57, or canned low-sodium chicken broth

1. Rinse the rice in several changes of cold water and drain. In a large saucepan, combine the rice, salt, and water. Bring to a boil over moderate heat. Cover, reduce the heat, and cook at a gentle boil, adding more water if needed, until the rice is tender. This can take from 35 to 60 minutes. Drain well and set aside.

2. Heat the oven to 350°. Spread the cubed bread out onto a large baking sheet and bake in the middle of the oven, stirring occasionally, until uniformly crisp and golden, about 40 minutes. Leave the oven on.

3. Meanwhile, in a large frying pan, heat the oil over moderate heat. Add the onion, scallions, and celery, and cook, stirring occasionally, until soft and golden, about 10 minutes. Add the carrots, marjoram, rosemary, thyme, and pepper. Reduce the heat to low, cover, and cook for 10 minutes. Using a slotted spoon, transfer the vegetables to a large bowl.

4. Add the mushrooms to the frying pan and increase the heat to moderately high. Cook, stirring occasionally, until all of the liquid evaporates, about 7 minutes. Transfer the mushrooms to the bowl.

5. Heat the oven to 350°. Butter a deep 4-quart baking dish and a large square of aluminum foil.

6. In a medium saucepan, melt the butter over moderate heat. Add the flour and cook, whisking, for 1 minute. Whisk in the stock. Still over moderate heat, bring to a boil, whisking. Reduce the heat and simmer,

stirring occasionally, until the sauce is thickened, about 5 minutes.

7. Add the sauce, toasted bread cubes, and wild rice to the bowl and toss. Spoon the dressing into the prepared baking dish. Cover with the foil, buttered-side down, and seal. Bake in the middle of the oven until hot, about 1 hour.

—JEAN ANDERSON

MAKE IT AHEAD
This stuffing is actually better if prepared a day ahead. Just cover and refrigerate. The next day, reheat the dish at 350° for about 1 hour.

STUFFING VS. DRESSING

As far as ingredients are concerned, stuffing and dressing are the same thing. Technically speaking, this seasoned mixture should be called stuffing if it will be put inside the cavity of a roasting bird, and dressing if it will be baked separately. All of our stuffing recipes can be made into dressing, and vice versa.

■ **To make stuffing into dressing**, put the mixture into a buttered baking dish, cover with buttered aluminum foil, and bake in a 350° oven until steaming hot, about 40 minutes.

■ **To make dressing into stuffing**, obviously enough, put the mixture into your bird and proceed with the roasting. Any stuffing that does not fit in the bird can be baked as dressing.

CHESTNUT DRESSING

Chestnuts are especially popular around the holidays. Maybe it's the image of them roasting on an open fire that teases our taste buds. Or maybe it's just that chestnuts are harvested in the fall. Whatever the reason, this dressing is delicious.

MAKES ABOUT 12 CUPS

- 2 pounds fresh chestnuts
- 2 cups Chicken Stock, page 57, or canned low-sodium chicken broth
- 12 tablespoons butter
- 6 ribs celery, chopped fine
- 2 onions, chopped fine
- 10 cups fresh bread crumbs
- 2 teaspoons dried marjoram
- 1 teaspoon dried thyme
- 2 teaspoons salt
- 1 teaspoon fresh-ground black pepper

1. Cut an "X" through the shell on the flat end of each chestnut. Drop the chestnuts in a large saucepan of boiling water and cook for 5 minutes. Drain. Remove the shells and brown skins while the chestnuts are still hot. Cut the chestnuts in half.

2. In a medium saucepan, bring the Chicken Stock to a simmer over moderate heat. Add the peeled chestnuts and cook until just tender, about 8 minutes. Drain, reserving the stock.

3. In a large saucepan, melt 8 tablespoons of the butter. Add the celery, onions, and 1½ cups of the reserved stock. Cook over moderately high heat until the stock has boiled away, about 15 minutes. Do not allow the vegetables or the butter to brown.

4. Heat the oven to 425°. Butter a 3-quart baking dish and a sheet of aluminum foil. In a small saucepan, melt the remaining 4 tablespoons butter over moderately low heat. In a large bowl, combine the celery-and-onion mixture with the bread crumbs. Add the chestnuts, melted butter, marjoram, thyme, salt, and pepper. Mix well. If the dressing is too dry, add the remaining reserved stock.

5. Spoon the dressing into the prepared baking dish. Cover with the buttered foil and bake in the middle of the oven until warmed through, 20 to 30 minutes.

—CAMILLE GLENN

MAKE IT AHEAD
The chestnuts can be peeled and simmered up to 2 days ahead. Cover and refrigerate until ready to use.

VENETIAN STUFFING

With the nuttiness of chestnuts, the sweetness of prunes and port, and the sharpness of Parmesan, this is a combination not to be missed.

MAKES ABOUT 8 CUPS

1½   pounds fresh chestnuts

3   cups Beef Stock, page 101, or canned low-sodium beef broth

3   cups cubed good-quality white bread

½   cup milk

3   tablespoons butter

4   ribs celery, chopped

1   onion, chopped

½   pound ground veal

½   pound ground pork

2   tablespoons chopped fresh parsley

1   teaspoon dried thyme

3   tablespoons tawny port

1   cup pitted prunes, quartered

½   cup grated Parmesan cheese

· 4   eggs, beaten to mix

1   tablespoon salt

½   teaspoon fresh-ground black pepper

1. Heat the oven to 400°. Cut an "X" through the shell on the flat end of each chestnut. Put the chestnuts on an ungreased baking sheet and bake until the shell at each "X" lifts away from the chestnut, about 20 minutes. Peel the chestnuts as soon as they are cool enough to handle.

2. In a medium saucepan, combine the chestnuts and the stock. Bring to a boil. Reduce the heat and simmer until all the liquid is absorbed, about 40 minutes. Puree the chestnuts in a food mill or food processor.

3. Put the bread in a large bowl. Pour the milk over the bread and let soak for 10 minutes, stirring occasionally.

4. In a large frying pan, melt the butter over moderately low heat. Add the celery and onion and cook until softened, about 8 minutes. Transfer the vegetables to the bowl. Stir in the pureed chestnuts, the veal, pork, parsley, thyme, port, prunes, Parmesan, eggs, salt, and pepper.

—Silvio Pinto

RICH CHICKEN-LIVER STUFFING

Because it is so rich and moist, this stuffing tastes almost like a mousse. Its creamy texture will melt in your mouth.

MAKES ABOUT 4 CUPS

¼ cup rendered goose fat or butter

2 onions, chopped

3 cups fresh bread crumbs

½ cup chopped fresh parsley

¾ pound chicken livers

1 each goose gizzard and goose liver, or an additional ¼ pound chicken livers

2 teaspoons salt

1 teaspoon dried oregano

2 eggs, beaten to mix

1. In a large frying pan, heat the rendered goose fat over moderately low heat. Add the onions and cook, stirring occasionally, until translucent, about 5 minutes.

2. Add the bread crumbs and parsley. Cook, stirring occasionally, until lightly toasted, about 5 minutes. Remove from the heat and let cool for 15 minutes.

3. Put the chicken livers, goose gizzard, and goose liver in a food processor. Add the bread-and-onion mixture, the salt, oregano, and eggs. Pulse to chop, 10 to 12 times.

—LYDIE MARSHALL

COUNTRY-HAM AND WILD-MUSHROOM DRESSING

Designed to bake separately from the holiday bird, this dressing can accompany meat as well. You have the option of moistening it with the bird's pan juices or the mushroom-soaking liquid. Either one makes a delicious dressing.

MAKES ABOUT 12 CUPS

- 2 cups Chicken Stock, page 57, or canned low-sodium chicken broth
- 1½ ounces dried porcini or other dried mushrooms
- 10 cups fresh bread crumbs
- 6 tablespoons butter
- ½ pound Smithfield or other ham, cut into ½-inch cubes
- 2 onions, chopped
- 1 teaspoon dried thyme
- 1 cup chopped flat-leaf parsley
- ½ teaspoon salt
- 1 teaspoon fresh-ground black pepper
- 1½ cups of pan juices from the roasting bird or reserved mushroom-soaking liquid

1. In a small saucepan, bring the stock to a boil. Add the dried mushrooms. Soak until softened, about 20 minutes.

2. Put the bread crumbs in a large bowl. In a medium frying pan, melt 2 tablespoons of the butter over moderate heat. Add the ham. Cook, stirring, until browned, about 4 minutes. With a slotted spoon, transfer the ham to the bowl with the bread.

3. Melt the remaining 4 tablespoons butter in the frying pan. Add the onions and thyme, cover, and cook, stirring occasionally, until the onions are soft and light brown, about 10 minutes. Transfer to the bowl.

4. Butter a 4-quart baking dish and a sheet of aluminum foil. Remove the mushrooms from the stock and strain the liquid into a bowl through a sieve lined with a paper towel. Rinse the mushrooms well to remove any remaining grit. Add the mushrooms to the bread mixture. Reserve the soaking liquid for basting the dressing, or for adding to gravy or soup.

5. Add the parsley, salt, and pepper to the dressing and mix well. Transfer to the prepared baking dish.

6. Heat the oven to 325°. Spoon the pan juices or mushroom-soaking liquid evenly over the dressing. Cover with the buttered foil and bake until the dressing is steaming and the sides and bottom are crunchy and brown, about 45 minutes.

—MICHAEL MCLAUGHLIN

Old-Fashioned Corn Bread

All kinds of stuffings can be made with this firm, basic corn bread. For the best results when making stuffing, turn the slightly cooled corn bread out onto a rack and let air-dry uncovered for a day or two at room temperature (or three days in the refrigerator) before crumbling.

MAKES ABOUT 10 CUPS CRUMBLED BREAD

- 2 cups flour
- 2 cups cornmeal
- 2 tablespoons baking powder
- 1 tablespoon sugar
- 1½ teaspoons salt
- 2 eggs, beaten to mix
- 2 cups milk
- ½ cup cooking oil or bacon drippings

1. Heat the oven to 400°. Butter a 9 by 13-inch baking pan.

2. In a large bowl, combine the flour, cornmeal, baking powder, sugar, and salt. Make a well in the center. In a large bowl, whisk the eggs, milk, and oil until blended. Pour the egg mixture into the well of the dry ingredients and stir until just combined. The batter will be slightly lumpy.

3. Transfer the batter to the prepared pan and bake in the middle of the oven until the top is golden and a toothpick stuck in the center comes out clean, about 30 minutes. Let the bread cool on a rack for 10 minutes.

—Jean Anderson

MAKE IT AHEAD
You can keep the corn bread 2 or 3 days or freeze it for up to a month.

KITCHEN TIP

If you're making a stuffing that calls for half a recipe of Old-Fashioned Corn Bread, either divide the ingredients in half and bake in a buttered nine-inch round cake pan, or make the whole recipe and enjoy some of the bread for breakfast.

chapter 7
SWEET POTATOES, PUMPKIN & SQUASH

Gratin of Sweet Potatoes Flambéed with Bourbon, page 137

SPICED BUTTERNUT SQUASH

Butternut squash is a winter vegetable that lends itself to a wide range of preparations. Here it's pureed and spiced for the season. Also pictured is Glazed Roasted Shallots and Garlic, page 152.

SERVES 8

- 4 pounds butternut squash, peeled, seeded, and cut into chunks
- 1 cup Chicken Stock, page 57, or canned low-sodium chicken broth
- 3 cups water
- 6 tablespoons butter, cut into pieces
- ½ teaspoon ground ginger
- ¼ teaspoon ground mace
- ¼ teaspoon ground coriander
  Pinch cayenne
  Salt and fresh-ground black pepper
- 1 tablespoon lemon juice, more to taste
- 3 tablespoons crème fraiche or sour cream

1. In a large saucepan, combine the butternut squash, stock, and water. Bring to a boil over high heat. Reduce the heat to moderately low and simmer, partially covered, until the squash is tender, about 20 minutes. Reserve ¼ cup of the cooking liquid and drain the squash.

2. Heat the oven to 350°. Combine the cooked squash, the butter, ginger, mace, coriander, cayenne, 1 teaspoon salt, ¼ teaspoon black pepper, the lemon juice, and the reserved cooking liquid. Puree half of the mixture in a food processor or blender.

Transfer the puree to a 3-quart baking dish. Repeat with the remaining squash mixture. Stir in the crème fraiche and season with additional lemon juice, salt, and pepper to taste. Bake the puree until heated through, about 30 minutes.

—SHEILA LUKINS

MAKE IT AHEAD
The recipe can be prepared 2 days in advance. Cover and refrigerate. Return the squash to room temperature before baking, or add a few minutes to the baking time.

BAKED SQUASH
WITH BUTTER AND MAPLE SYRUP

Maple syrup lends a distinct sweetness and seems to heighten the buttered-squash flavor. For a special effect, serve the squash in their own scooped-out skins.

SERVES 8

4 pounds acorn or butternut squash, halved lengthwise and seeded

   Salt and fresh-ground black pepper

3 tablespoons butter

3 tablespoons pure maple syrup

1. Heat the oven to 400°. Put the squash, cut-side down, on a baking sheet. Bake until tender, about 40 minutes. Turn the squash over and bake another 5 minutes to dry the flesh. Scoop the flesh into a bowl, add 1 teaspoon salt and 1/4 teaspoon pepper, and mash with a potato masher until fairly smooth. Season with more salt and pepper to taste.

2. In a small saucepan, combine the butter and maple syrup and heat gently, stirring, until the butter is melted, about 2 minutes. Stir 3 tablespoons of the syrup mixture into the squash. Serve with the rest of the syrup drizzled over the top.

—MARION CUNNINGHAM

MAKE IT AHEAD The recipe can be prepared several days ahead. Reheat on top of the stove or in a 350° oven.

CARROT AND SQUASH PUREE

Carrots and butternut squash make a delicate and ever-so-slightly sweet puree.
It will complement almost any roast bird or meat, both in flavor and texture.

SERVES 8

12 carrots, peeled and cut into 1-inch chunks

1 butternut squash (about 2 pounds), peeled, seeded, and cut into 1-inch chunks

½ cup light cream or half-and-half

¼ pound butter

Salt

1 teaspoon grated nutmeg

Fresh-ground black pepper

1. In a large saucepan, combine the carrots, squash, and enough salted water to cover. Cover the pan and bring the mixture to a boil. Reduce the heat and simmer, partially covered, until the vegetables are tender, about 20 minutes. Drain well.

2. Puree the vegetables in a food processor or blender. Transfer the puree to a large mixing bowl and stir in the cream, butter, 1 teaspoon salt, the nutmeg, and ¼ teaspoon pepper. Taste and add more salt and pepper if needed.

—MARTHA STEWART

BUTTERNUT SQUASH

Smooth and buckskin-colored, with a long neck and a bulbous bottom, butternut squash is the workhorse of the winter-squash family. It tastes good and is readily available; its smooth, thin skin is easily peeled; and its slender neck, which is free of seeds, is simple to cut into pieces. The squash doesn't have dramatic sweetness, which makes it perfect for pairing with other foods

—DEBORAH MADISON

SWEET-POTATO AND BUTTERNUT-SQUASH PUREE

For the dieters among us, here's a no-fat puree. Moist butternut squash and richly flavored sweet potatoes join forces to create a tasty, colorful dish.

SERVES 12

4 pounds sweet potatoes (about 4)

1 butternut squash (about 2 pounds), halved lengthwise and seeded

Salt and fresh-ground black pepper

1. Heat the oven to 400°. Prick the sweet potatoes in several places with a fork. Put the squash, cut-side down, and the sweet potatoes on a baking sheet. Bake until tender, about 1 hour. Let cool slightly.

2. Transfer the pulp from the sweet potatoes and squash to a food processor. Add 1½ teaspoons salt and ½ teaspoon pepper and puree. Taste and add more salt and pepper if needed.

MAKE IT AHEAD
The recipe can be prepared several days ahead. Reheat on top of the stove or in a 350° oven, covered, for about 20 minutes.

YAMS VS. SWEET POTATOES

Despite what many people think, yams and sweet potatoes are not the same thing. **Yams** are tropical tubers that are very large (two pounds or more), with rough brown or black-brown skin and white or orange flesh. They're starchier, blander, and less sweet than sweet potatoes. True yams can most often be found in Latin American markets. **Sweet potatoes** come in many different varieties. Their skin is tan or reddish-brown, and the flesh is orange, white, or yellow. These can be found in any supermarket.

GRATIN OF PUMPKIN

Pumpkin tastes so good in savory dishes, it's a shame to use it only in pies. If fresh pumpkin is not available, butternut or acorn squash—as well as frozen or canned pumpkin puree—can be substituted. This gratin is pictured on page 80. For added elegance, bake the puree in individual gratin dishes.

SERVES 8

1 4-pound piece pumpkin, cut into 3-inch pieces and peeled

1 cup heavy cream

1 cup milk

⅛ teaspoon grated nutmeg

Salt and fresh-ground black pepper

6 eggs, beaten to mix

½ cup grated Swiss cheese

2 tablespoons grated Parmesan cheese

1. Put the pumpkin in a large saucepan and cover with water. Bring to a boil over high heat. Reduce the heat to low, cover, and simmer until tender, about 20 minutes. Drain well. Puree the pumpkin in a food processor or blender while still hot.

2. Heat the oven to 375° and butter a shallow 2-quart baking dish. In a large mixing bowl, combine the pureed pumpkin, the cream, milk, nutmeg, 2 teaspoons salt, and ¼ teaspoon pepper. Taste and add more salt and pepper if needed. Beat in the eggs, one at a time, then stir in the Swiss cheese.

3. Pour the mixture into the prepared baking dish and sprinkle the Parmesan on top. Set the dish in a larger pan and add enough hot water to reach halfway up the sides of the baking dish. Bake until the gratin is set, about 40 minutes, or 20 minutes if using individual gratin dishes.

—JACQUES PEPIN

MAKE IT AHEAD

The gratin can be assembled up to a day ahead. Store it in its baking dish, covered, in the refrigerator. Let the gratin return to room temperature before baking, or add a few minutes to the cooking time.

GRATIN OF SWEET POTATOES FLAMBEED WITH BOURBON

You can bring this dish to the table dramatically aflame or let the flames die down in the kitchen. The point is to burn off the raw alcohol flavor.

SERVES 8

- 4 pounds sweet potatoes (about 4)
- 4 tablespoons butter, at room temperature
- 1 teaspoon salt
- ¼ teaspoon fresh-ground black pepper
- 2 tablespoons sugar
- ⅓ cup bourbon

1. Put the sweet potatoes in a large pot of cold salted water and bring to a boil over moderately high heat. Cook until the sweet potatoes are just tender around the edges but still firm in the center, about 15 minutes. Drain and rinse under cold water. Peel the sweet potatoes when they are cool enough to handle.

2. Heat the oven to 475°. Butter a large shallow baking dish. Cut the sweet potatoes into ¼-inch slices and arrange the slices in the baking dish, overlapping slightly. Dot the potatoes with the butter and sprinkle with the salt, pepper, and sugar.

3. Bake the sweet potatoes for 20 minutes. Reduce the heat to 350° and bake until the potatoes are tender and lightly glazed, about 20 minutes longer.

4. Pour the bourbon into a small saucepan. Warm over low heat for about 20 seconds, then carefully ignite the bourbon and pour it over the sweet potatoes.

SWEET-POTATO SHAM

Sweet potatoes change as the season progresses. In early fall, they are full of moisture and cook quickly; later in the year they may need a few extra minutes of cooking time. This sweet side-dish recipe comes to us from Texas.

SERVES 8 TO 10

4½   pounds sweet potatoes

 4   tablespoons butter, softened

½   cup granulated sugar

½   cup brown sugar

 1   egg

½   cup milk

½   teaspoon grated nutmeg

½   teaspoon cinnamon

 1   teaspoon salt

1. Heat the oven to 350°. Put the sweet potatoes in a large pot and add enough salted water to cover. Bring to a boil, reduce the heat to moderately low, and cook until the potatoes are soft, about 40 minutes. Drain well.

2. When the potatoes are cool enough to handle, peel them and transfer to a large bowl. Using a potato masher or fork, mash the sweet potatoes until smooth.

3. In a medium bowl, mix the butter, the granulated sugar, and the brown sugar. Whisk in the egg until blended, add the milk, and mix well. Add this mixture to the mashed sweet potatoes, stir, and season with the grated nutmeg, the cinnamon, and the salt.

4. Put the potatoes in a large baking dish and smooth the top. Bake until heated through, about 30 minutes.

—Susan Herrmann Loomis

MAKE IT AHEAD
The sham can be cooked a day ahead, covered, and refrigerated. Return to room temperature and reheat in a 350° oven.

SWEET POTATOES WITH CIDER AND BROWN SUGAR

Inspired by a Jeffersonian menu, this especially easy and tasty version of a trusty Thanksgiving standby may become traditional in your house.

SERVES 8

  4 pounds sweet potatoes (about 4), peeled and cut into 1-inch chunks

2½ cups apple cider

 ½ cup dark-brown sugar

  8 tablespoons butter

  1 2-inch piece of cinnamon stick

1. In a large saucepan, combine the sweet potatoes, cider, brown sugar, 6 tablespoons of the butter, and the cinnamon stick. Bring to a boil over moderate heat. Reduce the heat to moderately low, partially cover, and cook, stirring occasionally, until the potatoes are very tender, about 20 minutes.

2. Heat the oven to 350°. Let the mixture cool slightly and then remove the cinnamon stick. Puree the potatoes and liquid in batches in a food processor. Transfer the puree to a 3-quart baking dish. Dot the surface of the potatoes with the remaining 2 tablespoons butter and bake, stirring once or twice, until heated through, about 30 minutes.

—MICHAEL MCLAUGHLIN

MAKE IT AHEAD
The potatoes can be prepared several days before serving; cover with aluminum foil and refrigerate. Return to room temperature before baking or increase the cooking time by a few minutes.

SHERRIED SWEET POTATOES

The sugar here is just enough to glaze the sweet potatoes beautifully without turning them into candy.

SERVES 8

- 4 pounds sweet potatoes (about 4)
- ⅓ cup sugar
- 1 teaspoon salt
- ⅓ cup medium-dry sherry, such as amontillado
- 4 tablespoons butter, cut into pieces

1. Heat the oven to 350°. In a large saucepan, cover the sweet potatoes with salted water and bring to a boil over high heat. Reduce the heat to moderate and simmer until the potatoes are tender but still firm, about 30 minutes. Drain well.

2. When the potatoes are cool enough to handle, peel them. Cut the potatoes in half lengthwise. Put the halves in a large baking dish and sprinkle with the sugar and salt. Drizzle the sherry over the potatoes and dot with the butter. Bake until the potatoes are light brown and the glaze is bubbling, about 20 minutes.

—CAMILLE GLENN

MAKE IT AHEAD
The sweet potatoes can be simmered 1 day ahead. Wrap the cooled potatoes in foil and refrigerate until ready to peel.

SWEET-POTATO AND TURNIP PUREE

Turnips temper the sweetness of the potatoes, and egg whites lighten this airy and sophisticated side dish.

SERVES 10

- 3 pounds sweet potatoes (about 3)
- 2 pounds turnips, peeled and quartered
- 2 tablespoons dark brown sugar
- 4 tablespoons butter
  Salt
  Pinch grated nutmeg
- 3 egg whites

1. Heat the oven to 400°. Prick the sweet potatoes in several places with a fork and bake until soft, about 1 hour. Reduce the oven temperature to 350°.

2. Meanwhile, put the turnip quarters in a large saucepan of salted water. Bring to a boil, reduce the heat, and simmer until the turnips are tender, about 25 minutes. Drain the turnips. Butter a shallow 3-quart baking dish.

3. When the sweet potatoes are cool enough to handle, peel them, cut into chunks, and transfer to a food processor. Add the turnips, brown sugar, butter, 1½ teaspoons salt, and the nutmeg. Puree and season to taste.

4. Beat the egg whites until they hold firm peaks when the beaters are lifted. Fold into the sweet potato-turnip puree. Transfer the mixture to the prepared baking dish and bake until heated through, about 30 minutes.

—LEE BAILEY

MAKE IT AHEAD
The recipe can be prepared through Step 3 up to 4 hours ahead. Set aside, covered, at room temperature until ready to proceed.

141

chapter *8*
OTHER SIDE DISHES

Pearl Onions in Creamy Onion Sauce, page 159

BRIOCHE AND OYSTER PUDDING

Slices of lightly buttered brioche form the perfect base for this creamy pudding. Adding oysters makes it even more indulgent.

SERVES 8

- 6 tablespoons butter, softened
- 1 leek, white and light-green parts only, chopped and washed well
- ¼ cup chopped celery
- ¼ pound smoked ham, such as Black Forest, chopped coarse
- 12 parsley stems
- 1 sprig fresh thyme, or ⅛ teaspoon dried
- 1½ cups milk
- 1 cup heavy cream
- 6 brioche rolls (about 10 ounces total), ends trimmed, sliced ⅜ inch thick
- 2 whole eggs
- 3 egg yolks
- 2 tablespoons chopped fresh chives
- 1½ tablespoons chopped fresh parsley
- ½ teaspoon salt
- 5 drops hot-pepper sauce
- 1 dozen shucked oysters, chopped, liquor reserved

1. Heat the oven to 350°. In a large frying pan, melt 1 tablespoon of the butter. Add the leek, celery, ham, parsley stems, and thyme, and cook over moderate heat, stirring occasionally, until the leek softens, about 5 minutes. Add the milk and the heavy cream. Bring to a boil, reduce the heat, and simmer gently for 45 minutes.

2. Meanwhile, lightly butter both sides of the brioche slices using 4 tablespoons of the butter. Put them on a baking sheet and toast in the oven until lightly browned, turning once, about 15 minutes. Leave the oven on. Butter a 9-inch springform pan with the remaining 1 tablespoon butter. Arrange the brioche in the pan in three overlapping rows.

3. Strain the milk mixture into a bowl. Press the solid ingredients to get as much liquid as possible. In a medium bowl, beat the whole eggs and yolks. Slowly whisk in 1 cup of the milk mixture in a thin stream. Whisk in the remainder. Add the chives, parsley, salt, hot sauce, and oysters with their liquor.

4. Wrap the outside of the springform pan in a double sheet of aluminum foil. Pour the oyster mixture into the pan and distribute the oysters evenly. Put the pan in a roasting pan and pour in enough hot water to reach about one-third up the sides of the springform. Bake until a knife stuck in the center comes out clean, 35 to 40 minutes.

5. Remove the foil and let rest for 10 minutes. Run a knife around the edge and remove the outer ring of the pan. Using a wide metal spatula, transfer the pudding to a serving platter. Serve warm or room temperature.

—ANNE DISRUDE

CRESCENT ROLLS

For tender, flaky rolls, make a soft dough, work it as little as possible, and allow plenty of time for slow rising.

1   cup milk

¼   pound butter, at room temperature

1   package dry yeast (about 2¼ teaspoons)

½   cup sugar

4½ cups flour, more for kneading

2   eggs

1   teaspoon salt

1. In a small pan, bring the milk and butter to a simmer over moderate heat. Pour into a large bowl and let stand until lukewarm. Stir in the yeast and sugar and then 1 cup of the flour. Add the eggs, one at a time, whisking well after each addition. Add the salt and one more cup of flour. Mix with a wooden spoon until the dough is elastic and smooth, about 6 minutes. Alternatively, mix the dough with an electric mixer at medium-high speed for 3 minutes.

2. Work in the remaining 2½ cups flour until the dough is a little firmer, but still very soft. Turn the dough out onto a floured surface and knead just until smooth, about 2 minutes. Put the dough in an oiled bowl, cover, and let rise in a warm place until doubled, about 2 hours.

3. Punch down the dough, turn it out onto a floured surface, and divide it in half. Roll each half into a 16-inch round. Cut each round into quarters, then each quarter into four wedges. Beginning at the wide ends, roll up the wedges. Tuck the points underneath so they won't pop up during rising and baking, and turn the ends toward the middle to form crescents.

4. Arrange the rolls 2 inches apart on three lightly floured baking sheets. Cover the rolls with kitchen towels and set aside to rise in a warm place until nearly doubled, about 4 hours.

5. Heat the oven to 350°. Bake the rolls in three batches in the middle of the oven until golden, 10 to 12 minutes.

—SUSAN HERRMANN LOOMIS

POTATO PUREE WITH SCALLIONS

Mashed potatoes, by any name, are always a favorite. This puree, delicately flavored with scallions, is sure to bring smiles to all the faces around the table.

SERVES 6

2 pounds baking potatoes (about 4), peeled and cut into 1½-inch chunks

¼ pound butter, at room temperature

1 cup half-and-half or light cream, more if needed

2 scallions including green tops, chopped

Salt and fresh-ground black pepper

1. Put the potatoes in a medium saucepan of salted water. Bring to a boil, reduce the heat, and simmer until tender, 15 to 20 minutes. Drain and transfer the potatoes to a mixing bowl.

2. Add the butter and ½ cup of the half-and-half to the potatoes. Using an electric mixer, beat until smooth, gradually adding enough additional half-and-half to make a creamy puree. Blend in the scallions and season with salt and pepper to taste.

—KEN HOM

BAKED WILD RICE
WITH CARROTS AND MUSHROOMS

The earthy flavors of wild rice, mushrooms, and carrots make this an especially nice dish for fall and winter celebrations.

SERVES 6 TO 8

2½ cups Chicken Stock, page 57, or canned low-sodium chicken broth

¾ teaspoon salt

1 cup wild rice, rinsed well

6 slices bacon, cut crosswise into thin strips

1 onion, chopped

2 carrots, cut into ¼-inch dice

¼ pound mushrooms, diced

½ teaspoon dried thyme

½ teaspoon dried marjoram

⅛ teaspoon fresh-ground black pepper

1½ tablespoons butter, more if needed

1. In a medium saucepan, bring the Chicken Stock to a boil. Add the salt and wild rice. When the stock returns to a boil, cover, reduce the heat, and cook at a gentle boil until the rice is tender, about 40 minutes. Remove from the heat; do not drain.

2. Butter a 2-quart baking dish. In a large frying pan, fry the bacon until crisp. Remove the bacon. Pour off all but 3 tablespoons of the fat.

3. Add the onion and carrots to the frying pan and cook, stirring, over moderate heat for 5 minutes. Add the mushrooms, thyme, marjoram, and pepper, and cook for 2 minutes longer. Transfer the rice and its liquid to the frying pan. Add the reserved bacon and toss.

4. Heat the oven to 350°. Transfer the rice mixture to the prepared baking dish. Cover and bake until the rice is tender, 25 to 30 minutes. Dot the surface of the rice with the butter and toss.

—JEAN ANDERSON

MAKE IT AHEAD
The recipe can be completed ahead of time through Step 3. Transfer the mixture to the baking dish, cover tightly, and refrigerate. Either bring to room temperature before proceeding or add a few minutes to the baking time.

FRAGRANT BARLEY

With pasta bow-ties, toasted pine nuts, and a confetti of carrots and mint, these pearly grains belong on the most festive tables. The dish is pictured on page 90.

SERVES 12

3 tablespoons olive oil

1 cup pine nuts

4 carrots, cut into ¼-inch dice

1 large onion, chopped

2 cups pearl barley

1 quart Beef Stock, page 101, or canned low-sodium beef broth

½ cup dried currants (optional)

1 cinnamon stick (optional)

1 teaspoon salt

½ teaspoon fresh-ground black pepper

2 cups water

½ pound bow-tie pasta

2 tablespoons chopped fresh mint

1. In a large frying pan, heat the oil over moderately low heat. Add the pine nuts and cook, stirring, until just golden, about 5 minutes. Remove and reserve. Add the carrots and onion to the pan and cook, stirring occasionally, until the onion is soft, about 5 minutes. Add the barley and cook, stirring, for 2 minutes.

2. Add the stock, currants, cinnamon, salt, pepper, and water. Increase the heat to high. Bring to a boil. Reduce the heat, cover, and simmer until the liquid is absorbed and the barley is tender, about 55 minutes.

3. Meanwhile, in a large pot of boiling, salted water, cook the bow-tie pasta until just done, about 11 minutes. Drain and rinse with cold water.

4. Stir the cooked pasta, the pine nuts, and 1 tablespoon of the mint into the barley. Heat until the pasta is warm, about 5 minutes. Serve sprinkled with the remaining 1 tablespoon mint.

—SHEILA LUKINS

PARSLIED CARROTS

Cooked carrots shine with a gloss of butter and a sprinkling of chopped fresh parsley for a simple and tasty side dish.

SERVES 8

2½ pounds carrots, peeled and cut diagonally into ½-inch chunks

4 tablespoons butter

Salt

¼ cup chopped fresh parsley

Bring a large saucepan of salted water to a boil. Add the carrots and boil until tender, about 10 minutes. Drain. Add the butter to the pan and toss to coat the carrots. Season with salt to taste, add the chopped parsley, and mix well.

—MARION CUNNINGHAM

MAKE IT AHEAD
Boil, butter, and season the carrots in advance, if you like. At the last minute, reheat them and add the parsley.

STEAMED BRUSSELS SPROUTS AND RED GRAPES

What reminds us more of the holiday season than red and green? You can put together this colorful side dish in just minutes.

SERVES 6 TO 8

1½ pounds brussels sprouts, cut in half from top to stem end

2 cups seedless red grapes

2½ tablespoons butter

1 tablespoon lemon juice

½ teaspoon salt

¼ teaspoon fresh-ground black pepper

In a steamer basket over boiling water, steam the brussels sprouts, covered, until tender, about 15 minutes. Add the grapes and steam 1 minute longer; drain well. Put the brussels sprouts and the grapes in a serving bowl, add the butter, lemon juice, salt, and pepper, and toss well.

GLAZED ROASTED SHALLOTS AND GARLIC

A sprinkling of sugar brings out the nutty sweetness of shallots and garlic. When tender, they're quickly sautéed with butter for the final caramelized glaze. The shallots are pictured on page 130.

SERVES 10 TO 12

3¾ pounds large shallots, peeled

2 heads garlic, separated into cloves, cloves peeled

¾ cup Chicken Stock, page 57, or canned low-sodium chicken broth

2 tablespoons lemon juice

2 tablespoons sugar

1 teaspoon salt

½ teaspoon fresh-ground black pepper

3 tablespoons butter

1. Heat the oven to 375°. Put the shallots and garlic in a single layer in a shallow baking dish. In a small saucepan, combine the Chicken Stock and lemon juice and bring to a boil over high heat. Pour the hot stock over the shallots and garlic and sprinkle with the sugar, salt, and pepper. Cover with aluminum foil and bake for 45 minutes. Remove the foil, stir gently, and bake uncovered until the shallots are very tender, 25 to 30 minutes.

2. In a large frying pan, melt 1½ tablespoons of the butter over moderate heat. Add half of the shallots and garlic and half of their cooking liquid. Increase the heat to moderately high and cook, shaking the pan frequently, until the shallots and garlic are golden brown and caramelized all over, about 5 minutes. Transfer to a serving dish. Rinse out the pan and repeat with the remaining butter, shallots, garlic, and cooking liquid.

—SHEILA LUKINS

MAKE IT AHEAD Prepare the dish several days in advance, cool, cover, and refrigerate. Let it return to room temperature before reheating in a 375° oven for 10 minutes.

BRAISED RED CABBAGE WITH MAPLE-GLAZED CHESTNUTS

Braised red cabbage not only has a delicious subtle sweetness but also a gorgeous color. It needs acidity—provided here by apple cider and wine vinegar—to bring out that magenta hue.

SERVES 8

- 1 pound fresh chestnuts
- 1 head red cabbage (about 2 pounds), shredded
- 4 cloves garlic, minced
- 4 large shallots, cut into thin slices
- ½ pound Canadian bacon, cut into ½-inch dice
- 1 teaspoon caraway seeds
- ¼ teaspoon grated nutmeg
- ½ teaspoon salt
- ¼ teaspoon fresh-ground black pepper
- 2 cups apple cider
- ½ cup red-wine vinegar
- 2 cups milk
- 2 cups water
- 1 teaspoon vanilla extract
- 3 tablespoons butter
- ⅓ cup maple syrup

1. Heat the oven to 350°. Cut an "X" through the shell on the flat end of each of the chestnuts. Put the chestnuts on a baking sheet. Bake the chestnuts until the shell at each "X" lifts away from the chestnut, 10 to 15 minutes. Peel the chestnuts while they are still warm.

2. In a large pot, combine the shredded red cabbage, the garlic, shallots, Canadian bacon, caraway seeds, nutmeg, salt, pepper, apple cider, and vinegar. Bring to a boil over moderately high heat. Reduce the heat, cover, and simmer, stirring occasionally, until the cabbage is tender and the liquid is reduced to ½ cup, about 2 hours.

3. Meanwhile, in a medium saucepan, combine the chestnuts with the milk and water. Bring to a boil. Reduce the heat, add the vanilla, cover, and simmer until the chestnuts are just tender, about 40 minutes. Drain well, rinse under warm water, and drain again.

4. In a large frying pan, melt the butter. Add the chestnuts and the maple syrup and cook over moderately high heat, stirring frequently, until the chestnuts are glazed and light brown, about 8 minutes. Serve the chestnuts over the hot cabbage.

MAKE IT AHEAD
You can complete the recipe through Step 3 at least 3 days ahead. Refrigerate the cabbage and chestnuts separately. Reheat the cabbage and proceed with the recipe.

CABBAGE WITH PINE NUTS

Since it cooks for less than half a minute, the cabbage here retains its lovely pale-green color and a slightly crisp texture. Toasted pine nuts look pretty on top and add their sweet, nutty flavor.

SERVES 8

½ cup pine nuts

1 head green cabbage, chopped

4 tablespoons butter, melted

2 tablespoons lemon juice

Salt

1. In a small frying pan, toast the pine nuts over moderately low heat, stirring frequently, until golden brown, about 4 minutes. Or toast them in a 350° oven for about 6 minutes.

2. Meanwhile, bring a large pot of salted water to a boil. Add the cabbage and return to a boil. Cook for 20 seconds, then drain well in a colander. Return the cabbage to the pan. Stir in the butter and lemon juice. Season the cabbage with salt to taste and toss well to combine. Serve sprinkled with the toasted pine nuts.

—MARION CUNNINGHAM

FIELD SALAD WITH MUSHROOMS AND WALNUTS

Field salad, mâche, or lamb's lettuce—whatever you call it, it makes a flavorful salad. If it's unavailable, you can substitute a mixture of greens.

SERVES 12

½	pound mushrooms, stems removed
1	tablespoon lemon juice
1	tablespoon Dijon mustard
	Salt
1	teaspoon fresh-ground black pepper
¼	cup peanut oil
1½	cups walnut pieces
1½	tablespoons butter, melted
1½	tablespoons red-wine vinegar
6	tablespoons olive oil
9	cups mâche or a mixture of greens such as Boston lettuce, romaine, and arugula

1. Heat the oven to 400°. Slice the mushroom caps horizontally about ¼ inch thick. Stack the slices and cut them into ¼-inch sticks.

2. In a medium bowl, combine the lemon juice, mustard, ¼ teaspoon salt, and ½ teaspoon of the pepper. Add the peanut oil slowly, whisking. Add the mushrooms and toss to combine.

3. On a baking sheet, toss the walnuts with the melted butter. Sprinkle with salt and toast in the preheated oven until golden brown, about 10 minutes.

4. In a large bowl, combine the vinegar, ¼ teaspoon salt, and the remaining ½ teaspoon pepper. Whisk in the olive oil. Just before serving, put the salad greens in the bowl and toss. Arrange the salad on serving plates. Put mushrooms in the center of each salad and scatter walnuts over the top.

—JACQUES PEPIN

MAKE IT AHEAD
Prepare the mushrooms up to 3 hours ahead, if you like. Cover with plastic wrap and set aside at room temperature. You can toast the nuts well in advance. Let cool, then store them in an airtight container. The dressing can also be made ahead; refrigerate until ready to use.

MIXED SALAD WITH KUMQUATS AND PECANS

Sliced fresh kumquats add a tart, orangey zip to this winter salad. Marinating them in the dressing for half an hour softens their skins nicely.

SERVES 8 TO 10

- 3 tablespoons wine vinegar
- 1 tablespoon Dijon mustard
- 1 clove garlic, crushed
- 1/4 teaspoon salt
- 1/4 teaspoon fresh-ground black pepper
- 1/2 cup olive oil
- 10 fresh kumquats, cut into thin slices, seeds removed
- 1 1/2 cups pecans
- 1 head romaine lettuce, torn into pieces (about 1 1/2 quarts)
- 1 head red-oak-leaf lettuce, torn into pieces (about 2 quarts)
- 1 small red onion, cut into thin rings
- 4 Belgian endives, two cut into thin slices, two separated into leaves

1. Heat the oven to 400°. In a large bowl, combine the wine vinegar, Dijon mustard, garlic, salt, and pepper. Add the oil slowly, whisking. Add the kumquats to the dressing and set aside to marinate for 30 minutes.

2. Meanwhile, spread the pecans on a baking sheet. Toast until the nuts are fragrant, about 5 minutes. Let cool. Break the pecans into large pieces.

3. Just before serving, add the lettuces, onion, the sliced endive, and the toasted pecans to the kumquats. Toss well to combine. Serve with the endive spears arranged around the salad.

MAKE IT AHEAD

Make the dressing one day ahead, if you like, but don't add the kumquats until 30 minutes before serving time. You can also clean and dry the lettuces the day before serving. Wrap them loosely in paper towels, pack them in a roomy plastic bag, and refrigerate until needed.

PEARL ONIONS IN CREAMY ONION SAUCE

Frozen pearl onions are a terrific holiday timesaver. They're already peeled, and so you start the recipe one step ahead of the game.

SERVES 8

- 8 tablespoons butter
- 1 cup dry bread crumbs
- 3 onions, chopped fine
- ¼ cup flour
- 2 cups milk
- 2 teaspoons salt
- ½ teaspoon fresh-ground black pepper
- 2 16-ounce packages frozen pearl onions

1. Heat the oven to 350°. Melt 4 tablespoons of the butter in a medium frying pan. Pour the melted butter into a small bowl and stir in the dry bread crumbs. Set this mixture aside.

2. Melt the remaining 4 tablespoons butter in the frying pan. Add the chopped onions and cook over moderately low heat, stirring occasionally, until the onions are translucent, about 5 minutes.

3. Sprinkle the flour over the onions in the pan and cook, whisking, for 1 minute. Slowly add the milk, whisking. Increase the heat to moderate and cook, whisking constantly, until the onion sauce comes to a boil. Boil for 1 minute. Stir in the salt and the pepper.

4. Put the pearl onions in a 2-quart baking dish. Pour the onion sauce over them and mix well, spreading the onions into an even layer. Sprinkle the buttered bread crumbs over the top. Bake until the topping is crisp and the sauce is bubbling around the edges, 40 to 50 minutes.

—MARION CUNNINGHAM

CRANBERRY WALNUT RELISH

Crunchy walnuts, tangy cranberries and orange, and mellow pear make an easy, refreshing, no-cook relish. The fruit isn't even peeled, so you can really make this recipe in no time.

MAKES ABOUT 3 CUPS

- 1 juice orange, scrubbed, halved, seeded, and chopped coarse
- 1 pear, quartered and cored
- 2¼ cups cranberries
- ½ cup walnut halves
- ½ cup sugar

Put the orange, pear, cranberries, and walnuts in a food processor and pulse to chop, 20 to 30 seconds. Do not overprocess. Alternatively, pass the ingredients through a meat grinder. Stir in the sugar.

JELLIED CRANBERRY SAUCE

Homemade cranberry sauce has a fresh, tart flavor. It's so easy to make, you may never go back to store-bought.

MAKES ABOUT 3 CUPS

- 2¼ cups water
- 1 12-ounce package fresh cranberries (about 3 cups)
- 1½ cups sugar
- ⅛ teaspoon salt

1. In a medium saucepan, bring the water to a boil. Add the cranberries and boil over moderately high heat, stirring occasionally, for 20 minutes.

2. Puree the cranberries in a food processor and strain. Return the puree to the pan and cook over low heat, stirring frequently, for 3 minutes. Add the sugar and salt and cook until the sugar dissolves, about 2 minutes. Transfer to a bowl, let cool, and refrigerate until gelled.

—MARION CUNNINGHAM

MAKE IT AHEAD
You can prepare the sauce 1 week in advance. Keep refrigerated until ready to use.

CANDIED QUINCES

Quinces look like yellowish-green apples. They are very tart and need lots of sugar to bring out their wonderful flavor. Candied quinces, pictured on page 70, are delicious with any roasted bird but are especially perfect with goose.

SERVES 6 TO 8

2   lemons, halved

4   pounds quinces

2   cups sugar

2   tablespoons butter

1. Squeeze the juice from one of the lemons into a large bowl half-filled with cold water. One at a time, peel, quarter, and core the quinces and add them to the bowl.

2. In a large saucepan, combine 6 cups of water with the sugar and the juice of the remaining lemon. Bring to a boil over high heat, stirring to dissolve the sugar. Remove the quinces from the water and add them to the syrup. Reduce the heat to moderate and cook, uncovered, until the quinces are soft and the liquid is very syrupy, about 1 hour. Drain the quinces, reserving the syrup for another use (see "Quince Syrup," right).

3. Shortly before serving, melt the butter in a large frying pan over moderate heat. Add the candied quinces and cook, stirring, until warmed through, 2 to 3 minutes.

—LYDIE MARSHALL

MAKE IT AHEAD
The dish can be made through Step 2 a week ahead. Cover and refrigerate.

QUINCE SYRUP

The reserved syrup can be refrigerated in a one-pint jar for several months. When cold, the syrup becomes a jelly, which you can spread on toast or melt again and use to glaze fruit tarts, ham, or a roasting bird.

chapter 9
COOKIES

Linzer Wreaths, page 166

Granny's Molasses Spice Cookies

Everyone's Granny west of the Mississippi, it seems, had a recipe for some version of these cookies. As the cookies bake, they puff up, heave a sigh, and then collapse as flat as can be. They have a cracked surface and a sugary sheen. Be careful not to overbake them, for burnt molasses tastes very bitter.

MAKES ABOUT 4 DOZEN

6 ounces unsalted butter

$\frac{1}{4}$ cup molasses

1 teaspoon vanilla extract

2 cups flour

$1\frac{1}{3}$ cups sugar

2 teaspoons baking soda

2 teaspoons ground ginger

2 teaspoons cinnamon

$\frac{1}{4}$ teaspoon grated nutmeg

$\frac{1}{4}$ teaspoon ground cloves

$\frac{1}{4}$ teaspoon salt

1 large egg

1. Heat the oven to 375°. In a small saucepan, melt the butter over low heat. Remove from the heat and add the molasses and vanilla. Set aside to cool.

2. In a medium bowl, whisk together the flour, 1 cup of the sugar, the baking soda, ginger, cinnamon, nutmeg, cloves, and salt.

3. Add the egg to the butter mixture and whisk to mix. With a wooden spoon, stir the butter mixture into the dry ingredients. Cover the dough with plastic wrap and refrigerate until firm, about 15 minutes.

4. Put the remaining $\frac{1}{3}$ cup sugar in a small bowl. Shape the dough into 1-inch balls. Toss the balls in the sugar to coat completely and put them about 2 inches apart on ungreased baking sheets.

5. Bake the cookies in the middle of the oven until the bottoms just begin to brown, about 10 minutes. Let the cookies cool on the baking sheets for 5 minutes, then transfer to a rack to cool.

—Peggy Cullen

MAKE IT AHEAD
You can make these cookies a week to 10 days in advance and keep them in an airtight container.

LINZER WREATHS

Hazelnut linzer dough is baked into small, rimmed cookies that are then filled with raspberry jam. The end result is a perfect little wreath of pastry holding a shiny red pool—just right for a holiday cookie tray.

MAKES 2 DOZEN

- 1 cup hazelnuts
- 1½ cups plus 2 tablespoons flour
- 6 ounces unsalted butter, at room temperature
- ¾ cup sugar
- ½ teaspoon vanilla extract
- 1 large egg, at room temperature
- ¾ teaspoon baking powder
- ¼ teaspoon salt
- ¾ teaspoon cinnamon
- ⅓ cup raspberry jam

1. Heat the oven to 350°. Put the hazelnuts on a baking sheet and toast them in the oven until the skins crack and loosen and the nuts are golden brown, about 15 minutes. Wrap the hot hazelnuts in a kitchen towel and firmly rub them together to loosen most of the skins. Discard the skins. Let the nuts cool.

2. In a food processor, grind the hazelnuts to a powder with the 2 tablespoons flour. Avoid processing too long, or the nut oil will separate from the meat.

3. Using an electric mixer, cream the butter with the sugar and vanilla until fluffy, about 5 minutes. Beat in the ground nuts. Add the egg and beat until combined, scraping the bowl occasionally.

4. In a small bowl, whisk together the remaining 1½ cups flour, the baking powder, salt, and cinnamon. Add to the butter mixture in two batches, mixing until just combined. Wrap the dough and chill at least 2 hours or overnight.

5. Divide the dough in half. On a lightly floured surface, roll half the dough about ¼ inch thick. Using a 2-inch round cookie cutter, stamp out circles. Put each circle on the bottom of an ungreased ½-cup muffin cup. Repeat with the remaining dough scraps to fill twenty-four cups.

6. Divide the remaining dough into twenty-four equal pieces and shape each into a 6-inch log, about ½ inch thick. Using a small knife, cut each log into twelve slices, each about ½ inch thick. Roll each slice into a small ball. Press twelve balls around the edge of each dough circle. The fit should not be too tight. Alternatively, roll the reserved dough into twenty-four logs about 5 inches long and put each log around the edge of a circle. Or, let the dough soften and, using a pastry bag fitted with a ¼-inch plain tip, pipe the dough around the edge of each circle.

7.   Bake the cookies in the middle of the oven until golden brown and firm, about 17 minutes. Transfer them to a rack. While the cookies are still hot, drop about ½ teaspoon of raspberry jam into the center of each wreath. Let cool.

—PEGGY CULLEN

MAKE IT AHEAD
Once baked, these little wreaths can be stored in an airtight container for a week to 10 days.

VARIATIONS

■ Use another flavor of jam, such as apricot, blackberry, or blueberry, in the centers of the cookies. You can also make a colorful combination by filling half the cookies with one type of jam and the other half with another.

■ Use another nut, such as blanched almonds or walnuts, in place of the hazelnuts. Reduce the toasting time to about ten minutes. The cookies will taste different but just as good, and you'll save a few minutes since there's no skin to remove from the nuts.

■ Dust the cookies with a little bit of confectioners' sugar once they're cool. It will look like snow has fallen on the wreaths.

FRUITCAKE COOKIES

As with any good fruitcake, there is only enough batter here to hold the fruit together. The fruit is dried rather than candied; sticky Medjool dates and moist, plump figs are our first choices, but you can substitute other fruits such as raisins or prunes. These cookies, pictured on page 164, are best eaten a day after they are baked, when the flavors have had a chance to develop.

MAKES ABOUT 2 DOZEN

- 10 tablespoons unsalted butter, at room temperature
- $1/3$ cup dark-brown sugar
- $1/2$ teaspoon cinnamon
- $1/2$ teaspoon ground ginger
- $1/4$ teaspoon grated nutmeg
  Pinch salt
- 1 cup plus 2 tablespoons flour
- $1/2$ cup whole unblanched almonds
- 4 dried figs, cut into $1/2$-inch pieces (about $1/2$ cup)
- 4 large dates, preferably Medjool, cut into $1/2$-inch pieces (about $1/2$ cup)
- $1/2$ cup pecans, chopped coarse
- 2 tablespoons honey
- 2 tablespoons plus $1\frac{1}{2}$ teaspoons rum, preferably dark
- 1 large egg, at room temperature, beaten to mix
- $2/3$ cup confectioners' sugar

1. Using an electric mixer, cream 6 tablespoons of the butter with the brown sugar, cinnamon, ginger, nutmeg, and salt until fluffy, about 3 minutes. Add $3/4$ cup of the flour, mixing until just combined. Wrap the dough and refrigerate for 15 minutes.

2. Heat the oven to 400°. Put the almonds on a baking sheet and toast them in the oven for 5 minutes. Let cool and then chop coarse. Put the almonds in a large bowl and stir in the figs, dates, and pecans.

3. Using an electric mixer, cream the remaining 4 tablespoons butter with the honey and 1 teaspoon of the rum until fluffy, about 5 minutes. Add the egg and beat until combined, scraping the bowl occasionally. Add the remaining 6 tablespoons flour, mixing until just combined. Fold the dried fruit and nuts into this batter until they're completely coated. Set the fruitcake batter aside.

4. Butter two baking sheets. On a lightly floured surface, roll the chilled dough about $1/4$ inch thick. Using a 2-inch fluted cookie cutter, stamp out rounds. Reroll the scraps and repeat. Put the cookies about 1 inch apart on the prepared baking sheets. Mound 1 tablespoon of the fruitcake batter on each.

5. Bake the cookies in the middle of the oven until they begin to brown on top, about 10 minutes. Meanwhile, sift the confectioners' sugar into a bowl. Stir in the remaining 2 tablespoons plus $1/2$ teaspoon rum until smooth.

6. When the cookies are baked, drizzle about ½ teaspoon of the rum glaze over each one. Return to the oven and bake until the glaze bubbles and cracks, about 1 minute. Let the cookies cool on the baking sheet for about 5 minutes and then transfer them to a rack to cool.

—PEGGY CULLEN

MAKE IT AHEAD
You can keep these cookies in an airtight container for up to 2 weeks.

VARIATIONS

■ Use another liquor, such as brandy or bourbon, in place of the rum.

■ For a quicker version, omit the individual pastry rounds. Drop tablespoons of the fruitcake batter directly into buttered mini-muffin pans. You can also drop tablespoons of batter about one inch apart onto a buttered baking sheet. Bake the mini-fruitcakes for the same length of time as specified in the recipe and drizzle with the rum glaze in the same way. The little fruitcakes aren't as fancy as the cookies, but they taste delicious.

CRANBERRY PISTACHIO BISCOTTI

With flecks of dried cranberries and pistachios, these new-style biscotti, pictured on page 164, look and taste like Christmas. They're perfect with Cranberry Raspberry Sorbet, page 237, or with coffee.

MAKES ABOUT 3 DOZEN

1¾ cups flour

1 cup plus 1 teaspoon sugar

½ teaspoon baking powder

¼ teaspoon salt

½ cup dried cranberries

4 tablespoons cold unsalted butter, cut into ½-inch pieces

1 teaspoon vanilla extract

1½ cups shelled, unsalted pistachios

2 large eggs, beaten to mix

1. Heat the oven to 350°. Butter a large baking sheet.

2. Put the flour, 1 cup of the sugar, the baking powder, and the salt in a food processor and pulse once or twice to mix. Add the cranberries. Pulse until chopped coarse. Add the butter and vanilla. Pulse until the mixture is the texture of coarse meal.

3. Add the pistachios and the eggs and pulse ten times. Scrape down the sides of the bowl and pulse until the dough is evenly moistened, about five more times.

4. On a lightly floured surface, shape the dough into four logs about 8 inches long. Put the logs about 2 inches apart on the prepared baking sheet. With your hands, flatten the logs to a width of 2 inches and sprinkle with the remaining 1 teaspoon sugar.

5. Bake the logs in the middle of the oven until golden brown, about 25 minutes. Transfer the logs to a rack to firm up slightly, about 15 minutes.

6. Transfer the logs to a work surface. Using a sharp knife and a quick single motion, cut diagonally into ½-inch slices. Put the slices on the baking sheet and bake until just beginning to brown, about 7 minutes. Transfer the biscotti to a rack to cool.

—PEGGY CULLEN

MAKE IT AHEAD
Like all biscotti, these keep well in an airtight container for up to 2 weeks.

CHOCOLATE-DIPPED SNOWBALLS

Somewhere between a cookie and a candy, these flourless macaroons are crunchy on the outside, moist and chewy on the inside. The slight bitterness of semisweet chocolate is the perfect foil for the sweet coconut.

MAKES ABOUT 2 DOZEN

2½ cups unsweetened medium shredded coconut*

 1 tablespoon plus 2 teaspoons cornstarch

¾ cup sugar

 2 tablespoons unsalted butter, cut into pieces

¼ cup light corn syrup

 1 teaspoon vanilla extract

¼ teaspoon salt

 2 large egg whites, beaten to mix

 5 ounces semisweet chocolate, chopped

*Available at health-food stores

1. Heat the oven to 375°. Butter and flour a baking sheet. In a medium bowl, combine the shredded coconut and the cornstarch. Set aside.

2. In a medium stainless-steel saucepan, combine the sugar, butter, corn syrup, vanilla, and salt. Bring to a boil over high heat, stirring constantly. Boil for 10 seconds, remove from the heat, and stir in the coconut mixture. Add half the egg whites and stir until thoroughly combined. Stir in the remaining egg whites. The mixture will form a ball. Return to high heat and cook, stirring, for 30 seconds. Let cool slightly.

3. With moistened hands, roll the mixture into 1-inch balls. Put the balls about 1 inch apart on the prepared baking sheet.

4. Bake in the middle of the oven for 5 minutes. Rotate the baking sheet and continue cooking until the tops begin to turn golden brown, about 5 minutes longer. Let the cookies cool completely on the pan.

5. Put the chocolate in a double boiler over simmering water. When the chocolate is nearly melted, remove from the heat. Stir until completely smooth. Set aside to cool, stirring occasionally. It's ready for dipping when a small drop feels cool on your skin.

6. Line a baking sheet with parchment or waxed paper. Using your fingers, hold a snowball near the top and dip the bottom half into the cooled chocolate. Gently shake off the excess and lightly scrape the bottom over the rim of the bowl. Put the dipped snowball, chocolate-side up, on the paper. Chill the finished snowballs for just 5 minutes to set the chocolate. Store at room temperature.

—PEGGY CULLEN

MAKE IT AHEAD
You can keep the snowballs in an airtight container for about a week.

GILDED CHOCOLATE SHORTBREAD

The trick to baking a good shortbread with a tender, buttery bite is to use just enough flour to prevent the cookies from spreading while in the oven. Confectioners' sugar, rather than granulated, also helps them hold their shape. These shortbread cookies are shaped with crescent-moon and star cutters. To really gild the lily, brush on powdered 24-karat gold dust before the cookies are baked.

MAKES ABOUT 3 DOZEN

- ½ pound unsalted butter, at room temperature
- 1 cup confectioners' sugar
- ½ cup unsweetened cocoa powder
- 1 teaspoon vanilla extract
- ¼ teaspoon salt
- 2 cups flour

  24-karat gold dust (optional; see "Pure Gold," below)

1. Using an electric mixer on medium speed, cream the butter with ¾ cup of the confectioners' sugar, the cocoa, vanilla, and salt until just blended, about 30 seconds.

2. With the mixer on low speed, add the flour to the butter mixture in three batches, mixing until just combined. Wrap the dough and chill for 1 hour.

3. Heat the oven to 325°. Sprinkle a work surface with 2 tablespoons of the confectioners' sugar. Roll half the dough until it's just under ½ inch thick. Using crescent-moon and star cutters or whatever shape you like, stamp out cookies and put them about 1 inch apart on unbuttered

baking sheets. Combine the scraps and set aside. Repeat with the remaining piece of dough, using the remaining 2 tablespoons confectioners' sugar, if necessary, to prevent the dough from sticking. Reroll all the scraps and repeat.

4. Using a small, stiff paintbrush or a flat pastry brush, lightly paint the surface of each cookie with the gold dust.

5. Bake the cookies in the middle of the oven until firm and beginning to crisp on the bottom, about 15 minutes. Do not overbake. Let the cookies cool on the baking sheet for 5 minutes and then transfer to a rack to cool.

—PEGGY CULLEN

PURE GOLD

Gold dust, which is edible, can be found at art-supply stores or at stores specializing in cake-decorating equipment.

GINGERBREAD COOKIES

One of America's favorites, these gingerbread cookies are the old-fashioned kind that you roll out into gingerbread people, or any shape you like. A hint of cardamom makes this version extra special. The cookies are delicious plain, but especially fun and festive decorated with icing, seeds, nuts, or dried fruit.

MAKES ABOUT 2 DOZEN

- 3 cups flour
- 2½ teaspoons ground ginger
- 1¼ teaspoons cinnamon
- ½ teaspoon ground cardamom
- ½ teaspoon grated nutmeg
- ¼ teaspoon ground cloves
- ½ teaspoon baking soda
- ¼ teaspoon salt
- ¾ cup molasses
- ¼ pound unsalted butter, at room temperature
- ½ cup sugar
- 2 tablespoons water
- 1 large egg, at room temperature

  Royal Icing, opposite page (optional)

  Nuts, seeds, raisins, or other dried fruits, for decoration (optional)

1. In a large bowl, whisk together the flour, ginger, cinnamon, cardamom, nutmeg, cloves, baking soda, and salt.

2. In a small saucepan, heat the molasses over low heat until bubbles begin to form around the edge. Remove from the heat and stir in the butter, 1 tablespoon at a time, until it is completely incorporated.

Scrape the mixture into a large bowl. Stir in the sugar and water. Stir in the egg until completely incorporated.

3. Make a well in the center of the flour mixture and pour in the molasses mixture. Gradually stir in the flour mixture until blended. Turn the dough out onto a floured surface. Knead gently until smooth. Pat into a 6-inch disk. Wrap and chill overnight.

4. Heat the oven to 350°. Butter two baking sheets. On a lightly floured surface, roll half the dough to ⅛ inch thick. (Keep the rest wrapped until ready to use.) Using cookie cutters, stamp out cookies. Put them about ½ inch apart on the prepared baking sheets. If you like, brush the cookies with icing. Or, brush them with a little water and press on the nuts, seeds, and/or dried fruit.

5. Bake the cookies in the middle of the oven until firm and slightly puffed, about 10 minutes. Transfer them to a rack to cool and then decorate with icing, if you like.

—LINDA MERINOFF

MAKE IT AHEAD
You can make the dough up to 3 days ahead. Once baked, the cookies keep well in an airtight container for up to 2 weeks.

ROYAL ICING

This easy-to-make icing hardens as it dries, so it's ideal for decorating. You can brush or pipe it onto the cookies before or after baking.

MAKES ABOUT 1 CUP

- 1 large egg white, at room temperature
- 1¾ cups plus 2 tablespoons confectioners' sugar, sifted, more if needed
- ⅛ teaspoon cream of tartar
- 1½ teaspoons lemon juice
  Food coloring (optional)

1. In a large bowl, combine all the ingredients except the food coloring. Using a hand-held electric mixer, beat the mixture at high speed until fluffy, thick, and shiny, about 3 minutes.

2. Divide the icing into small amounts and adjust the consistency as needed. To thin for painting, beat in water; for a stiffer icing that holds its shape when piped, add more confectioners' sugar. Tint the icing with the food coloring. Cover tightly to keep the icing from drying out.

—PEGGY CULLEN

MAKE IT AHEAD
You can make the icing and refrigerate it in an airtight container for up to 1 week.

COOKIE DECORATING TIPS

- You can pipe an outline around a baked or unbaked cookie and then fill in by brushing with thinned icing of a different color.

- To make hair for gingerbread people or animals, knead a little extra flour into a bit of the dough and then squeeze the dough through a garlic press.

- Paint or pipe icing onto baked or unbaked cookies. Before the icing dries, sprinkle it with tinted sugar, sugar glitter, or dragées, or dust with confectioners' sugar.

- For hanging ornaments, pierce unbaked cookies with the blunt end of a bamboo skewer, or with a chopstick. Repierce after baking, while still warm.

- For a ribbon border, make holes around the edge of an unbaked cookie with a skewer or chopstick. Pierce again after baking. Weave a ribbon through the holes.

—PEGGY CULLEN

LEBKUCHEN

Honey and spices are the characteristic ingredients in these traditional German cookies. The rich, satisfying flavor of lebkuchen explains why it's held its popularity since medieval times.

MAKES ABOUT 6 DOZEN

1 cup plus 2 tablespoons sliced blanched almonds, plus more (optional) for decorating

3¾ cups flour

1½ teaspoons baking powder

1 tablespoon cinnamon

½ teaspoon ground cloves

½ teaspoon ground anise seeds

½ teaspoon grated nutmeg

½ teaspoon ground ginger

1 teaspoon ground cardamom

1¼ cups honey or molasses

¼ pound unsalted butter

½ cup candied fruit, chopped fine

1. In a food processor, grind the almonds to a powder. Set aside.

2. In a large bowl, whisk together the flour, baking powder, cinnamon, cloves, anise, nutmeg, ginger, and cardamom.

3. In a large saucepan, heat the honey and butter until the butter melts and the mixture just comes to a boil. Don't let it continue to boil, or the cookies may become too hard. Remove from the heat and let cool for about 1 minute. With a wooden spoon, stir in the ground almonds and the candied fruit, stirring vigorously to break up any clumps of fruit and to combine thoroughly.

4. Add the flour mixture, stir for a moment, and then turn out onto a floured surface. Knead until smooth. The dough should be very soft but not sticky. Wrap and let sit overnight at room temperature.

5. Heat the oven to 375°. Butter and flour two large baking sheets. On a lightly floured surface, roll the dough as thin as possible. Using decorative cutters, stamp out cookies and put them about 1 inch apart on the prepared baking sheets. If you like, gently press sliced almonds into the cookies for decoration.

6. Bake the cookies in the middle of the oven until crisp and brown, about 7 minutes. Transfer to a rack to cool.

MAKE IT AHEAD The honey helps the cookies last; in fact, they're best 2 or 3 weeks after baking when they have softened and the flavors of the spices have mingled and ripened. Store in an airtight container.

LACY GINGER SNOWFLAKES

The caramel crunch of these elegant, lacy cookies complements the chewy bite of candied ginger and pineapple. The ginger should be soft enough to tear, and the candied pineapple should be moist and pliable.

MAKES ABOUT 2 DOZEN

½ cup instant rolled oats

½ cup flour

⅓ cup chopped crystallized ginger

⅓ chopped candied pineapple

4 tablespoons unsalted butter, cut into ½-inch pieces

¼ cup light-brown sugar

¼ cup light corn syrup

1 teaspoon ground ginger

1 teaspoon rum, preferably dark

1. Heat the oven to 350°. In a medium bowl, combine the oats and the flour. Add the crystallized ginger and the pineapple and toss to coat thoroughly with the flour.

2. In a medium saucepan, combine the butter, brown sugar, corn syrup, ground ginger, and rum. Bring to a boil over high heat, stirring, until the butter is completely melted, about 2 minutes. Stir the hot syrup into the dry ingredients and let cool, stirring occasionally, until the batter is somewhat stiff, about 5 minutes.

3. Butter two baking sheets. With moistened hands, roll the dough into 1-inch balls. Put the balls about 3 inches apart on the prepared baking sheets.

4. Bake the cookies in the middle of the oven until the edges are golden, about 8 minutes. The centers will look somewhat underbaked, but they will continue to cook on the hot baking sheet. Let the cookies cool on the baking sheet until they begin to harden, about 3 minutes. Transfer to a rack to cool completely.

—PEGGY CULLEN

HEAVENLY PUFF ANGELS

Gingerbread-girl cutters and frozen puff pastry are the secrets here. Just attach pastry wings for a unique and delicious cookie.

MAKES 9 ANGELS

1 1-pound sheet frozen all-butter puff-pastry dough, thawed

About 1 cup sugar, more if needed

1. Line two baking sheets with parchment paper. On a lightly sugared surface, unfold the puff pastry and sprinkle ¼ cup of the sugar on each side. Cut off an 8 by 6-inch rectangle.

2. Sprinkle each side of the rectangle with 1 tablespoon of the sugar. With one of the long sides toward you, fold in the top and bottom edges about ½ inch toward the center. Gently pat the folds flat, keeping the sides and the corners square, and sprinkle with 1 tablespoon sugar. Fold in the top and the bottom edges again so that they meet in the center. Gently flatten and sprinkle with another tablespoon of the sugar. Fold over where the top and the bottom meet and gently press the layers together. Wrap and chill the folded dough for 20 minutes.

3. Using a 5-inch gingerbread-girl cutter, stamp out nine cookies from the remaining puff pastry. Cut the cookies as close together as possible, reversing the cutter each time. Sprinkle generously with more sugar to prevent sticking. Put the cookies on the prepared baking sheets, leaving as much space as possible between them. With a fork, prick each of the cookies in six places.

4. Heat the oven to 425°. Cut the folded dough crosswise into eighteen ¼-inch slices. (Reserve any remaining dough and, if you like, bake separately.) To make the wings, pinch the middle of the outer layer of dough on the rounded edge of each slice between your thumb and forefinger to flatten slightly. Use this flattened portion as a tab to tuck underneath the angel cookie at the shoulder; press firmly to attach the wing to the angel's body.

5. Bake the cookies in the middle of the oven until well-browned, puffed, and crisp, about 15 minutes. Let the angels cool completely on the pan and then gently peel off the parchment paper. Be careful to keep the wings intact.

—PEGGY CULLEN

MAKE IT AHEAD
Puff pastry is best when just baked, but you can assemble these cookies and freeze them ready-to-bake.

Spicy Nut Meringues

Flavored with cinnamon, cloves, and walnuts, these crisp and airy little cookies are a sweet holiday treat. They're quick to prepare and are a great addition to an assorted-cookie tray.

MAKES ABOUT 5 DOZEN

½   cup sugar

1   teaspoon cinnamon

⅛   teaspoon ground cloves

2   large egg whites, at room temperature

2   cups finely chopped walnuts

1. Heat the oven to 250°. Use nonstick baking sheets, or butter two baking sheets. In a small bowl, combine the sugar, cinnamon, and cloves.

2. In a large bowl, using an electric mixer, beat the egg whites on medium speed until they hold soft peaks. Increase the speed to high. Gradually beat in the sugar mixture. Continue beating until the whites hold very firm peaks when the beaters are lifted. Fold in the walnuts. Spoon 1-teaspoon mounds of the batter about ½ inch apart on the prepared baking sheets.

3. Bake the meringues for 1¼ hours and then turn off the oven. Open the oven door to allow the meringues to cool slowly.

MAKE IT AHEAD
The meringues keep perfectly in an airtight container for up to 3 weeks.

Variations

■ You can use other nuts, such as pecans, almonds, or hazelnuts, instead of the walnuts.

■ In place of the ground cloves, use one-quarter teaspoon grated nutmeg or ground ginger. Or replace one-quarter teaspoon of the cinnamon with grated nutmeg or ground ginger.

Storing Nuts

The best way to keep nuts so they won't become rancid is to freeze them. You can use the nuts directly from the freezer. Or, to bring out their flavor, toast them in a 350° oven for five minutes.

PFEFFERNUSSE

Spicy and cake-like with a delicious, thin lemon glaze, these cookies are the essence of holiday baked goods. So they'll hold their shape during baking, let the unbaked cookies dry overnight.

MAKES ABOUT 3 1/2 DOZEN

- ⅓ cup whole unblanched almonds
- 1½ cups plus 2 tablespoons flour, more if needed
- 1 teaspoon baking powder
- 1 tablespoon cinnamon
- ¼ teaspoon ground cloves
- ¼ teaspoon grated nutmeg
- ¼ teaspoon ground ginger
- 2 large eggs
- 1⅓ cups superfine sugar
- 1 tablespoon rum, more if needed
- 1 tablespoon minced candied fruit
- 1½ cups confectioners' sugar, more if needed
- 2 tablespoons lemon juice, more if needed

1. Butter two baking sheets. In a food processor, grind the almonds to a powder. Avoid processing too long, or the nut oil will separate from the meat. Set aside. In a large bowl, whisk together the flour, baking powder, cinnamon, cloves, nutmeg, and ginger.

2. In a large bowl, using a hand-held electric mixer or a whisk, beat together the eggs and superfine sugar. Set the bowl over a large saucepan that contains about an inch of simmering water. The water should not touch the bottom of the bowl. Beat the mixture until it mounds when the beaters are lifted, about 5 minutes. Remove from the heat. Beat for 3 minutes longer. Beat in the rum.

3. With a wooden spoon, fold the flour mixture into the egg mixture. Fold in the ground almonds and the candied fruit.

4. Turn the dough onto a lightly floured surface and knead until smooth, about 3 minutes. The dough should be quite soft. If the dough is too stiff, add a little more rum. If the dough is too wet, add a little more flour. Roll the dough into 1-inch balls and put them about 1 inch apart on the prepared baking sheets. Let the cookies dry, uncovered, at room temperature for 16 to 24 hours.

5. Heat the oven to 375°. In a small bowl, combine the confectioners' sugar and the lemon juice. Using a hand-held electric mixer or whisk, beat until completely smooth, about 10 minutes. The icing should just coat a spoon. If too thin, add a little more sugar; if too thick, a little more lemon juice.

6. Bake the cookies in the middle of the oven until firm and light brown, about 12 minutes. Don't worry if they crack during baking. Transfer the cookies to a rack and let cool to warm. Brush with the icing and let cool completely so that the icing sets.

chapter *10*
PIES & TARTS

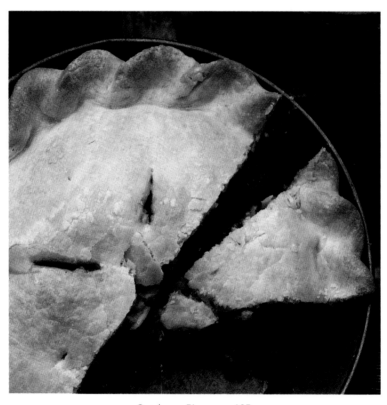

Cranberry Pie, page 185

CRANBERRY PIE

The cranberries are sweetened just enough to calm their tartness and let the other flavors in the filling come through.

MAKES ONE 9-INCH PIE

- 1 12-ounce package cranberries (about 3 cups)
- ½ cup golden raisins
- ⅓ cup chopped walnuts
- ¼ cup orange juice
- 3 tablespoons unsalted butter, melted
- ½ teaspoon grated orange zest
  Old-Fashioned Pie Dough, page 191
- 1 cup sugar
- ¼ cup flour
- 1 egg, beaten to mix with 2 teaspoons water

1. Heat the oven to 400°. In a food processor, chop the cranberries until the largest pieces are the size of peas, about 3 seconds. Transfer the cranberries to a medium bowl and add the raisins, walnuts, orange juice, melted butter, and orange zest. Stir until thoroughly combined.

2. On a lightly floured surface, roll half of the pie dough into a 12-inch round. Drape the dough over a 9-inch pie pan. Press it into the pan and against the sides. Leave the edges overhanging. Roll the remaining pie dough into another 12-inch round.

3. In a small bowl, combine the sugar and flour. Sprinkle ¼ cup of the mixture on the bottom of the pie shell. Mound the filling in the pie shell and sprinkle with the remaining sugar-and-flour mixture. Moisten the rim of the pie shell with water and cover with the dough round. Trim the edges of the dough ¾ inch from the rim of the pan. Roll both layers of the dough under and crimp the edge to seal. Brush the pie with the beaten egg and cut several steam vents in the top.

4. Put the pie on a baking sheet and bake in the middle of the oven until the pastry is golden and the filling bubbles up through the vents, about 50 minutes. Transfer to a rack and let cool completely.

—SUSAN HERRMANN LOOMIS

CRANBERRY ORANGE CREAM TART

A creamy custard flavored with orange liqueur is topped with walnuts, a sparkling layer of cooked cranberries, and candied orange zest in this exceptional and elegant tart.

MAKES ONE 10¹/₂-INCH TART

 4 large egg yolks, at room temperature

1¹/₂ cups sugar

 5 tablespoons plus 2 teaspoons cornstarch

1¹/₂ cups milk

 ¹/₂ vanilla bean, split lengthwise, or ³/₄ teaspoon vanilla extract

1¹/₂ tablespoons orange liqueur, such as Grand Marnier

 ¹/₂ cup heavy cream

 2 navel oranges

 1 cup plus 2 tablespoons water, more if needed

 1 12-ounce package cranberries (about 3 cups)

 Tart Shell, opposite page

 ¹/₂ cup chopped walnuts

1. In a medium bowl, beat the egg yolks and ¹/₂ cup of the sugar with an electric mixer on medium-high speed until pale in color, 3 to 5 minutes. Beat in 4 tablespoons of the cornstarch until smooth. In a small saucepan, bring the milk and the vanilla bean, if using, just to a boil. Strain and gradually whisk the hot milk into the egg mixture.

2. Pour into a medium saucepan. Bring to a boil over low heat, stirring frequently. Reduce the heat and simmer, stirring, until the custard thickens and is smooth, about 1 minute. Pour into a medium bowl and beat until fluffy and cooled to room temperature, about 5 minutes. Add the vanilla extract, if using, and the orange liqueur.

3. In a medium bowl, beat the heavy cream just until it holds stiff peaks when the beaters are lifted. Fold into the cooled custard, cover, and chill.

4. Using a vegetable peeler, strip off the zest from the oranges. Cut the zest into matchstick strips. Squeeze the juice from the oranges. You should have 1 cup; if there is less, add enough water to make 1 cup.

5. In a small pot of boiling water, blanch the zest for 3 minutes. Drain and return the zest to the pot. Add the remaining 1 cup sugar and 1 cup of the water and bring to a boil. Reduce the heat and simmer until the syrup is reduced to ¹/₂ cup, about 20 minutes. With a slotted spoon, removed the zest and spread the strips flat on a piece of waxed paper.

6. Add the orange juice to the syrup and bring to a boil. Add the cranberries, reduce the heat, and simmer for 10 minutes. Meanwhile, in a small bowl, combine the remaining 1 tablespoon plus 2 teaspoons

cornstarch and 2 tablespoons water. Add this mixture to the cranberries, stirring, until the liquid thickens, about 1 minute. Pour into a shallow bowl and let cool to room temperature.

7. Fill the Tart Shell with the custard. Scatter the walnuts over the custard and top with the cranberry mixture. Sprinkle the candied orange zest around the edge. Chill the tart until ready to serve.

TART SHELL

MAKES ONE 10½-INCH SHELL

1½ cups flour
1½ tablespoons sugar
¼ teaspoon salt
6 tablespoons cold unsalted butter, cut into pieces
3 tablespoons vegetable shortening
3 tablespoons cold water, more if needed

1. In a medium bowl, combine the flour, sugar, and salt. Cut the butter and shortening into the flour until the mixture resembles coarse meal. Sprinkle the water on top and stir until just combined. If it doesn't hold together when pressed, add more water, a teaspoon at a time. Press the dough into a flat disk and wrap tightly. Chill for 30 minutes.

2. Heat the oven to 425°. On a lightly floured surface, roll the dough into a 13-inch round. Drape it over a 10½-inch tart pan, press it into the pan and against the sides, and trim it even with the rim of the pan. Prick the bottom of the shell every inch or so with a fork. Freeze until firm, about 5 minutes.

3. Press a double thickness of aluminum foil against the dough. Bake for 12 minutes. Reduce the heat to 375°. Remove the foil from the pan and bake until the crust is golden brown, about 15 minutes longer. Let cool.

APPLE QUINCE PIE

Adding quince to all-American apple pie both intensifies the flavor and, because of the high pectin content of the fruit, provides body. Fall is the season for quince; look for large, aromatic fruit with smooth skin.

MAKES ONE 9-INCH PIE

- 2 pounds tart apples (about 4), such as Granny Smith, peeled, cored, and cut into ½-inch slices
- 2 quinces (about 1 pound), peeled, cored, and cut into ⅛-inch slices

  Zest and juice of 1 lemon
- ¾ cup sugar
- 1 tablespoon flour

  Old-Fashioned Pie Dough, page 191
- 3 tablespoons unsalted butter

1. Heat the oven to 400°. In a large bowl, toss together the apples, quinces, lemon zest, lemon juice, sugar, and flour.

2. On a lightly floured surface, roll half of the pie dough into a 12-inch round. Drape the dough over a 9-inch pie pan. Press it into the pan and against the sides. Leave the edges overhanging. Roll the remaining pie dough into another 12-inch round.

3. Mound the filling in the pie shell and dot with the butter. Moisten the rim of the pie shell with water and cover with the dough round. Trim the edges of the dough ¾ inch from the rim of the pan. Roll both layers of the dough under and crimp the edge to seal. Cut several steam vents in the top of the pie.

4. Bake the pie in the lower third of the oven for 25 minutes. Reduce the heat to 350°. Bake until the pastry is golden brown and the fruit is tender when pierced through one of the vents, about 35 minutes longer. Transfer to a rack and let cool for at least 2 hours before serving.

—MICHAEL JAMES

PEAR AND GINGER PIE

Very often the flavor of a fruit pie is obscured by too many spices. This one has only fresh ginger, which adds a piquant note. You can serve the pie warm or at room temperature.

MAKES ONE 9-INCH PIE

Old-Fashioned Pie Dough, page 191

1/3 cup sugar

3 tablespoons flour

2½ pounds pears (about 5)

1 1-inch piece fresh ginger, peeled and grated

2 tablespoons unsalted butter

1 egg, beaten to mix with a pinch of salt

1. Heat the oven to 450°. On a lightly floured surface, roll half of the pie dough into a 12-inch round. Drape the dough over a 9-inch pie pan. Press it into the pan and against the sides. Leave the edges overhanging.

2. In a small bowl, combine the sugar and flour. Sprinkle 2 tablespoons of this mixture on the bottom of the pie shell.

3. Peel, quarter, and core the pears. Cut each quarter crosswise into five or six slices. Put the pears in a large bowl and toss with the ginger. Add the remaining sugar-and-flour mixture and toss. Pour this filling into the pie shell. Dot with the butter.

4. On a lightly floured surface, roll the remaining pie dough into a 12-inch round.

Moisten the rim of the pie shell with water and cover with the dough round. Trim the edges of the dough ¾ inch from the rim of the pan. Roll both layers of the dough under and crimp the edge to seal. Brush the pie with the beaten egg and cut several steam vents in the top.

5. Put the pie on a baking sheet and bake in the lower third of the oven for 15 minutes. Reduce the heat to 350° and bake until the pastry is golden brown and the filling bubbles up through the vents, about 35 minutes longer. Let cool.

—NICHOLAS MALGIERI

189

MEATLESS MINCE PIE WITH BOURBON

Raisins, currants, apples, orange, spices, and bourbon make a deliciously full-flavored mince pie. For an over-the-top-dessert, serve it with whipped cream or vanilla ice cream.

MAKES ONE 9-INCH PIE

1 pound tart apples (about 2), such as Granny Smith, peeled and cored

⅔ cup golden raisins

⅓ cup currants

¼ cup bourbon

¼ cup apple cider or apple juice

3 tablespoons lemon juice

1 navel orange, unpeeled, cut into eight pieces

⅔ cup sugar

½ teaspoon salt

½ teaspoon cinnamon

½ teaspoon ground mace

¼ teaspoon ground cloves

¼ teaspoon ground ginger

2 tablespoons molasses

1 tablespoon flour

4 tablespoons unsalted butter

Old-Fashioned Pie Dough, opposite page

1. Heat the oven to 400°. In a food processor, chop the apples fine. Put them in a large bowl, add the raisins, currants, bourbon, cider, and lemon juice, and toss. In the food processor, puree the orange and add it to the apple mixture with the sugar, salt, cinnamon, mace, cloves, ginger, molasses, and flour. Stir until thoroughly combined.

2. In a small pan, melt the butter over low heat. Cook until the butter is golden brown, about 5 minutes. Stir the butter into the apple mixture.

3. On a lightly floured surface, roll half of the pie dough into a 12-inch round. Drape the dough over a 9-inch pie pan. Press it into the pan and against the sides. Leave the edges overhanging. Roll the remaining pie dough into a 12-inch round. Using a fluted dough cutter or a knife, cut the dough into ½- to ¾-inch-wide strips.

4. Pour the filling into the pie shell. Moisten the rim of the pie shell with water and weave the strips of dough into a lattice. Trim the edges of the dough ¾ inch from the rim of the pan. Roll both layers of the dough under and crimp the edge to seal.

5. Put the pie on a baking sheet and bake in the lower third of the oven for 25 minutes. Reduce the heat to 350° and bake until the pastry is golden brown and the filling is bubbling, about 45 minutes longer. Transfer to a rack and let cool completely before serving.

—MICHAEL JAMES

OLD-FASHIONED PIE DOUGH

MAKES ENOUGH DOUGH FOR ONE 9-INCH PIE

2¼ cups flour

¾ teaspoon salt

¾ cup vegetable shortening

5 tablespoons cold water, more if needed

1. In a medium bowl, combine the flour and the salt. Cut the shortening into the flour until the mixture resembles very coarse meal with some pieces of shortening still the size of corn kernels.

2. Sprinkle the water on top and stir the dough until just combined. If it doesn't hold together when pressed, add more water. Be stingy with the water, though; too much will make the pastry tough.

3. Shape the dough into two flat disks. Wrap tightly. Refrigerate for at least 30 minutes.

FLAKY PIE SHELL

MAKES ONE 9-INCH PIE SHELL

1½ cups flour

¼ teaspoon salt

½ cup vegetable shortening

3 tablespoons cold water, more if needed

1. Heat the oven to 425°. In a medium bowl, combine the flour and the salt. Using your fingertips, rub in the shortening until the mixture resembles very coarse meal with some pieces of shortening the size of corn kernels still visible.

2. Sprinkle the ice water on top of the flour mixture and stir just until combined. If the dough doesn't hold together when pressed, add additional water. Be stingy with the water, though; too much will make the pastry tough. Press the dough into a flat disk.

3. On a lightly floured surface, roll out the dough into a 12-inch round. Drape the dough over a 9-inch pie pan and press the dough into the pan and against the sides. Trim the edge of the dough ¾ inch from the rim of the pan. Roll the dough under and crimp. Prick the bottom of the shell every inch or so with a fork. Freeze until firm, about 5 minutes. Press a double thickness of aluminum foil against the dough.

4. Bake in the upper third of the oven for 6 minutes. Remove the foil and bake until golden brown, about 8 minutes longer. Transfer to a rack and let cool completely.

—MARION CUNNINGHAM

FUDGE PIE

Creamy, sweet, and chocolatey—that says it all. Whipped cream would make a nice, luxurious finishing touch.

MAKES ONE 9-INCH PIE

¼ pound unsalted butter

2 ounces unsweetened chocolate, chopped

2 large eggs, beaten to mix

1 cup sugar

¼ cup flour

¼ teaspoon salt

2 teaspoons vanilla extract

Flaky Pie Shell, page 191

1. Heat the oven to 350°. In a small saucepan, melt the butter with the chocolate, stirring frequently until smooth. Remove from the heat and let cool.

2. In a medium bowl, whisk together the eggs, sugar, flour, salt, and vanilla. Beat until smooth. Whisk in the chocolate mixture and beat until thoroughly combined.

3. Pour the filling into the pie shell. Bake the pie in the middle of the oven until just set, about 30 minutes. Let cool.

—MARION CUNNINGHAM

MELTING CHOCOLATE IN A MICROWAVE

A microwave oven is handy for melting chocolate, whether alone or in combination with butter. Put chopped chocolate and butter, if using, into a microwave-safe container and microwave at medium until the chocolate turns shiny, 1½ to 4 minutes. (Remove white and milk chocolate after 1½ minutes.) Stir the chocolate until completely melted. Do not overheat, or it may become grainy.

MAPLE PECAN PIE

For this pecan pie, you make a caramelized filling of sugar, cream, eggs, and maple syrup. It's rich, gooey, and altogether heavenly. Serve it with whipped cream.

MAKES ONE 9-INCH PIE

1½ cups heavy cream

¾ cup sugar

¾ cup pure maple syrup

2 large eggs, beaten to mix

2 teaspoons vanilla extract

2 cups pecan halves

Cornmeal Pie Shell, below

1. Heat the oven to 400°. In a large saucepan, bring the cream and sugar to a simmer over moderate heat. Reduce the heat and simmer for 25 minutes, whisking occasionally, until the mixture turns a light caramel color. Remove from the heat and whisk in the maple syrup, eggs, and vanilla. Stir in the pecans. Pour the filling into the pie shell.

2. Bake the pecan pie in the lower third of the oven until the filling is nearly set and the top is well browned, about 25 minutes. Let cool.

—MICHAEL JAMES

CORNMEAL PIE SHELL

MAKES ONE 9-INCH PIE SHELL

1 cup plus 2 tablespoons flour

¼ cup cornmeal

½ teaspoon salt

6 tablespoons vegetable shortening

¼ cup cold water, more if needed

1. In a medium bowl, combine the flour, cornmeal, and salt. Cut the shortening into the flour until the mixture resembles very coarse meal with some pieces still the size of corn kernels. Sprinkle the water on top and stir just until combined. If the dough doesn't hold together when pressed, add more water a teaspoon at a time. Press into a flat disk; wrap tightly. Refrigerate at least 30 minutes. On a lightly floured surface, roll the dough into a 12-inch round. Drape over a 9-inch pie pan and press into the pan and against the sides. Trim the edge ¾ inch from the rim of the pan. Roll under and crimp the edge. Prick the bottom every inch or so with a fork. Freeze until firm, about 5 minutes.

2. Heat the oven to 450°. Press a double thickness of aluminum foil against the dough. Bake in the lower third of the oven until partially done and beginning to brown, about 10 minutes. Remove the foil. Let cool.

PUMPKIN CUSTARD PIE

Light and airy, with a subtle pumpkin taste and delicate edge of cinnamon, this pie is perfect for Thanksgiving.

MAKES ONE 9-INCH PIE

- 1 cup Fresh Pumpkin Puree, right, or canned pumpkin puree
- 2 large eggs, separated, at room temperature
- 1⅓ cups milk
- 6 tablespoons granulated sugar
- 6 tablespoons light-brown sugar
- 1 tablespoon butter, melted
- ¾ teaspoon vanilla extract
  Pinch salt
- 3 tablespoons flour
  Flaky Pie Shell, page 191
- ¼ teaspoon cinnamon

1. Heat the oven to 425°. In a medium bowl, whisk together the pumpkin puree and the egg yolks until combined. Whisk in the milk, the granulated and light-brown sugars, the butter, vanilla, and salt. Sift the flour over the pumpkin mixture and whisk until smooth.

2. In a medium bowl, using an electric mixer on medium speed, beat the egg whites until they mound slightly. Increase the speed to high and continue beating until the whites hold soft peaks when the beaters are lifted. Gently whisk them into the pumpkin mixture. Pour the filling into the pie shell. Sprinkle with the cinnamon.

3. Bake the pie in the middle of the oven for 10 minutes. Reduce the heat to 350° and bake until the custard is just set but still jiggles in the center when the pie pan is touched, about 25 minutes. Let cool.

—SUSAN HERRMANN LOOMIS

FRESH PUMPKIN PUREE

MAKES ABOUT 1 CUP

Peel ¾ pound of pumpkin and cut into large chunks. In a medium pot with a steamer basket, bring about 1 inch of water to a boil. Put the pumpkin in the basket, cover, and steam until very soft, about 15 minutes. Puree the pumpkin in a food processor. Transfer the puree to a medium saucepan and cook over moderately high heat until it is thick enough to hold its shape on a spoon, about 8 minutes.

PUMPKIN CHEESECAKE IN A GINGERSNAP CRUST

If you like both pumpkin pie and cheesecake, you'll love this combination. A small slice of this rich and creamy pie feels like an extravagant treat.

MAKES ONE 10-INCH PIE

½ cup pecan halves, plus more for decoration

2 tablespoons granulated sugar

1 cup gingersnap crumbs (from about 20 cookies)

5 tablespoons unsalted butter, melted

1 pound cream cheese, at room temperature

⅔ cup brown sugar

½ cup sour cream, at room temperature

1 cup Fresh Pumpkin Puree, page 195, or canned pumpkin puree

1 teaspoon cinnamon

Pinch ground cloves

Pinch ground ginger

3 large eggs, at room temperature

1. Heat the oven to 325°. In a food processor, chop the ½ cup of pecan halves with the granulated sugar until fine. Put the chopped nuts into a large bowl and stir in the gingersnap crumbs. Pour in the butter and stir to combine. Put the cookie-crumb-and-pecan mixture into a 10-inch pie pan and press it evenly against the bottom and sides of the pan to make a crust. Bake the crust in the middle of the oven for 10 minutes. Let cool.

2. In a large bowl, beat the cream cheese and brown sugar with an electric mixer until soft and smooth, about 3 minutes. Add the sour cream, pumpkin, cinnamon, cloves, and ginger, and beat until just combined. Beat in the eggs one at a time.

3. Put the pie crust on a baking sheet and pour in the filling. Bake in the middle of the oven until the filling is just set, about 45 minutes. Transfer to a rack and let cool. Decorate the pie with additional pecan halves.

MAKE IT AHEAD
Because its cookie-crumb crust won't get soggy like a regular pie crust, the cheesecake can be made a day in advance and refrigerated.

SWEET-POTATO PIE

Flavored with maple syrup, cinnamon, and nutmeg, this is a delicious variation on a traditional Thanksgiving dessert. Whipped cream is the perfect accompaniment.

MAKES ONE 9-INCH PIE

¾ pound sweet potatoes (about 2)

1 cup milk

2 large eggs, separated, at room temperature

⅓ cup plus 2 tablespoons granulated sugar

2 tablespoons pure maple syrup

½ teaspoon vanilla extract

¼ teaspoon cinnamon

¼ teaspoon grated nutmeg

    Salt

¼ pound unsalted butter

    Cornmeal Pie Shell, page 194

    Confectioners' sugar, for dusting

1. Heat the oven to 400°. Prick the potatoes in several places with a fork and bake until tender when pierced, about 1 hour. Let cool. Peel and cut into large chunks.

2. In a food processor or blender, puree the sweet potatoes, gradually adding the milk to make a smooth puree. Add the egg yolks, ⅓ cup of the sugar, the maple syrup, vanilla, cinnamon, nutmeg, and ¼ teaspoon salt. Whir until combined, about 1 minute.

3. In a small saucepan, melt the butter over low heat and cook until golden brown, about 5 minutes. Add the butter to the sweet-potato mixture and whir until thoroughly combined.

4. In a medium bowl, using an electric mixer, beat the egg whites on medium speed until they hold soft peaks. Increase the speed to high and gradually beat in the remaining 2 tablespoons sugar. Continue beating until the whites hold firm peaks when the beaters are lifted. Fold the sweet-potato mixture into the egg whites.

5. Pour the filling into the pie shell. Bake the pie in the middle of the oven for 20 minutes. Reduce the heat to 350° and bake until the filling is just set and the crust is browned, about 20 minutes. Let cool. Dust the top with confectioners' sugar.

—MICHAEL JAMES

MAKE IT AHEAD
You can bake the sweet potatoes a day ahead and keep them in the refrigerator.

chapter *11*
CAKES

Ali Baba, page 209

COCONUT CAKE WITH DIVINITY FROSTING

Here's a delicious old-fashioned butter cake that's flavored with coconut both inside and out. Fresh fruit is the perfect accompaniment.

MAKES ONE 10-INCH CAKE

3 cups flour

¼ teaspoon baking soda

½ pound unsalted butter, at room temperature

3 cups sugar

6 large eggs, at room temperature

1 cup sour cream

½ teaspoon vanilla extract

1 teaspoon coconut extract

Divinity Frosting, next page

4 cups unsweetened shredded coconut, preferably fresh

1. Heat the oven to 350°. Butter and flour a 10-inch tube pan or a 3-quart Bundt pan. In a medium bowl, whisk together the flour and baking soda.

2. In a large bowl, using an electric mixer, cream the butter and sugar until fluffy, about 5 minutes. Beat in the eggs one at a time, beating well after each one.

3. Fold the flour mixture and the sour cream into the butter mixture alternating in three batches, beginning with the flour. Do not overmix. Stir in the vanilla and coconut extracts. Pour the batter into the pan.

4. Bake the cake in the middle of the oven until a toothpick stuck in the center comes out clean, about 1¼ hours. Cool completely in the pan. Remove from the pan and frost. Sprinkle the coconut over the frosting.

—LEE BAILEY

MAKE IT AHEAD
You can bake the cake several days in advance and keep it, unfrosted and well wrapped, in the refrigerator. Frost the cake the day you plan to serve it. ➤

SUGAR-COOKING TIPS

■ Whenever a thermometer, spoon, or other piece of equipment comes out of the syrup, it should go into water to melt any crystals. Keep a measuring cup or a jar of water near the burner for this purpose, and to wet the pastry brush, too.

■ Check the accuracy of your candy thermometer by putting it in boiling water. It should register 212°.

■ Use a thermometer with a metal clip that attaches to the side of the pan so the bulb won't touch the bottom of the pan. Read the thermometer at eye level.

—PEGGY CULLEN

DIVINITY FROSTING

MAKES ABOUT 3 CUPS

    2 cups sugar

 ¼ teaspoon cream of tartar

 ½ cup plus 1 tablespoon water

    3 large egg whites, at room temperature

1½ teaspoons vanilla extract

1. In a medium, heavy saucepan, combine the sugar, cream of tartar, and water. Bring to a boil over moderately high heat and boil, stirring to dissolve the sugar. Brush the inside of the pan with a pastry brush dipped in water to dissolve any crystals. Keep boiling, without stirring, until the syrup reaches the soft-ball stage, about 8 minutes. A candy thermometer should register 238°.

2. Meanwhile, in a large bowl, using an electric mixer on medium speed, beat the egg whites until they hold soft peaks when the beaters are lifted. Increase the speed to medium high and continue beating until the whites hold firm peaks when the beaters are lifted.

3. Beat a third of the syrup into the egg whites in a thin stream. Return the remaining syrup to the heat and boil until it reaches the firm-ball stage, about 5 minutes. A candy thermometer should register 248°. Beat half of this syrup into the egg whites. Boil the remaining syrup until it reaches the hard-ball stage, about 5 minutes. A candy thermometer should register 265°. Beat into the egg whites. Add the vanilla. Beat until thick but spreadable, about 3 minutes.

GINGER ANGEL FOOD CAKE

Fresh ginger adds a spicy kick to this light and fluffy angel food cake. For the most ethereal results, bake the cake on a day of low humidity.

MAKES ONE 10-INCH CAKE

   1   cup cake flour
1½   cups sugar
   1   4-inch piece fresh ginger, peeled and quartered
   2   cups egg whites (about 16 large), at room temperature
1½   teaspoons cream of tartar
 ½   teaspoon salt

1. Heat the oven to 350°. In a medium bowl, whisk together the flour and ¾ cup of the sugar.

2. In a food processor, combine the ginger and ¼ cup of the sugar. Process to a thick paste.

3. In a large bowl, using an electric mixer on medium speed, beat the egg whites until foamy. Beat in the cream of tartar and salt. Increase the speed to high and gradually beat in the remaining ½ cup sugar, 1 tablespoon at a time. Continue beating until the whites hold soft peaks when the beaters are lifted, about 8 minutes.

4. Sift the dry ingredients into the egg whites in two batches, beating on low speed until just combined. Do not overmix. Add the ginger paste and blend on the lowest speed. Scrape the batter into an ungreased 10-inch tube pan. With a rubber spatula, cut through the center of the batter to eliminate air pockets.

5. Bake the cake in the middle of the oven until a toothpick stuck in the center comes out clean, about 35 minutes. Invert the pan until the cake is completely cool. Run a long, thin knife around the side of the cake and unmold it onto a serving plate.

—MARION CUNNINGHAM

WHY USE CAKE FLOUR?

Low in gluten and ground finer than other flours, cake flour produces a light and delicate-textured cake. This flour is particularly useful for making angel food cake, with its characteristic airy structure.

Pecan Bourbon Torte
with Bourbon Buttercream Frosting

With its rich, creamy frosting and its piped chocolate and candied-violet decoration, this dense nut torte is a picture of European elegance.

MAKES ONE 9-INCH CAKE

1½ cups pecans

4 large eggs, at room temperature, separated

1 cup sugar

3 tablespoons bourbon

Bourbon Buttercream Frosting, opposite page

1½ ounces semisweet chocolate, for decoration (optional)

Candied violets, for decoration (optional)

1. Heat the oven to 325°. Butter the bottom of a 9-inch springform pan. In a food processor, grind the pecans to a powder. Avoid processing too long, or the nut oil will separate from the meat. Set aside.

2. In a large bowl, using an electric mixer on medium-high speed, beat the egg yolks, sugar, and bourbon until pale in color, 3 to 5 minutes.

3. In another large bowl, using clean beaters, beat the egg whites on medium speed until they hold soft peaks. Increase the speed to high and continue beating the whites until they hold firm peaks when the beaters are lifted. Spoon the whites onto the beaten egg-yolk mixture, sprinkle with the ground pecans, and fold just until combined. Pour the batter into the prepared pan and smooth the top.

4. Bake the cake in the middle of the oven until the center springs back when touched lightly, about 30 minutes. Cool the cake in the pan. Remove the cake from the pan and spread the frosting on the top and sides. Refrigerate for 30 minutes.

5. Melt the chocolate in a double boiler, stirring frequently, until smooth. Remove from the heat and let cool 5 minutes. Fill a paper cone (see "Making a Paper Cone," opposite page) with the chocolate and fold the top of the cone over to seal. Cut to make a ⅛-inch opening in the tip and, holding the cone with one hand and guiding it with the other, let the chocolate fall onto the cake in concentric circles. Decorate with the candied violets.

6. Refrigerate the cake if not serving immediately. Let sit at room temperature 15 to 20 minutes before serving.

—Maria Piccolo and Rosalee Harris

Bourbon Buttercream Frosting

MAKES ABOUT 2 1/2 CUPS

- 1/3 cup sugar
- 2 tablespoons water
- 3 large egg yolks
- 1 tablespoon bourbon
- 1/4 teaspoon vanilla extract
- Pinch of salt
- 6 tablespoons unsalted butter, at room temperature

1. In a small, heavy pot, combine the sugar and water. Bring to a boil over moderately high heat, stirring to dissolve the sugar. Brush the inside of the pan with a pastry brush dipped in water to dissolve any crystals. Keep boiling, without stirring, until the syrup reaches firm-ball stage, 5 to 7 minutes. A candy thermometer should register 248°.

2. Meanwhile, in a medium bowl, using an electric mixer on medium-high speed, beat the egg yolks, bourbon, vanilla, and salt until pale in color, 3 to 5 minutes. Beat in the hot syrup in a thin stream. Continue beating until cooled to room temperature, about 3 minutes.

3. Beat in the butter in two batches. Continue beating on low speed until smooth. Refrigerate until thick enough to spread, about 30 minutes.

Making a Paper Cone

Cut a twelve-inch square of parchment or waxed paper and fold it in half diagonally to make a triangle. Roll it up tightly to form a cone. The tip of the cone will be centered on the long side of the triangle. Tape the outside so the cone doesn't unroll.

Poppy-Seed Tante Cake with Cream-Cheese Frosting

Made solely with egg whites—no yolks—this cake has a stark white color that is a striking contrast to the blue-black poppy seeds.

MAKES ONE 9-INCH CAKE

2/3 cup milk

1 vanilla bean, split lengthwise, or 1 1/2 teaspoons vanilla extract

2/3 cup poppy seeds

1 2/3 cups cake flour

2 teaspoons baking powder
  Salt

6 ounces unsalted butter, at room temperature

1 1/4 cups superfine sugar

4 large egg whites, at room temperature
  Cream-Cheese Frosting, opposite page

1. In a small pot, bring the milk and the vanilla bean, if using, almost to a boil. Pour into a small bowl, add the poppy seeds, and let cool. Scrape the seeds from the vanilla bean, if using, into the milk and discard the pod. Add the vanilla extract, if using.

2. Heat the oven to 325°. Butter a 9-inch springform pan. In a medium bowl, whisk together the flour, baking powder, and 1/2 teaspoon salt.

3. In a large bowl, using an electric mixer on high speed, cream the butter until fluffy, about 2 minutes. Gradually beat in 1 cup of the sugar and continue beating until very fluffy, about 5 minutes longer. Fold the dry ingredients and the milk mixture into the butter mixture alternating in three batches each, beginning with the dry ingredients. Do not overmix.

4. In a medium bowl, using clean beaters, beat the egg whites with a pinch of salt on medium speed until they hold soft peaks. Gradually beat in the remaining 1/4 cup sugar, 1 teaspoon at a time, increasing the speed to high before adding the last 2 teaspoons sugar. Continue beating until the whites hold stiff peaks when the beaters are lifted. Fold a quarter of the whites into the butter mixture first to lighten it. Then gently fold in the remaining egg whites until just combined. Scrape the batter into the prepared pan.

5. Bake in the middle of the oven until a toothpick stuck in the center comes out clean, about 50 minutes. Let the cake cool in the pan for 10 minutes. Remove the cake from the pan and let cool on the rack.

6. Using a long serrated knife, trim the crusty top of the cake. Slice the cake horizontally into three even layers; set aside the middle layer to use as the unfrosted top.

Spread ¾ cup of the frosting on the bottom cake layer. Add the top layer and frost. Top the cake with the middle layer. Spread a thin layer of the frosting on the sides of the cake to hold the crumbs. Refrigerate for 10 minutes and then spread enough of the frosting on the sides to cover completely. If you like, put the remaining frosting in a pastry bag fitted with a star tip and pipe a border around the top edge of the cake.

—PEGGY CULLEN

MAKE IT AHEAD
You can make and frost the cake a day in advance. Keep it, covered, in the refrigerator (see "Covering the Frosted Cake," below). Remove the cake from the refrigerator about 30 minutes before you're ready to serve it. Or, bake the cake a day ahead, wrap well, and then frost it the day you plan to serve it.

COVERING THE FROSTED CAKE

If you don't have a cake cover, stick toothpicks into the top of the cake and loosely cover with plastic wrap. That way you won't spoil the frosting. When you remove the toothpicks, use a small knife and some frosting from near the bottom of the cake to patch the holes.

CREAM-CHEESE FROSTING

MAKES ABOUT 2 1/2 CUPS

11 ounces cream cheese, at room temperature

½ pound unsalted butter, at room temperature

1 vanilla bean, split lengthwise, or 1½ teaspoons vanilla extract

¾ cup confectioners' sugar, sifted

1. In a large bowl, using an electric mixer, beat the cream cheese until fluffy, about 5 minutes. With the mixer on low speed, gradually beat in the butter until thoroughly combined, about 4 minutes.

2. Scrape the seeds from the vanilla bean, if using, into the cream-cheese mixture, or add the vanilla extract. Add the confectioners' sugar and continue to beat on low speed, scraping the bowl frequently, until thoroughly combined, about 2 minutes. Refrigerate the frosting if making it ahead of time. Let return to room temperature before using.

ALI BABA

A light yeast cake soaked with Grand Marnier syrup, decorated with candied fruit, and served with whipped cream, this dessert resembles a large version of the more familiar individual rum babas. It's a specialty in France for Christmas and New Year's.

MAKES ONE 9-INCH CAKE

- ¼ cup lukewarm milk, plus 1 tablespoon cold milk
- ⅓ cup plus 1½ cups sugar
- 2 teaspoons dry yeast
- 2 large eggs, at room temperature, beaten to mix
- 7 tablespoons unsalted butter, at room temperature
- 1½ cups flour
- ½ teaspoon salt
- 1½ cups water
- ¼ cup plus 4 teaspoons Grand Marnier, or other orange liqueur
- ½ cup chopped mixed candied fruit, for decoration

  Grand Marnier Whipped Cream, next page

1. In a large bowl, combine the ¼ cup lukewarm milk, 1 teaspoon of the sugar, and the yeast. Let stand until the mixture bubbles, about 5 minutes. Add the eggs and butter and stir until combined.

2. In another large bowl, combine the flour, 2 tablespoons of the sugar, and the salt. With a wooden spoon, gradually stir the flour mixture into the yeast mixture, 2 to 3 tablespoons at a time. The dough should be loose and sticky. With the spoon or with your hands, beat the dough against the side of the bowl until smooth and elastic, about 5 minutes. Alternatively, you can mix and beat the dough in an electric mixer: Make the yeast mixture in the bowl of a standing electric mixer fitted with a dough hook. Add the flour mixture, 2 to 3 tablespoons at a time, and beat on low speed, scraping the bottom of the bowl occasionally. Increase the speed to medium and continue beating until the dough is elastic, about 5 minutes.

3. Cover the bowl with plastic wrap and set in a warm place until the dough has doubled in bulk, about 1½ hours.

4. Heat the oven to 400°. Butter a 1-quart ring mold and coat the bottom and sides with 1 tablespoon of the sugar. Punch down the dough. Divide the dough into six even pieces and put them, evenly spaced, in the prepared ring mold. Cover the mold and set in a warm place until the dough rises to the rim, about 45 minutes.

5. Sprinkle the dough with 1 tablespoon of the sugar. Bake the cake in the middle of the oven until golden brown, about 20 minutes. Let cool in the pan for 5 minutes. ➤

6. Meanwhile, in a small pot, combine 1½ cups of the sugar and the water. Bring to a boil over high heat, stirring to dissolve the sugar. Remove from the heat and add ¼ cup of the Grand Marnier.

7. Unmold the cake; if necessary, loosen the edges with a small knife. Return the hot cake to the mold. Prick the top of the cake all over with a fork and gradually drizzle ½ cup of the warm syrup over the cake. Invert the cake onto a serving plate, remove the mold, and prick the top of the cake with a fork. Drizzle the cake with another ½ cup of the syrup. Let cool. Add the remaining 4 teaspoons Grand Marnier to the syrup left in the pan and let cool.

8. In a small pot, combine the 1 tablespoon cold milk and the remaining 1 tablespoon sugar. Bring to a boil over moderate heat, stirring to dissolve the sugar. Brush this glaze all over the cake. Decorate the top with the candied fruit. Just before serving, fill the center of the cake with the whipped cream. Pass the remaining syrup.

—LYDIE MARSHALL

MAKE IT AHEAD

You can whip the cream up to 3 hours in advance. Keep it covered in the refrigerator. You may need to whisk it for 30 seconds just before serving if it has separated slightly.

GRAND MARNIER WHIPPED CREAM

MAKES ABOUT 3 CUPS

1½ cups heavy cream

2 tablespoons sugar

2 tablespoons Grand Marnier or other orange liqueur, more to taste

In a large bowl, whip the cream, sugar, and Grand Marnier just until the cream holds firm peaks when the beaters are lifted.

BUCHE DE NOEL

A traditional favorite during the holiday season in France, this Christmas log is an orange cake-roll filled with chocolate rum buttercream. Frosting that looks like bark and meringue mushrooms make the cake look like a log that's fallen in the woods and is sprouting fungi.

MAKES ONE 12-INCH LOG

SPONGE CAKE:

- ¾ cup whole blanched almonds
- ¾ cup plus 2 tablespoons granulated sugar
- 3 large eggs, separated, at room temperature
- 2 teaspoons grated orange zest
- 2½ tablespoons orange juice
- ¼ teaspoon almond extract
- ½ cup cake flour
- Confectioners' sugar, for dusting

MUSHROOMS AND BUTTERCREAM:

- 1⅓ cups granulated sugar
- ½ cup water
- 3 large egg whites, at room temperature
- ⅛ teaspoon cream of tartar
- Pinch salt
- ¾ pound semisweet chocolate, chopped
- ⅓ cup strong coffee
- 2 tablespoons rum, preferably dark, more to taste
- 1 tablespoon vanilla extract
- 8 tablespoons unsalted butter, at room temperature
- 3 tablespoons unsweetened cocoa powder

SPUN SUGAR (OPTIONAL):

- 1 cup granulated sugar
- ⅓ cup water
- 3 tablespoons light corn syrup

DECORATION:

- Confectioners' sugar, for dusting
- Unsweetened cocoa powder, for dusting

1. For the cake, heat the oven to 375°. Butter a 12 by 18-inch jelly-roll pan and line with parchment or waxed paper. Butter and flour the paper. In a food processor, grind the almonds and 3 tablespoons of the granulated sugar to a powder. Avoid processing too long, or the nut oil will separate from the meat.

2. In a large bowl, using an electric mixer on medium-high speed, beat the egg yolks and ½ cup of the granulated sugar until pale in color and thick, about 5 minutes. Beat in the ground almonds, the orange zest, the orange juice, and the almond extract. Slowly sift and fold in the flour until just combined.

3. In a medium bowl, using clean beaters, beat the egg whites on medium speed

until they hold soft peaks. Increase the speed to high and gradually beat in the remaining 3 tablespoons granulated sugar. Continue beating until the whites hold firm peaks when the beaters are lifted. Fold a quarter of the egg whites into the egg-yolk mixture to lighten it. Gently fold in the remaining egg whites until just combined. Scrape the batter into the prepared pan and spread in an even layer.

4. Bake the cake until it is just beginning to brown, about 8 minutes. Do not bake too long or the cake will crack when it is rolled. Meanwhile, spread a damp dish towel that's larger than the pan on a work surface. Cover with a sheet of waxed paper about the same size. Dust the waxed paper with confectioners' sugar. Invert the warm cake onto the prepared towel and peel the paper off the bottom of the cake. Dust the cake with confectioners' sugar. With the short edge toward you, roll the cake with the towel into a log. Put the cake on a rack and let cool.

5. For the mushrooms, reduce the oven temperature to 200°. Butter and flour a baking sheet. In a medium, heavy saucepan, combine the 1⅓ cups granulated sugar and the ½ cup water. Bring to a boil over moderately high heat and boil, stirring to dissolve the sugar. Brush the inside of the pan with a pastry brush dipped in water to dissolve any sugar crystals and continue to boil, without stirring, until the syrup reaches the soft-ball stage, 5 to 8 minutes. A candy thermometer should register 238°.

6. Meanwhile, in a medium bowl, using clean beaters, beat the 3 egg whites, the cream of tartar, and the salt on medium speed until they mound slightly. Increase the speed to medium-high and continue beating until the whites hold soft peaks when the beaters are lifted. Beat in the hot syrup in a thin stream and continue beating until the meringue is thick and cool, 5 to 8 minutes.

7. Spoon about a quarter of the meringue into a pastry bag fitted with a ⅜-inch plain tip and pipe eight to ten domes on the prepared baking sheet to make "mushroom caps." Hold a ⅛-inch plain tip over the end of the other tip and pipe out eight to ten ¾-inch-high conical shapes for the "mushroom stems." Bake the meringues until they are dry and can easily be removed from the baking sheet, about 1 hour.

8. For the buttercream, melt the chocolate with the coffee in a double boiler, stirring frequently, until smooth. Remove from the heat and let cool completely. Beat the melted chocolate, rum, vanilla, and 4 tablespoons of the butter into the remaining meringue. Transfer two-thirds of the mixture to a medium bowl and refrigerate; this is the frosting. Beat the remaining 4 tablespoons butter into the remaining chocolate mixture, which will be used as the filling.

9. To assemble the log, unroll the cake and spread with the (unchilled) chocolate filling, leaving a ½-inch margin on all sides. Roll the cake back up to form a log. Cut a

diagonal slice from each end of the log. Carve out a slight indentation on the top of the log and insert an end-piece to simulate a bump or knot. Put the cake on a serving plate and slip waxed paper under the sides and ends to catch any frosting spills.

10.   Beat the 3 tablespoons cocoa powder into the (chilled) chocolate frosting. Spread all but 1 tablespoon of the frosting evenly on the cake, leaving the two ends uncovered. Run a fork lengthwise along the frosting to simulate bark.

11.   To assemble the mushrooms, using a small sharp knife, pierce a small hole in the bottom of each mushroom cap. Insert a dab of the reserved frosting and gently press the pointed end of a meringue stem into place. Repeat with the remaining mushroom caps, frosting, and stems.

12.   For the spun sugar, if using, put newspapers on the floor covering an area of at least 4 square feet. Over the newspapers, balance a dowel or broom handle between the backs of two chairs. Fill a large bowl halfway with ice water and get out two forks.

13.   In a small, heavy saucepan, combine the 1 cup granulated sugar, $\frac{1}{3}$ cup water, and the light corn syrup. Bring to a boil, stirring to dissolve the sugar. Brush the inside of the pan with a pastry brush dipped in water to dissolve any sugar crystals and continue to boil, without stirring, until the sugar turns a light amber color. Remove from the heat and carefully lower the pan

into the ice water. Stir the mixture slowly with one of the forks until it thickens slightly, about 20 seconds. Remove the pan from the ice water. The mixture should be a little thinner than honey.

14.   Hold both of the forks in the same hand, back to back, and dip them into the sugar syrup. Let the excess drip off. Rapidly swing the forks back and forth over the dowel. If the syrup is the right temperature, long, thin strands will fall from the forks and lie over the dowel. If the syrup is too thin, it will need to cool slightly; if it is too thick, reheat it briefly. Continue until you have used all the sugar mixture.

15.   To decorate the log, top with clusters of the mushrooms. Dust the log with the confectioners' sugar to resemble snow, and dust the tops of the mushrooms with the cocoa. Remove the waxed paper from under the cake. Drape the spun sugar decoratively over the log.

—JULIA CHILD

MAKE IT AHEAD
You can keep the unfilled cake, rolled up and wrapped well, in the refrigerator for up to 3 days, or store it in the freezer for up to a month.

GINGER GENOISE WITH WHIPPED CREAM AND CANDIED ORANGE PEEL

Molasses, brown sugar, and ground ginger add deep color and rich taste to this classic French sponge cake. Filled and frosted with a preserved-ginger and orange whipped cream, it makes a light yet full-flavored dessert. You can make your own candied orange zest for decoration or buy a good-quality brand of candied orange peel.

MAKES ONE 9-INCH CAKE

⅔ cup flour

2 teaspoons ground ginger

3 large eggs, at room temperature

¼ cup molasses

2 tablespoons dark-brown sugar

½ teaspoon vanilla extract

1½ tablespoons unsalted butter, melted and cooled

1 cup heavy cream

3 tablespoons confectioners' sugar

1 tablespoon orange liqueur, such as Grand Marnier

1 tablespoon minced preserved ginger*, plus thin slices of preserved ginger for decoration

2 teaspoons grated orange zest

Candied Orange Zest, opposite page

*Available at specialty-food stores

1. Heat the oven to 350°. Butter and flour a 9-inch springform pan. In a medium bowl, whisk together the flour and the ground ginger.

2. In a large bowl, using a hand-held electric mixer or a whisk, beat the eggs, molasses, and brown sugar for 1 minute. Set the bowl over a large saucepan that contains about an inch of simmering water. The water should not touch the bottom of the bowl. Beat the egg mixture until just warm, about 3 minutes. Remove the bowl from the saucepan and continue beating until the eggs hold soft peaks when the beaters are lifted, about 7 minutes. Beat in the vanilla.

3. Sift the dry ingredients into the egg mixture in three batches, folding until almost combined. Add the butter and fold until all the ingredients are just combined. Do not overmix. Pour the batter into the prepared pan.

4. Bake in the middle of the oven until the center springs back when touched lightly, about 25 minutes. Cool the cake in the pan for 5 minutes. Unmold the cake onto a rack and let cool.

5. In a medium bowl, whip the cream, confectioners' sugar, and orange liqueur just

until the cream holds firm peaks when the beaters are lifted. Fold in the minced ginger and the grated orange zest.

6. Using a long serrated knife, slice the cake in half horizontally. Shortly before serving, spread half the whipped cream on the bottom layer. Cover with the second layer and spread the remaining whipped cream on top. Decorate the cake with the Candied Orange Zest and slices of ginger.

—MARIA PICCOLO

CANDIED ORANGE ZEST

MAKES ABOUT ¼ CUP

1 navel orange
¾ cup sugar
¼ cup water

1. Using a zester, scrape all the zest from the fruit. You should have very thin, delicate strips.

2. In a small pot, bring the sugar and water to a boil. Add the zest. Reduce the heat and cook at a gentle boil until the zest is translucent, about 10 minutes. Strain and cool. Transfer the zest to a rack and let dry at least 1 hour.

CRANBERRY JELLY ROLL

You'll appreciate this excellent cake roll; it's simple to make because the eggs are beaten together rather than separately. Tart and sweet, it makes a good ending to a rich meal. Top it with whipped cream, if you like.

MAKES ONE 15½-INCH ROLL

½ cup cake flour

½ teaspoon baking powder

¼ teaspoon salt

5 large eggs, at room temperature

½ cup granulated sugar

1 teaspoon vanilla extract

Confectioners' sugar, for dusting

Cranberry Jelly, opposite page, at room temperature

1. Heat the oven to 350°. Butter a 15½ by 10½ by 1-inch jelly-roll pan and line with parchment or waxed paper. Butter and flour the paper. In a medium bowl, whisk together the flour, baking powder, and salt.

2. In a large bowl, using an electric mixer, beat the eggs and the granulated sugar on high speed until pale and fluffy, about 4 minutes. Gradually beat in the dry ingredients and the vanilla, on low speed, until almost incorporated. Fold the mixture until just combined. Scrape the batter into the prepared pan and spread in an even layer.

3. Bake the cake in the middle of the oven until golden brown, about 12 minutes. Do not bake too long or the cake will crack when rolled. Meanwhile, spread a dish towel that's larger than the pan on a work surface. Dust the towel with confectioners' sugar. Invert the warm cake onto the prepared towel and peel off the paper. With the long side toward you, roll the cake with the towel into a log. Transfer to a rack and let cool.

4. Gently unroll the cake and spread with the jelly. Roll the cake up again. Dust with confectioners' sugar.

—MARION CUNNINGHAM

MAKE IT AHEAD
You can make the jelly in advance and keep it in the refrigerator.

CRANBERRY JELLY

MAKES ABOUT 1¼ CUPS

1½ cups water
½ pound cranberries (about 2 cups)
1 cup sugar
⅛ teaspoon salt

1. In a medium saucepan, bring the water to a boil over moderately high heat. Add the cranberries and let boil, stirring occasionally, for 20 minutes.

2. Puree the cranberries in a food processor or blender. Strain and press the fruit firmly to get all the juice and fruit puree. Pour the puree back into the pan and cook over low heat, stirring frequently, for 3 minutes. Add the sugar and salt and cook until the sugar dissolves, about 2 minutes. Pour the jelly into a bowl and refrigerate until set.

DUSTING WITH CONFECTIONERS' SUGAR

An easy way to sprinkle cakes with confectioners' sugar is to put the sugar in a strainer, preferably one with a fine mesh. Hold the strainer over the cake and tap it against your hand so that the sugar sifts evenly onto the surface.

PRUNE CAKE

Studded with chopped prunes and layered with brown sugar and walnuts, this moist Bundt cake is great to have on hand during the holidays. There's no need for frosting here; a sprinkling of granulated sugar on the cooled cake makes a quick and easy finish.

MAKES ONE 10-INCH CAKE

²⁄₃ cup brown sugar

1 teaspoon cinnamon

½ cup chopped walnuts

½ cup plus 2 teaspoons granulated sugar

3 large eggs, at room temperature

1 cup milk, at room temperature

¼ pound unsalted butter, melted

2½ cups flour

1 tablespoon baking powder

½ teaspoon salt

¾ pound pitted prunes (about 2 cups), chopped

1. Heat the oven to 350°. Butter and flour a 3-quart Bundt pan or 10-inch tube pan. In a small bowl, combine the brown sugar, cinnamon, and walnuts.

2. In a large bowl, whisk together ½ cup of the granulated sugar, the eggs, milk, and melted butter until thoroughly combined. In a medium bowl, whisk together the flour, baking powder, and salt. Add to the egg mixture and beat with a wooden spoon until smooth. Fold in the prunes.

3. Spread a third of the batter in the bottom of the prepared pan. Sprinkle half of the brown-sugar mixture over the batter. Spread another third of the batter on top. Sprinkle with the remaining brown-sugar mixture. Spread the remaining batter on top.

4. Bake the cake in the middle of the oven until a toothpick stuck in the center comes out clean, about 1 hour. Let cool in the pan for 10 minutes. Remove the cake from the pan and let cool completely on a rack. Sprinkle the remaining 2 teaspoons granulated sugar over the top.

—MARION CUNNINGHAM

MAKE IT AHEAD
The prunes in this cake help it to stay moist. You can make the cake several days in advance and keep it, well wrapped, at room temperature.

DOUBLE-VANILLA POUND CAKE WITH WALNUT BUTTER

Not your average pound cake, this one's flavored with brown sugar, nutmeg, and both vanilla seeds and vanilla extract. With a sweet walnut butter to accompany it, this is the ultimate tea cake.

MAKES ONE 9-INCH LOAF

- 2¼ cups flour
- 1½ teaspoons baking powder
- ½ teaspoon baking soda
- Salt
- ¼ teaspoon grated nutmeg
- 10 ounces unsalted butter, at room temperature
- 1 cup brown sugar
- 1 vanilla bean, split lengthwise
- 2 large eggs, separated, at room temperature
- 2 teaspoons vanilla extract
- 1 cup plain yogurt
- ½ cup walnuts
- 2 tablespoons confectioners' sugar

1. Heat the oven to 350°. Butter a 9 by 5-inch loaf pan. In a medium bowl, whisk together the flour, baking powder, baking soda, ½ teaspoon salt, and the nutmeg.

2. In a large bowl, using an electric mixer, cream 6 ounces of the butter and the brown sugar until fluffy, about 5 minutes. Scrape the seeds from half of the vanilla bean into the butter mixture. Beat in the egg yolks and 1½ teaspoons of the vanilla extract until thoroughly combined.

3. Fold the dry ingredients and the yogurt into the butter mixture alternating in three batches, beginning with the dry ingredients and mixing until just combined.

4. In a medium bowl, using clean beaters, beat the egg whites on medium speed until they hold soft peaks. Increase the speed to high and continue beating until the whites hold stiff peaks when the beaters are lifted. Fold a quarter of the egg whites into the butter mixture to lighten it. Gently fold in the remaining egg whites until just combined. Scrape the batter into the prepared pan.

5. Bake the cake in the middle of the oven until a toothpick stuck in the center comes out clean, about 1 hour and 10 minutes. Let cool in the pan for 30 minutes. Remove the cake from the pan and let cool completely on a rack.

6. Meanwhile, in a food processor, chop the walnuts. Add the remaining 4 ounces butter and the confectioners' sugar and process for 10 seconds. Scrape the seeds

from the remaining vanilla-bean half into the walnut butter. Add the remaining ½ teaspoon vanilla extract and a pinch of salt and process until thoroughly combined, 5 to 10 seconds longer. Refrigerate the walnut butter. Remove it from the refrigerator about 20 minutes before serving. Slice the cake and serve accompanied with the butter.

—MARIA PICCOLO

MAKE IT AHEAD
The cake tastes even better the next day when the flavors have had a chance to mellow. You can make the cake several days in advance and keep it, well wrapped, at room temperature. Or freeze it for up to one month. You can keep the walnut butter for several days in the refrigerator, or up to a month in the freezer.

PINEAPPLE CRUMBCAKE

Butter cake covered with pineapple and lots of crumb topping is delicious either warm or at room temperature. You can also make the cake with other fruits such as apricots, peaches, nectarines, or plums.

MAKES ONE 10-INCH CAKE

2½ cups flour

1 teaspoon baking powder

½ pound unsalted butter, at room temperature

1¼ cups sugar

1 large egg, at room temperature

3 large egg yolks, at room temperature

1 teaspoon vanilla extract

1 medium peeled and cored pineapple, cut into quarters lengthwise, then cut crosswise into ½-inch slices

¼ teaspoon cinnamon

1. Heat the oven to 350°. Butter a 10-inch springform pan. Cover the bottom with a round of parchment or waxed paper. In a medium bowl, whisk 1¼ cups of the flour with the baking powder.

2. In a large bowl, using an electric mixer, cream ¼ pound of the butter and ¾ cup of the sugar until fluffy, about 5 minutes. Add the whole egg and beat until thoroughly combined. Beat in the egg yolks one at a time, beating well after each one. Beat in the vanilla.

3. Gently fold the flour mixture into the butter mixture until combined. Scrape the batter into the prepared pan and spread in an even layer. Arrange the pineapple slices on the batter in concentric circles, overlapping slightly, leaving a 1-inch margin around the edge. (Don't worry if the pineapple mounds slightly in the center; the top will even out as the cake bakes.)

4. In a small pot, melt the remaining ¼ pound butter. Let cool slightly. In a medium bowl, combine the remaining 1¼ cups flour and ½ cup sugar and the cinnamon. Add the melted butter and rub into the flour mixture until it forms pea-size crumbs. Sprinkle the crumbs evenly over the pineapple.

5. Bake the cake in the middle of the oven until a toothpick stuck in the center comes out clean, about 55 minutes. Let cool in the pan for 15 minutes. Turn the cake out onto a plate and peel off the paper. Invert the cake onto a rack to cool at least slightly before serving.

—NICHOLAS MALGIERI

DARK APPLESAUCE FRUITCAKES

These moist, dark fruitcakes are filled with an assortment of dried, not candied, fruit. Make them at least a week ahead so the flavors have time to meld.

MAKES TEN 5 BY 3-INCH LOAVES

- 3 cups unsweetened applesauce
- ½ pound unsalted butter, cut into chunks
- 1¼ cups sugar
- ½ cup molasses
- ⅓ cup honey
- 1 15-ounce box golden raisins (about 2¾ cups)
- 1 15-ounce box dark raisins (about 2¾ cups)
- 1 cup currants
- 1 cup dried sour cherries, or another 1 cup currants
- 1 cup dried apricots, chopped
- 2 cups walnut halves, chopped, plus more for decoration
- 2 cups pecan halves, chopped, plus more for decoration
- 4½ cups flour
- 1 tablespoon plus 1 teaspoon baking soda
- 2 teaspoons cinnamon
- 1 teaspoon grated nutmeg
- 1 teaspoon ground allspice
- 1 teaspoon salt
- ½ teaspoon ground cloves
- ½ cup brandy

1. In a medium stainless-steel saucepan, heat the applesauce over moderate heat. Add the butter and stir until the butter is melted and the applesauce comes to a boil, about 5 minutes. Add the sugar, molasses, and honey, and cook, stirring, until the sugar dissolves, about 1 minute longer. Pour into a large bowl and let cool completely. Add the raisins, currants, cherries, apricots, chopped walnuts, and chopped pecans.

2. Heat the oven to 275°. Butter and flour ten 5 by 3 by 2-inch loaf pans (available in disposable foil). In a large bowl, whisk together the flour, baking soda, cinnamon, nutmeg, allspice, salt, and cloves. Fold the dry ingredients into the applesauce mixture until just combined. Divide the batter among the prepared pans and smooth the surfaces with a rubber spatula dipped in water. Arrange walnut and pecan halves on the tops.

3. Bake the fruitcakes in the middle of the oven until a toothpick stuck in the centers comes out clean, about one hour. Let the cakes cool in the pans for 1 hour. Unmold them and let cool on racks. Brush the brandy on all sides of the fruitcakes. Wrap tightly first in plastic wrap, then in aluminum foil. Keep in a cool, dry place for at least 1 week.

—GRACE STUCK

chapter 12
FROZEN DESSERTS

Frozen Praline Meringue, page 227

FROZEN PRALINE MERINGUE

Meringue layers filled with praline ice cream and frosted with rum-whipped cream stack up to a classic French ice-cream cake. The balance of textures and flavors is superb.

MAKES ONE 10-INCH CAKE

5	large egg whites, at room temperature
1½	cups granulated sugar
1½	cups sliced blanched almonds
1	pint vanilla ice cream
3	cups heavy cream
¼	cup confectioners' sugar
1½	tablespoons rum, preferably dark
	Candied violets or rose petals, for decoration

1. Heat the oven to 200°. Butter two 11 by 17-inch baking sheets. Cut two pieces of parchment paper the same size as the baking sheets. Using a pencil, draw a 10-inch circle in the center of each piece of parchment paper. Turn the parchment paper over, make sure the circles are visible, and then put each piece of paper on one of the prepared baking sheets.

2. Using an electric mixer, beat the egg whites on medium speed until they hold soft peaks. Increase the speed to high and continue beating until the whites hold stiff peaks when the beaters are lifted. Gradually beat in 1 cup of the granulated sugar over a 10-second period, and beat for 10 seconds longer. Some of the sugar should remain granular to make a tender meringue.

3. Spoon the meringue into a large pastry bag fitted with a 1-inch plain tip. Pipe the meringue in a spiral onto the pieces of parchment paper, beginning at the center of each circle and ending at the edge, to make two 10-inch disks. Alternatively, spread the meringue onto the parchment paper with a spatula.

4. Bake the meringues until hard, about 4 hours. Turn the heat off but leave the meringues in the oven until cool.

5. Lightly oil a baking sheet. In a medium, heavy saucepan, cook the remaining ½ cup granulated sugar over moderately high heat, stirring occasionally with a wooden spoon as the sugar closest to the sides of the pan begins to melt. Stir the melting sugar into the dry sugar in the center. Let cook until the sugar turns a medium-brown caramel color and all of the sugar crystals dissolve, about 6 minutes. Stir in the almonds; the sugar will harden somewhat. Continue cooking until the sugar melts again and the almonds brown, about 2 minutes longer. Pour onto the oiled baking sheet and let cool. Break the praline into pieces.

6. Put the vanilla ice cream in a large bowl and let soften slightly. Meanwhile, in a food processor, grind the praline pieces to

a powder. Fold the praline powder into the softened ice cream and freeze to firm it slightly, about 30 minutes.

7. In a large bowl, whip the heavy cream, confectioners' sugar, and rum just until the cream holds firm peaks when the beaters are lifted. Chill the whipped cream.

8. Peel the paper from the meringues. Trim the meringues, using a cake pan as a guide, to make them the same size and uniformly round. Crumble the trimmings and set aside. Put one of the meringue disks on a serving plate. Spread the ice cream on the meringue in an even layer. Spread 1½ cups of the whipped cream over the ice cream. Sprinkle reserved meringue trimmings over the whipped cream and top with the second meringue disk, flat-side up. Spread 2¾ cups of the whipped cream on the top and sides of the cake.

9. Spoon the remaining whipped cream into a pastry bag fitted with a star tip. Pipe rosettes along the base and top edge of the cake. Gently press the candied violets into the rosettes and put the cake, uncovered, in the freezer. Freeze until firm, at least 3 hours. About 30 minutes before serving, put the cake in the refrigerator to soften slightly.

—JACQUES PEPIN

MAKE IT AHEAD
You can make and decorate the cake and then store it in the freezer for 2 or 3 weeks. Be sure that it's well frozen before you wrap it first in plastic wrap and then in two layers of aluminum foil. The foil keeps the cake from absorbing any flavors from the freezer.

228

COFFEE ALMOND-CRUNCH TART

A crunchy cookie-like tart shell, coffee amaretto ice cream, and a drizzle of chocolate add up to a perfect finale to any holiday meal. With its store-bought ice-cream filling, the dessert is easy to make, too.

MAKES ONE 10- OR 11-INCH TART

- 2 cups whole blanched almonds
- ¾ cup flour
- ¼ cup sugar
- ½ teaspoon grated nutmeg
- 4 tablespoons cold unsalted butter, cut into pieces
- 1 large egg
- ¼ teaspoon almond extract
- ¼ pound semisweet chocolate, chopped fine
- 1 quart coffee ice cream
- 1 tablespoon amaretto

1. Heat the oven to 350°. Butter a 10- or 11-inch tart pan. Toast the almonds in the oven until golden brown, about 8 minutes. Let cool.

2. In a food processor, chop 1 cup of the toasted almonds with the flour, sugar, and grated nutmeg until fine. Add the butter and pulse until the butter is well distributed, about five times. Add the egg and the almond extract and process until the dough begins to come together, about 10 seconds. Remove the dough and wipe out the bowl. Press the dough into the prepared tart pan to evenly cover the bottom and sides. Freeze until firm, about 20 minutes. Press a double thickness of aluminum foil against the dough.

3. Increase the oven temperature to 400°. Bake the shell in the middle of the oven for 20 minutes. Remove the foil. Bake until golden brown, about 5 minutes longer. Sprinkle half of the chocolate over the bottom of the shell and, as it melts, spread it with a pastry brush. Let the shell cool to room temperature.

4. Put the ice cream into a large bowl and let soften slightly. Meanwhile, in a food processor, grind the remaining 1 cup toasted almonds to a paste, about 2 minutes. Using a hand-held electric mixer or a whisk, beat the almond paste and the amaretto into the ice cream. Continue beating until thoroughly combined, about 1 minute. Put the ice-cream mixture in the tart shell, smooth the top, and freeze for at least 30 minutes.

5. Melt the remaining chocolate in a double boiler. Using a paper cone (see "Making a Paper Cone," page 205), pipe it onto the tart in a decorative pattern. Or, drizzle it on the tart with a fork. Cover the tart with plastic wrap. Freeze until firm, at least 3 hours. About 20 minutes before serving, put in the refrigerator to soften slightly.

—DORIE GREENSPAN

FROSTY LIME PIE

Frozen lime mousse in a graham-cracker crust makes a light yet satisfying dessert. For a Christmas color scheme, decorate the pie with fresh strawberries.

MAKES ONE 8-INCH PIE

1¼ cups graham-cracker crumbs

1 cup superfine sugar

4 tablespoons unsalted butter, at room temperature

5 large eggs, separated, at room temperature

2 teaspoons grated lime zest

⅔ cup lime juice (from about 6 limes)

⅛ teaspoon salt

1½ cups heavy cream

2 tablespoons granulated sugar

1 pint Sugared Strawberries, opposite page (optional)

1. Heat the oven to 350°. In a medium bowl, combine the graham-cracker crumbs and ¼ cup of the superfine sugar. Add the butter and stir or rub it into the crumbs until thoroughly combined. Put the crumb mixture into an 8-inch pie pan and press it evenly against the bottom and sides of the pan to make a crust. Bake the crust in the middle of the oven for 10 minutes. Let cool.

2. In a large bowl, using a hand-held electric mixer, beat the egg yolks to combine. Set the bowl over a large saucepan that contains about an inch of simmering water. The water should not touch the bottom of the bowl. Beat the egg yolks, gradually adding ½ cup of the superfine sugar, until the mixture is thick and forms a ribbon trail on the surface when the beaters are lifted, about 10 minutes. Add the lime zest and lime juice and continue cooking, stirring with a wooden spoon, until the mixture is thick enough to coat the spoon, about 8 minutes longer. Do not let the mixture boil. Pour the filling into a large bowl and let cool.

3. In another large bowl, using clean beaters, beat the egg whites with the salt on medium speed until they hold soft peaks. Increase the speed to high and gradually beat in the remaining ¼ cup superfine sugar. Continue beating until the whites hold firm peaks when the beaters are lifted. Stir a third of the whites into the lime filling to lighten it. Gently fold in the remaining egg whites until just combined. Pour the filling into the crumb crust.

4. Bake the pie in the middle of the oven until the top just begins to brown, about 15 minutes. Let cool. Freeze the pie until firm, at least 6 hours.

5. About 10 minutes before serving, remove the pie from the freezer and let sit at room temperature to soften slightly. In a large bowl, whip the cream and the granulated sugar until the cream holds firm peaks when the beaters are lifted. Spread the

whipped cream on the pie and decorate with the strawberries.

—PEARL BYRD FOSTER

MAKE IT AHEAD
Once the pie is firm, you can wrap it well and keep it frozen for 2 to 3 weeks.

SUGARED STRAWBERRIES

Depending on their size, leave the strawberries whole or cut them into halves or quarters. Just before serving, toss them with sugar and immediately arrange them on the pie.

VARIATIONS

■ Top the pie with raspberries instead of the Sugared Strawberries. You'll still get that Christmas-y look. Berries and mint leaves also look pretty on top.

■ For a cool, monochromatic color scheme, use thin slices of lime instead of the strawberries.

ICY FRESH-CRANBERRY PIE

Vanilla ice cream studded with bits of cranberry and orange and mounded in a cinnamon graham-cracker crust—this pie captures the essence of the season. It takes minimal time to prepare and makes beautiful, festive slices.

MAKES ONE 9-INCH PIE

1½ cups graham-cracker crumbs

¼ cup confectioners' sugar

6 tablespoons butter, melted

½ teaspoon cinnamon

1 pint vanilla ice cream

2 thin-skinned oranges, unpeeled, cut into eight pieces and seeded

2 cups cranberries (about 8 ounces)

½ cup plus 1½ tablespoons granulated sugar

1 tablespoon lemon juice

1 cup heavy cream

1. Heat the oven to 350°. In a medium bowl, stir together the graham-cracker crumbs and the confectioners' sugar. Add the melted butter and the cinnamon and stir to combine. Put the graham-cracker-crumb mixture into a 9-inch pie pan and press it evenly against the bottom and sides of the pan to make a crust. Bake for 10 minutes. Let cool.

2. Put the ice cream in a large bowl and let soften slightly. In a food processor, chop the oranges and cranberries with ½ cup of the granulated sugar and the lemon juice. Fold the cranberry mixture into the ice cream and then put it in the pie shell. Freeze for 30 minutes. Cover with plastic wrap and freeze until firm, at least 3 hours longer.

3. About 20 minutes before serving, put the pie in the refrigerator to soften slightly. In a large bowl, whip the heavy cream and the remaining 1½ tablespoons granulated sugar just until the cream holds firm peaks when the beaters are lifted. Spread the whipped cream on the pie.

—PEARL BYRD FOSTER

MAKE IT AHEAD
You can make the pie through Step 2, and keep it, well wrapped, in the freezer for 2 to 3 weeks.

THICK-SKINNED ORANGES

If your oranges have thick skins, remove the skin before processing and cut off and discard the bitter white pith.

SPICED PUMPKIN ICE CREAM

Here's the answer if you want to feature pumpkin in something other than the traditional pie. The ice cream is great on its own, with Granny's Molasses Spice Cookies, page 165, or as an accompaniment to Maple Pecan Pie, page 194.

MAKES ABOUT 1½ QUARTS

  3 large egg yolks

  1 cup plus 2 tablespoons sugar

2¼ cups milk

1½ cups Fresh Pumpkin Puree, page 195, or canned pumpkin puree

1½ cups heavy cream

2¼ teaspoons cinnamon

2¼ teaspoons grated nutmeg

1. In a medium bowl, whisk the egg yolks with ¾ cup of the sugar until pale yellow, about 2 minutes.

2. In a medium saucepan, combine 1½ cups of the milk with the remaining 6 tablespoons sugar. Cook over moderate heat, stirring frequently with a wooden spoon, until the mixture comes to a simmer and the sugar is dissolved.

3. Pour the hot milk into the yolks in a thin stream, whisking. Pour the mixture back into the pan and cook over moderately low heat, stirring constantly, until just thick enough to coat a spoon, about 3 minutes. Do not let the custard boil or it may curdle. Strain into a bowl. Add the remaining ¾ cup milk, the pumpkin puree, the cream, cinnamon, and nutmeg, and whisk until thoroughly combined. Cover and refrigerate to cool.

4. Pour the custard into an ice-cream maker and freeze according to the manufacturer's instructions. Put a 2-quart container in the freezer to chill. Transfer the ice cream to the chilled container. Store the ice cream in the freezer until hard enough to scoop, about 30 minutes.

MAKE IT AHEAD
You can make the pumpkin custard a day or two before churning. Actually, this improves the ice cream because the flavors have a chance to meld. You can keep the finished ice cream for at least a week. Check it 15 minutes before serving. If it's too hard, let it soften slightly at room temperature.

PUMPKIN MAPLE ICE CREAM

Mellow pumpkin ice cream sweetened with maple syrup is a fine way to celebrate the harvest. Scooped into glasses and sprinkled with rum and walnuts, it becomes an original combination that's do-ahead and delicious.

MAKES ABOUT 1¼ QUARTS

    4 large egg yolks

1¼ cups pure maple syrup

1¼ cups milk

1¼ cups Fresh Pumpkin Puree, page 195, or canned pumpkin puree

1¼ cups heavy cream

1¾ teaspoons grated nutmeg

 ½ cup chopped walnuts

    3 tablespoons rum, preferably dark, or more to taste

1. In a large bowl, whisk the egg yolks and maple syrup until thoroughly combined.

2. In a large saucepan, bring the milk to a simmer, stirring frequently with a wooden spoon. Pour the hot milk into the egg yolks in a thin stream, whisking. Pour the mixture back into the pan and cook over moderately low heat, stirring constantly, until just thick enough to coat a spoon, about 3 minutes. Do not let the custard boil or it may curdle. Strain into a bowl. Add the pumpkin puree, the cream, and the nutmeg, and whisk until thoroughly combined. Cover and refrigerate to cool.

3. Pour the pumpkin custard into an ice-cream maker and freeze according to the manufacturer's instructions. Put a 1½-quart container in the freezer to chill. Transfer the ice cream to the chilled container. Put in the freezer until hard enough to scoop, about 30 minutes.

4. Meanwhile, heat the oven to 350°. Toast the walnuts in the oven until golden brown, about 8 minutes. Let cool. To serve, scoop the ice cream into bowls or stemmed glasses. Sprinkle with the rum and top with the walnuts.

MAKE IT AHEAD
You can prepare the ice-cream base a day before churning, and complete the ice cream at least a week ahead. Check it 15 minutes before serving. If it's too hard, let it soften slightly at room temperature.

MAPLE ICE CREAM

Maple syrup is boiled down to produce full-flavored and ultra-smooth ice cream. Enjoy it alone, or alongside a slice of fruit pie. Maple complements apple and blueberry especially well.

MAKES ABOUT 1 1/4 QUARTS

- 2 cups pure maple syrup
- 2 cups milk
- 2 cups heavy cream
- 4 large egg yolks

1. In a medium saucepan, bring the maple syrup to a boil over moderate heat. Reduce the heat to very low and simmer, stirring frequently, until reduced to 1 cup, about 45 minutes. The syrup will look like a combination of maple syrup and maple sugar. Let cool slightly.

2. Slowly whisk the milk and cream into the reduced syrup. Bring to a boil, stirring to dissolve the sugar.

3. In a medium bowl, whisk the egg yolks to combine. Pour the hot syrup mixture into the yolks in a thin stream, whisking. Pour the mixture back into the pan and cook over moderately low heat, stirring constantly, until just thick enough to coat a spoon, about 3 minutes. Do not let the custard boil or it may curdle. Strain into a bowl. Cover and refrigerate to cool.

4. Pour the maple custard into an ice-cream maker and freeze according to the manufacturer's instructions. Put a 1 1/2-quart container in the freezer to chill. Transfer the ice cream to the chilled container. Put in the freezer until hard enough to scoop, about 30 minutes.

—MICHAEL McLAUGHLIN

MAKE IT AHEAD
Prepare the ice-cream base a day ahead, if you like, and chill it in the refrigerator overnight. The finished ice cream can be kept at least a week. Check it 15 minutes before serving. If it's too hard, let it soften slightly at room temperature.

CRANBERRY RASPBERRY SORBET

With its glorious color and intense berry flavor, this sorbet is the ultimate light dessert of the season. For an elegant touch, pair it with Lacy Ginger Snowflakes, page 177.

MAKES ABOUT 1¼ QUARTS

- 1 12-ounce package cranberries (about 3 cups)
- 1½ cups water
- 1½ cups sugar
- 1 12-ounce package frozen unsweetened raspberries, thawed (1⅓ cups)

1. In a large, stainless-steel saucepan, bring the cranberries and water to a boil. Reduce the heat and simmer until the berries pop, about 5 minutes. Stir in the sugar and the raspberries and stir until the sugar dissolves, about 1 minute. Let cool. Strain the berry mixture into a stainless-steel or glass bowl. Press the fruit firmly to get all the juice and fruit puree. Discard the seeds. Cover the puree and refrigerate to cool.

2. Put a 1½-quart container in the freezer to chill. Pour the berry mixture into an ice-cream maker and freeze according to the manufacturer's instructions. Transfer the sorbet to the chilled container and store in the freezer until hard enough to scoop, about 30 minutes.

MAKE IT AHEAD
You can make the berry mixture 2 days ahead and churn it a day before serving. All homemade sorbet is best served relatively soon after it's churned. Store the sorbet in the freezer and check it about 15 minutes before serving. If it's too hard, let it soften slightly at room temperature.

FREEZING FRESH RASPBERRIES

If you want to have delicious, local raspberries during the winter months, freeze them. Put the berries on a baking sheet in a single layer and freeze until hard. Transfer them to plastic bags and freeze, airtight, for up to six months.

chapter *13*
OTHER DESSERTS

Peach and Ginger Trifle, page 241

PEACH AND GINGER TRIFLE

Layers of gingery angel food cake, lemon cream, peaches, and whipped cream make a delicious departure from traditional trifle. You can use other fruit in place of the peaches, such as raspberries or strawberries.

SERVES 12

Zest and juice of 2 large lemons

1/4 pound unsalted butter, cut into pieces

1 cup sugar

4 large eggs

2 cups heavy cream

Ginger Angel Food Cake, page 203

8 peaches, peeled and sliced, or two 1-pound bags unsweetened frozen sliced peaches, thawed

1. In a double boiler, combine the lemon zest, lemon juice, butter, and sugar. Cook, stirring occasionally, over simmering water until the butter melts and the sugar dissolves, about 5 minutes.

2. In a medium bowl, beat the eggs until thoroughly combined. Pour about one-third of the hot lemon mixture into the eggs in a thin stream, stirring. Pour the egg mixture back into the remaining lemon mixture in a thin stream, stirring. Continue cooking, stirring constantly, until the lemon curd is thick and steaming, about 3 minutes. Strain into a stainless-steel or glass bowl and chill.

3. In a large bowl, whip 1 cup of the cream until it holds firm peaks when the beaters are lifted. Fold the whipped cream into the curd until thoroughly combined.

4. Using a large serrated knife, slice the cake horizontally into three rings. Cut each ring into eight wedges. Line the bottom of a 3½- to 4-quart glass serving bowl with eight of the cake wedges. Spoon about half of the lemon cream over the cake. Reserve 1½ cups peach slices for the top. Put the remaining peach slices over the lemon cream. Line the sides of the bowl with eight more wedges of cake, overlapping if necessary. Put the remaining cake wedges over the peaches and press gently. Spoon the rest of the lemon cream over the cake and smooth the surface. Arrange the reserved peach slices decoratively on top. Refrigerate at least 6 hours before serving so that the cake softens and the flavors mellow.

5. In a large bowl, whip the remaining 1 cup heavy cream until it holds firm peaks when the beaters are lifted. Using a pastry bag fitted with a large star tip, pipe the whipped cream decoratively on the trifle, letting the peaches show. Or simply spoon the whipped cream over the trifle.

—MARION CUNNINGHAM

GINGER SABAYON

Orange juice, orange liqueur, and preserved ginger are the major players in this hot, fluffy mousse that you can whip up at the last minute. Preserved ginger comes packed in jars with its syrup, and is available in specialty stores. If you can't find the preserved variety, use three tablespoons minced crystallized ginger instead and omit the ginger syrup.

SERVES 6

- 8 large egg yolks
- 2 large eggs
- 1 cup sugar
- 1 cup orange juice (from about 2 oranges)
- ¼ cup orange liqueur, such as Grand Marnier
- 2 tablespoons minced preserved ginger
- 2 tablespoons preserved-ginger syrup

1. In a large bowl, using a hand-held electric mixer or a whisk, beat together all of the ingredients until thoroughly combined.

2. Set the bowl over a large saucepan that contains about an inch of simmering water. The water should not touch the bottom of the bowl. Beat the egg mixture until it mounds when the beaters are lifted, about 10 minutes. Remove from the heat and let the sabayon sit over the hot water for 1 minute. Divide the sabayon among six glasses or dessert goblets. Serve at once.

—JEAN ANDERSON

FRESH-FRUIT VARIATION

If you like, put fruit such as raspberries, strawberries, or peaches in the serving glasses and top them with the sabayon.

242

GOLDEN-SYRUP AND GINGER PUDDING

Moist and spicy, with a syrupy glaze, this steamed English pudding is served hot with custard sauce. You can make it with imported golden syrup, now found in many supermarkets, and preserved ginger, which is available at specialty stores. Or, make your own Golden Syrup, next page, and use three tablespoons crystallized ginger in place of the preserved variety (or just omit it).

SERVES 6

- ⅓ cup Golden Syrup, next page
- 1 cup plus 2 tablespoons flour
- 1 teaspoon baking powder
- 1 teaspoon ground ginger
- ¼ pound unsalted butter, at room temperature
- ½ cup sugar
- 2 eggs, beaten to mix
- 2 tablespoons milk
- 2 tablespoons preserved ginger, cut into ¼-inch dice (optional)

  Custard Sauce, next page

1. Butter a 1-quart glass or stainless-steel bowl and pour in the syrup. In a medium bowl, whisk together the flour, baking powder, and ground ginger. Bring water to a simmer for steaming the pudding.

2. In a large bowl, using an electric mixer, cream the unsalted butter and the sugar until fluffy, about 5 minutes. Beat in half of the beaten eggs. Stir half of the dry ingredients into this butter mixture. Stir in the remaining egg and then the remaining dry ingredients. Stir in the milk and the preserved ginger.

3. Scrape the batter into the bowl with the syrup. Cover with buttered waxed paper and aluminum foil, both pleated in the middle to allow for expansion. Crimp the edges tightly around the rim of the bowl or tie securely with string. Put the bowl in the center of a kitchen towel and tie the diagonal corners together over the bowl to make a sling. Holding the towel, lower the bowl into a pot that's larger than the bowl. Pour enough simmering water into the pot to reach about halfway up the sides of the pudding bowl.

4. Cover the pot and steam the pudding over moderate heat, replenishing with simmering water every half hour or so, until a toothpick stuck in the center comes out almost clean, about 1½ hours. Unmold the pudding with its syrup onto a plate. Cut into wedges and serve hot with the warm Custard Sauce. ➤

CUSTARD SAUCE

MAKES ABOUT 1 CUP

1 large egg
2 large egg yolks
2 tablespoons sugar
1 cup milk
½ teaspoon vanilla extract

1. In a small bowl, whisk the egg, egg yolks, and 1 tablespoon of the sugar until thoroughly combined.

2. In a double boiler, bring the milk almost to a simmer with the remaining 1 tablespoon sugar. Remove from the heat and stir about 2 tablespoons of the hot milk into the egg mixture. Pour the egg mixture into the remaining milk in a thin stream, stirring constantly. Cook over simmering water, stirring constantly with a wooden spoon, until just thick enough to coat a spoon, 3 to 5 minutes. Do not cook the custard too long or it may curdle. Transfer the top of the double boiler to a bowl of ice water to stop the cooking. Strain and stir in the vanilla. Serve warm.

MAKE IT AHEAD
You can make the sauce several days ahead and keep it in the refrigerator. Reheat the custard in a double boiler over simmering water, stirring, until just warm, about 5 minutes.

GOLDEN SYRUP

MAKES ABOUT ⅓ CUP

¼ cup sugar
1 tablespoon water
½ teaspoon white or white-wine vinegar
⅓ cup light corn syrup

1. Put the sugar in a small, heavy pot. Shake gently to make an even layer of sugar. Add the water and vinegar and cook, without stirring, over low heat for 5 minutes.

2. Raise the heat to moderate. Cook until the sugar turns a golden color, about 5 minutes longer. Remove from the heat and add the corn syrup. The mixture will bubble up, but do not stir. When the bubbles have subsided, after 2 or 3 minutes, stir with a wooden spoon until thoroughly mixed. Let cool to room temperature before using.

MAKE IT AHEAD
You can make the syrup weeks in advance and keep it, in a covered jar, at room temperature.

ORANGE-AND-HONEY BREAD PUDDING

Orange-flavored custard sweetened with honey sets this bread pudding apart.
If you like, after using their zest in the custard, peel and slice the oranges. Add
a little sugar and orange liqueur and serve the oranges alongside.

SERVES 8

¼ pound unsalted butter

½ day-old French baguette (a piece about
   8 inches long), cut into ¼-inch slices

2 cups milk

1 cup heavy cream

⅔ cup honey, preferably orange blossom

3 navel oranges

5 large eggs

1. Heat the oven to 325°. Bring water
to a simmer for the water bath. Melt the
butter. Dip one side of each piece of bread
into the butter and overlap the slices, buttered-side up, in a 1½-quart shallow baking
or gratin dish.

2. In a medium saucepan, combine the
milk, the heavy cream, and the honey. Using a vegetable peeler, strip off the zest from
the oranges and add it to the pan. Bring the
mixture to a boil over moderate heat. Remove the pan from the heat and let infuse
for 5 minutes.

3. In a large bowl, whisk the eggs until
thoroughly combined. Pour the hot milk
mixture over the eggs, whisking just until
combined. Strain this custard over the
bread in the baking dish.

4. Put the baking dish in a roasting pan
and pour in enough of the simmering water
to reach about halfway up the sides of the
dish. Carefully transfer the roasting pan to
the oven and bake until the pudding is just
set and the bread is golden brown, about 45
minutes. Remove the pudding from the
water bath and cool to warm or room temperature.

—NICHOLAS MALGIERI

MAKE IT AHEAD
You can make the pudding up to 4 hours
ahead and keep it at room temperature until ready to serve. Of course, you can refrigerate the pudding and keep it longer, but
the top won't remain crisp.

CHRISTMAS ORANGE-AND-CURRANT SHORTCAKES

When the cold winds blow, you'll welcome these shortcakes, inspired by hot cross buns with their felicitous pairing of orange and currants.

SERVES 6

- 2 cups flour
- 1 tablespoon baking powder
- ½ teaspoon salt
- ¼ teaspoon grated nutmeg
- ¾ cup superfine sugar
- ¼ cup cold unsalted butter, cut into pieces
- ¾ cup currants or raisins
- ⅔ cup plus 1 tablespoon milk
- 1½ cups orange juice (from about 3 oranges)
- ¼ cup kirsch
- 1 cinnamon stick
- 4 large navel oranges
- 1 cup heavy cream

1. Heat the oven to 375°. Line a baking sheet with aluminum foil. In a medium bowl, whisk together the flour, baking powder, salt, nutmeg, and 3 tablespoons of the sugar. Cut the butter into the flour until the mixture resembles coarse meal with some pieces of butter still the size of peas. Toss in the currants. Stir in the ⅔ cup milk just until the mixture forms a dough when pressed together.

2. On a lightly floured surface, knead the dough gently two or three times. Shape the dough into a 12-inch log and then pat it out into a 12 by 3-inch strip that's 1 inch thick. Using a 3-inch round cutter dipped in flour, stamp out four circles. Gather the scraps, pat them into a 1-inch thickness, and cut out two more rounds. Brush the tops with the remaining 1 tablespoon milk. Put the shortcakes on the prepared baking sheet and refrigerate for 10 minutes.

3. Bake the shortcakes until golden brown, about 30 minutes. Let cool on the baking sheet for 10 minutes and then transfer to a rack to cool completely.

4. In a medium stainless-steel saucepan, combine the orange juice, kirsch, ½ cup of the sugar, and the cinnamon stick. Bring to a boil over high heat. Reduce the heat to moderate and boil until reduced to 1 cup, about 10 minutes.

5. Using a stainless-steel knife, peel the oranges down to the flesh, removing all of the white pith. Cut the orange sections away from the membranes. Remove the orange syrup from the heat and discard the cinnamon stick. Let the syrup cool for about 5 minutes and then add the orange sections. The syrup will thin out when you add the oranges. ➤

6. In a medium bowl, whip the cream and the remaining 1 tablespoon sugar until the cream holds soft peaks when the beaters are lifted.

7. Shortly before serving, split the shortcakes in half. Spoon 1 tablespoon of the orange syrup onto each dessert plate. Put the bottom half of the shortcakes on the plates and spread with a ½-inch layer of whipped cream. Spoon 2 tablespoons of the oranges over the cream on each cake and then spread with another layer of cream. Cover with the shortcake tops. Spoon the remaining whipped cream over the shortcakes and top with the remaining orange sections.

—PEGGY CULLEN

MAKE IT AHEAD
You can prepare the shortcakes and oranges several hours ahead and keep them at room temperature. You can whip the cream ahead, too. Keep it, covered, in the refrigerator. Just before serving, you may need to whisk the cream for half a minute if it has started to separate.

Orange and Chocolate Mousse

Orange zest contributes a surprising amount of flavor to this airy mousse topped with bittersweet-chocolate curls. If you prefer your chocolate mousse plain, however, simply omit the orange.

SERVES 8

- 1 pound bittersweet chocolate, ¾ pound chopped
- 1½ cups milk
- 4 large egg yolks
- Grated zest of 1 orange
- ½ cup sugar
- ¼ cup water
- 6 large egg whites, at room temperature
- 1 cup heavy cream

1. Put the chopped chocolate in a food processor and pulse until ground fine, about 20 seconds. Leave the chocolate in the processor.

2. In a medium stainless-steel saucepan, combine the milk, egg yolks, and orange zest. Cook over moderate heat, whisking constantly, until slightly thickened, about 5 minutes. Do not let the custard boil. Strain. With the food processor running, pour the hot custard into the chocolate. Scrape the chocolate mixture into a large bowl.

3. In a small, heavy saucepan, combine the sugar and water. Bring to a boil over moderately high heat, stirring to dissolve the sugar. Brush the inside of the pan with a pastry brush dipped in water to dissolve any sugar crystals and continue to boil, without stirring, until the syrup reaches the soft-ball stage, about 10 minutes. A candy thermometer should register 238°.

4. Meanwhile, in a large bowl, using an electric mixer on medium speed, beat the egg whites until they mound slightly. Increase the speed to medium high and continue beating until the whites hold soft peaks when the beaters are lifted. Beat in the hot syrup in a thin stream. Continue beating until the meringue holds firm peaks when the beaters are lifted.

5. Fold a quarter of the meringue into the chocolate mixture to lighten it. Gently fold in the remaining meringue just until combined. Refrigerate until cool, about 15 minutes.

6. In a medium bowl, whip the cream until it holds firm peaks when the beaters are lifted. Fold the whipped cream into the cooled chocolate mixture and pour the mousse into a large serving bowl or eight individual soufflé dishes. Cover and refrigerate until set, about 4 hours.

7. Scrape a vegetable peeler along the remaining piece of chocolate to form curls. Top the mousse with the curls.

250

FIG AND HAZELNUT SHORTCAKES WITH RUBY-PORT SAUCE

Hazelnuts, figs, and mascarpone are the winter flavors of Italy. For this short-cake, dried figs are plumped in a port syrup, which is then reduced to a glistening sauce the color of Dorothy's ruby slippers. Even if you dislike anise, don't be afraid to use it here. It brings out the flavor of the toasted hazelnuts.

SERVES 6

- 1 cup hazelnuts
- 2 cups flour
- 1 cup plus 3 tablespoons superfine sugar
- 1 tablespoon anise seeds, chopped
- 1 tablespoon baking powder
- ½ teaspoon salt
- ¼ pound cold unsalted butter, cut into pieces
- ⅔ cup plus 1 tablespoon milk
- 1 vanilla bean, split lengthwise
- 12 dried figs
- 2 cups ruby port
- ½ cup heavy cream
- ½ pound mascarpone cheese (1 cup), at room temperature

1. Heat the oven to 350°. Put the hazelnuts on a baking sheet and toast them in the oven until the skins crack and loosen and the nuts are golden brown, about 15 minutes. Wrap the hot hazelnuts in a kitchen towel and firmly rub them together to loosen most of the skins. Discard the skins. Let the peeled hazelnuts cool and then chop them.

2. In a medium bowl, whisk together the flour, the 3 tablespoons superfine sugar, the anise seeds, baking powder, and salt. Cut the butter into the flour until the mixture resembles coarse meal with some pieces of butter still the size of peas. Toss in the hazelnuts.

3. Pour the ⅔ cup milk into a small bowl and scrape the seeds from the vanilla bean into the milk. Stir the milk mixture into the flour mixture just until it forms a dough when pressed together.

4. On a lightly floured surface, knead the dough gently two or three times. Shape the dough into a 12-inch log and then pat it out into a 12 by 3-inch strip that's 1 inch thick. Using a 3-inch round cutter dipped in flour, stamp out four circles. Gather the scraps, pat them out again to 1 inch thick, and cut out two more rounds. Brush the tops with the remaining 1 tablespoon milk. Put the shortcakes on a baking sheet lined with aluminum foil and refrigerate for 10 minutes.

5. Bake the shortcakes until golden brown, about 30 minutes. Let cool on the baking sheet for 10 minutes and then transfer to a rack to cool completely. ➤

6. Meanwhile, cut the stems off the figs. In a medium stainless-steel saucepan, combine the port and the remaining 1 cup superfine sugar. Bring to a boil over high heat and let boil to dissolve the sugar, about 3 minutes. Add the figs and bring back to a boil. Reduce the heat and simmer the figs until soft, about 20 minutes. Remove from the heat and let cool.

7. Meanwhile, in a medium bowl, whisk the cream and the mascarpone until slightly thickened. Remove the figs from the syrup. Cut each fig into quarters. Reserve the syrup.

8. Shortly before serving, split the short-cakes in half. Spoon about 1 tablespoon of the port syrup onto each of six dessert plates. Put the bottom halves of the short-cakes on the plates and spread each with 1/4 cup of the mascarpone cream. Arrange four fig quarters on the cream. Drizzle about 1 tablespoon of the syrup over the figs and top with about 3 tablespoons more cream. Put four more fig quarters on the cream and cover each with a shortcake top. Spoon the remaining cream on the shortcakes and drizzle the syrup over the tops.

—Peggy Cullen

MAKE IT AHEAD
The figs can be cooked several days ahead. Bring them back to room temperature before using. You can prepare the shortcakes several hours ahead and keep at room temperature, and combine the cream and mascarpone ahead and keep the mixture in the refrigerator. If it softens, whisk to thicken.

CHILLED BOURBON CUSTARD

This custard is a clone of English syllabub, a rich, frothy beverage for which the English designed beautiful syllabub cups, the size of demitasse cups but with two handles. You can serve the custard Southern-style in small cups topped with whipped cream, or use it as a sauce. It's delicious with Sweet-Potato Pie, page 197.

SERVES 6

2 cups milk

6 large egg yolks

¼ cup plus 1 tablespoon sugar

1 teaspoon flour

Pinch salt

1 cup heavy cream

1½ tablespoons bourbon, more to taste

1. In a medium saucepan, bring the milk almost to a simmer over moderately high heat, stirring frequently.

2. In a medium bowl, whisk the egg yolks, the ¼ cup sugar, the flour, and the salt until thick, about 5 minutes.

3. Pour the hot milk into the yolks in a thin stream, whisking. Pour the mixture back into the pan and cook over moderately low heat, stirring constantly, until it is just thick enough to coat a spoon, about 3 minutes. Do not let the custard boil or it may curdle. Strain into a bowl. Refrigerate until cold.

4. In a medium bowl, whip the cream and the remaining 1 tablespoon sugar until the cream holds soft peaks when the beaters are lifted. Stir the bourbon into the custard. Pour the custard into small cups and top with the whipped cream.

—CAMILLE GLENN

MAKE IT AHEAD
You can make the custard a day ahead and the whipped cream 2 to 3 hours in advance. Keep them both, well covered, in the refrigerator. Just before serving, put them in cups. You may need to whisk the cream for half a minute if it has begun to separate.

Chocolate Pecan Pudding with Bourbon Sauce

Midway between a chocolate cake and a soufflé, this pudding can be served right from the oven or allowed to cool slightly. Even when fully cooled, it is still delicious and moist, though it does sink a bit.

SERVES 6

¼ pound semisweet chocolate, chopped

3 tablespoons hot water

1½ cups pecans

⅓ cup sugar

¼ cup dry bread crumbs

¼ teaspoon cinnamon

¼ pound unsalted butter, at room temperature

1 tablespoon bourbon

5 large eggs, separated, at room temperature

Pinch salt

Bourbon Sauce, opposite page

1. Heat the oven to 350°. Butter a 1½-quart baking dish or 8-inch square pan.

2. In a double boiler, melt the chocolate with the 3 tablespoons hot water over hot but not simmering water, stirring frequently until smooth. Let cool.

3. In a food processor, chop the pecans. Remove ½ cup of the pecans and set aside. Add 1 tablespoon of the sugar to the remaining pecans and process the nuts to a powder. In a medium bowl, combine the ground pecans, the bread crumbs, and the cinnamon.

4. In a large bowl, using an electric mixer, cream the butter with half the remaining sugar until fluffy, about 5 minutes. Beat in the cooled chocolate and then the bourbon. Add the egg yolks, one at a time, beating until smooth. Stir in the ground pecan mixture. Bring water to a simmer for the water bath.

5. In another large bowl, using clean beaters, beat the egg whites with the salt on medium speed until they mound slightly. Increase the speed to medium-high and gradually beat in the remaining sugar. Continue beating until the whites hold soft peaks when the beaters are lifted. Fold one-quarter of the whites into the chocolate batter to lighten it. Gently fold in the remaining whites just until combined. Pour the batter into the prepared pan and smooth the top. Scatter the reserved chopped pecans over the batter.

6. Put the baking dish in a roasting pan and pour in enough of the simmering water to reach about halfway up the sides of the dish. Carefully transfer the roasting pan to

the middle of the oven and bake until the pudding is puffed and feels slightly firm when touched, about 30 minutes. Do not bake too long. Serve the pudding hot or let cool to warm or room-temperature. Spoon the pudding onto plates and drizzle each serving with several spoonfuls of the Bourbon Sauce. Pass the remaining sauce.

—NICHOLAS MALGIERI

MAKE IT AHEAD
You can make the pudding up to 8 hours ahead. Serve it at room temperature.

BOURBON SAUCE

MAKES ABOUT 2 CUPS

1½ cups milk
⅓ cup sugar
4 large egg yolks
2 tablespoons bourbon
1 teaspoon vanilla extract

1. In a medium saucepan, combine the milk and the sugar. Cook over moderate heat, stirring frequently with a wooden spoon, until the sugar dissolves and the mixture comes to a simmer, about 5 minutes.

2. In a medium bowl, whisk the egg yolks to combine. Pour the hot milk into the yolks in a thin stream, whisking.

3. Pour the mixture back into the pan and cook over moderately low heat, stirring constantly, until it is just thick enough to coat a spoon, about 30 seconds. Do not let the custard boil or it may curdle. Strain into a bowl and stir in the bourbon and vanilla. Let cool to warm.

MAKE IT AHEAD
You can make the sauce several days ahead and keep it, well covered, in the refrigerator. Reheat the sauce in a double boiler over simmering water, whisking, until warm, about 2 minutes.

INDIAN PUDDING
WITH BRANDY BUTTER SAUCE

Cornmeal is the base of this traditional New England dessert. Spiced, sweetened with molasses, and served warm with Brandy Butter Sauce, it's a natural for Thanksgiving. The pudding is also delicious with whipped cream or vanilla ice cream in place of the sauce.

SERVES 6

1½   quarts milk

1   cup cornmeal

2   large eggs

½   cup molasses

4   tablespoons unsalted butter, at room temperature

¼   cup sugar

1½   teaspoons cinnamon

1½   teaspoons grated nutmeg

½   teaspoon salt

¼   teaspoon baking powder

Brandy Butter Sauce, opposite page

1. Heat the oven to 300°. Butter a 1½- to 2-quart baking dish. In a large saucepan, bring the milk almost to a simmer.

2. In a medium bowl, whisk together the cornmeal, eggs, molasses, butter, sugar, cinnamon, nutmeg, salt, and baking powder until thoroughly combined. Pour the hot milk into this cornmeal mixture in a thin stream, whisking constantly. Pour the mixture back into the saucepan and cook over moderate heat, stirring, until it just begins to simmer, about 2 minutes. Pour the milk-and-cornmeal mixture into the prepared baking dish.

3. Fill a roasting pan with warm water and put it in the lower third of the oven. Put the pudding on the middle rack, above the water. Bake the pudding, replenishing the water if necessary, until set, 3½ to 4 hours. Serve warm with the brandy sauce.

MAKE IT AHEAD You can make the pudding a day ahead and keep it, covered, in the refrigerator. Reheat the pudding in a 350° oven until warmed through, about 20 minutes.

BRANDY BUTTER SAUCE

MAKES ABOUT 2 CUPS

- ¼ pound unsalted butter, at room temperature
- ¼ teaspoon salt
- 2 cups confectioners' sugar
- 2 tablespoons heavy cream, at room temperature
- 2 tablespoons cognac or other brandy

Using an electric mixer, cream the butter with the salt until fluffy, about 5 minutes. Beat in the confectioners' sugar, 1 tablespoon at a time, alternating with the cream and brandy, until smooth. The sauce should be thick like a frosting.

MAKE IT AHEAD
You can make the sauce several days in advance and keep it, well covered, in the refrigerator. Let it come to room temperature before serving.

APPLE PECAN SHORTCAKES WITH CARAMEL SAUCE

Inspired by two confections—sticky caramel apples and pecan buttercrunch—this dessert is delicious. The pecan-studded triangular shortcakes are split and filled with vanilla ice cream and apples in a buttery caramel sauce.

SERVES 6

- 2 cups flour
- 3 tablespoons brown sugar
- 1 tablespoon baking powder
- 1 teaspoon cinnamon
- ½ teaspoon salt
- 12 tablespoons cold unsalted butter, cut into pieces
- 1½ cups pecans, chopped
- ⅔ cup plus 1 tablespoon milk
- 1 teaspoon vanilla extract
- 1¾ pounds apples (about 4), peeled, cored, and cut into eight slices
- ¾ cup plus 1 tablespoon granulated sugar
- ¼ teaspoon lemon juice
- 2 tablespoons water
- ¾ cup heavy cream
- 1 pint vanilla ice cream

1. Heat the oven to 375°. Line a baking sheet with aluminum foil. In a medium bowl, whisk together the flour, brown sugar, baking powder, cinnamon, and salt. Cut in 8 tablespoons of the butter until the mixture resembles coarse meal with some pieces of butter still the size of peas. Toss in the pecans. Stir in the ⅔ cup milk and the vanilla just until the mixture forms a dough when pressed together.

2. On a lightly floured surface, knead the dough gently two or three times. Shape the dough into a 12-inch log and then pat it out into a 12 by 3-inch strip that is 1 inch thick. Cut the strip into six triangles. Brush the tops with the remaining 1 tablespoon milk. Put the shortcakes on the prepared baking sheet and refrigerate for 10 minutes.

3. Bake the shortcakes until golden brown, about 30 minutes. Let the shortcakes cool on the baking sheet for 10 minutes and then transfer to a rack to cool completely.

4. Meanwhile, in a large frying pan, melt the remaining 4 tablespoons butter. Add the apples and cook over high heat, stirring frequently, until the apples are lightly browned, about 4 minutes. Sprinkle the 1 tablespoon granulated sugar over the apples and continue cooking, stirring frequently, until the apples are tender and browned, about 4 minutes longer. Remove from the heat and set aside.

5. In a medium, heavy saucepan, using your fingers, rub the lemon juice thoroughly

into the remaining ¾ cup granulated sugar. Stir in the water until blended and bring to a boil over high heat. Brush the inside of the pan with a pastry brush dipped in water to dissolve any sugar crystals and continue to boil, without stirring, until the sugar turns a light amber color, about 5 minutes. Remove the pan from the heat and pour the cream into the caramel in a thin stream, whisking. Return the pan to the heat and continue whisking until thoroughly combined. Pour the warm caramel sauce into the apples and stir gently to coat the apples.

6. Shortly before serving, split the shortcakes in half. Put the bottom halves of the shortcakes on plates and cover each with several slices of apple and a little warm caramel sauce. Top with scoops of the ice cream and then drizzle with caramel sauce. Cover with the shortcake tops. Spoon the rest of the apple slices and caramel sauce over the shortcakes.

—Peggy Cullen

APPLE LAYER PUDDING

A pleasant change from apple pie, this steamed English pudding can also be made with pitted plums or sweetened rhubarb. Suet, or beef fat, is a traditional ingredient, but you can use one-quarter cup vegetable shortening instead.

SERVES 6

1 pound tart apples (about 2), such as Granny Smith, peeled, cored, and cut into ¼-inch slices

3 tablespoons lemon juice

1 teaspoon grated lemon zest

⅓ cup raisins

½ cup brown sugar

½ teaspoon cinnamon

1 cup plus 2 tablespoons flour, more if needed

1 teaspoon baking powder

¼ teaspoon salt

2 ounces cold grated suet (about ⅔ cup loosely packed)

6 tablespoons cold water, more if needed

Custard Sauce, page 244

1. Butter a 1-quart Pyrex or stainless-steel bowl. In a medium bowl, toss the apples with the lemon juice. Stir in the lemon zest, raisins, brown sugar, and cinnamon.

2. In a medium bowl, whisk together the flour, baking powder, and salt. Cut in the suet until the mixture resembles coarse meal. Sprinkle the water on top and stir until just combined. The dough should be soft but not sticky. Add more flour or water if needed.

3. Bring water to a simmer for steaming the pudding. Divide the dough into three slightly graduated pieces. On a lightly floured surface, roll out each piece to a ¼-inch-thick round. Put the smallest round in the bottom of the prepared bowl and top with half the apple mixture. Put the smaller of the remaining pastry rounds over the apples and, if necessary, trim to fit the bowl. Cover with the remaining apple mixture and any liquid from the apples. Top with the largest pastry round and trim to fit, if necessary.

4. Cover the bowl with buttered waxed paper and aluminum foil, both pleated in the middle to allow for expansion. Crimp the edges tightly around the rim of the bowl or tie securely with string. Put the bowl in the center of a kitchen towel and tie the diagonal corners together over the bowl to make a sling. Holding the towel, lower the pudding into a pot that's larger than the bowl. Pour enough of the simmering water into the pot to reach about halfway up the sides of the bowl.

5. Cover the pot and steam the pudding over moderate heat, replenishing with simmering water every half hour or so, for 2 hours. Run a knife around the edge of the pudding and unmold it onto a plate. Serve hot with the warm Custard Sauce.

APPLE QUINCE CRUMBLE WITH EGGNOG CUSTARD SAUCE

A crisp walnut topping covers apples and quince flavored with maple syrup and Calvados—a delectable combination. If you like, serve the crumble warm with a scoop of ice cream in place of the custard sauce.

SERVES 6

½   cup currants or raisins

¼   cup Calvados, applejack, or other apple brandy

⅓   cup plus 1 tablespoon flour

½   teaspoon ground allspice

½   teaspoon grated nutmeg

¼   teaspoon cinnamon

¼   teaspoon salt

2½   pounds tart apples (about 5), such as Granny Smith, peeled, cored, and cut into ¼-inch slices

1½   tablespoons lemon juice

1   large quince, peeled, cored, and cut into ¼-inch slices

⅓   cup pure maple syrup

½   cup rolled oats

½   cup brown sugar

¼   pound cold unsalted butter, cut into pieces

⅓   cup walnuts, chopped

Eggnog Custard Sauce, opposite page

1. Heat the oven to 375°. Butter a 2½-quart shallow baking dish. In a small stainless-steel pot, bring the currants and Calvados to a simmer. Set aside.

2. In a small bowl, combine the 1 tablespoon flour, the allspice, nutmeg, cinnamon, and salt. In a large bowl, combine the apples, lemon juice, quince, and maple syrup. Add the flour mixture and the Calvados with the currants to the apples. Toss until thoroughly combined. Put into the prepared baking dish.

3. In a large bowl, combine the oats, the brown sugar, and the remaining ⅓ cup flour. Cut in the butter until the mixture forms large crumbs. Stir in the walnuts. Top the fruit with this crumb mixture.

4. Bake the crumble in the middle of the oven until the topping is golden brown, about 1 hour. Let cool about 15 minutes. Serve warm with the eggnog sauce.

—RICHARD SAX

MAKE IT AHEAD
You can make the crumble up to 8 hours before serving and keep it, uncovered, at room temperature. To reheat, bake the crumble in a 325° oven until warmed through, about 15 minutes. Cover with aluminum foil partway through, if necessary, to keep the topping from getting too dark.

Eggnog Custard Sauce

MAKES ABOUT 2 1/2 CUPS

2½   cups milk
  1   vanilla bean, split lengthwise
  5   large egg yolks
 ⅓   cup sugar
  1   teaspoon amaretto, bourbon, or rum, preferably dark

1. In a medium saucepan, bring the milk and vanilla bean to a simmer over moderately high heat, stirring frequently. Remove from the heat, cover, and let infuse for 1 hour.

2. In a medium bowl, whisk the egg yolks and sugar until pale yellow, about 3 minutes.

3. Bring the milk back to a simmer and then pour the hot milk into the yolks in a thin stream, whisking. Pour the mixture back into the pan and cook over moderately low heat, stirring constantly, until it is just thick enough to coat a spoon, 1 to 3 minutes. Do not let the custard boil or it may curdle. Strain into a bowl. Scrape the seeds from the vanilla bean into the strained sauce. Let cool to room temperature and then stir in the amaretto.

MAKE IT AHEAD
You can make the sauce several days ahead, cover well, and refrigerate.

JAM ROLY-POLY

Here's a classic steamed pudding that's easy to prepare and looks festive with its spiral of plum jam. A spoonful of Custard Sauce on top completes the picture. If you like, replace the suet with one-quarter cup plus one tablespoon vegetable shortening.

SERVES 6

1½ cups flour, more if needed

1½ teaspoons baking powder

 ½ teaspoon salt

2½ ounces cold grated suet (about ¾ cup loosely packed)

 ⅔ cup water, more if needed

 ¾ cup plum jam, at room temperature
    Custard Sauce, page 244

1. Bring water to a simmer for steaming the pudding. In a medium bowl, whisk together the flour, baking powder, and salt. Cut in the suet until the mixture resembles coarse meal. Sprinkle the water on top; stir until just combined. The dough should be soft but not sticky. Add more flour or water if needed.

2. On a lightly floured surface, roll out the dough until it forms an 8 by 10-inch rectangle. Spread the dough with the plum jam, leaving a 1-inch margin of dough on all sides.

3. Moisten the edges of the dough with water. With the long side toward you, roll the dough into a log. Press along the seam and at both ends to seal in the jam.

4. Tear off a piece of aluminum foil 16 inches long. Put a piece of waxed paper the same size on top of the foil and butter the waxed paper. Put the jam roll lengthwise in the center of the paper. Fold the foil and waxed paper over and crimp the edges to seal, leaving room around the jam roll to allow for expansion.

5. Put the roll on a rack in a large steamer or pot. Add enough of the simmering water to come just below the rack. Lower the jam roll onto the rack. Cook, covered, replenishing the water every half hour or so, for 1½ hours. Remove the foil and waxed paper from the pudding and transfer it to a plate. Cut into slices and serve hot with the sauce.

WILD-RICE PUDDING WITH RAISINS

Sweetened with honey and flavored with orange liqueur, this rice pudding is a unique variation on a long-standing favorite. For an ideal garnish, marinate twelve orange sections in a little orange liqueur for about thirty minutes.

SERVES 6

1 cup wild rice

2½ cups water, more if needed

Pinch salt

½ cup raisins

2 tablespoons unsalted butter, at room temperature

3 tablespoons honey, more to taste

½ teaspoon grated nutmeg, more to taste

2 cups milk

2 large eggs, beaten to mix

2 tablespoons orange liqueur, such as Grand Marnier, more to taste

1 cup heavy cream

1. Rinse the rice well. In a medium pot, bring 1½ cups of the water to a boil over moderate heat. Add the rice and salt. Cover, reduce the heat, and cook at a gentle boil, adding more water if necessary, until the water is absorbed and the rice is tender. The cooking time can vary from 35 to 60 minutes. Remove ½ cup of the rice and reserve for garnish.

2. Meanwhile, in a small pot, bring the remaining 1 cup water and the raisins to a simmer. Continue cooking until plump, about 15 minutes. Add the raisins and their cooking liquid to the rice along with the butter, honey, and nutmeg. Stir until thoroughly combined.

3. Heat the milk in a medium bowl set over a saucepan filled with about an inch of simmering water. Add the rice mixture and stir in the eggs. Cook, stirring, until the mixture thickens, about 5 minutes. Do not let it boil. Remove from the heat and stir in the orange liqueur. Add more orange liqueur, honey, and nutmeg to taste.

4. In a large bowl, whip the cream until it holds firm peaks when the beaters are lifted. Serve the rice pudding warm or cold, topped with the whipped cream and the reserved rice.

—PEARL BYRD FOSTER

MAKE IT AHEAD
You can make the rice pudding a few days ahead and keep it, well covered, in the refrigerator. Serve the pudding cold.

CHRISTMAS BREAD PUDDING WITH AMARETTO SAUCE

Made with panettone, the traditional Italian Christmas bread, and a baked-on amaretto sauce, this bread pudding is an inspired finale to holiday dinners. If you can't get panettone, substitute a similar fruit-studded sweet bread.

SERVES 12

- 1   1-pound panettone, cut into 1-inch slices
- 1   quart light cream
- 3   large eggs
- 1   cup granulated sugar
- 1   tablespoon plus 2 teaspoons vanilla extract
- 1   teaspoon almond extract
- ¼   pound unsalted butter, cut into pieces
- 1   cup confectioners' sugar
- 3   tablespoons amaretto
- 2   large egg yolks

1. Heat the broiler. Put the bread slices on two baking sheets and toast, turning once, until lightly browned. Set aside to dry for at least one hour.

2. Tear the toasted panettone into 1½-inch pieces and put them in a large bowl. Add the cream and toss to moisten all the pieces. Let sit until all the cream is absorbed, about 1 hour.

3. Heat the oven to 325°. Butter a 9 by 13-inch baking dish. In a medium bowl, whisk the whole eggs, the granulated sugar, and the vanilla and almond extracts until thoroughly combined. Stir into the cream-soaked bread. Transfer the mixture to the prepared baking dish.

4. Bake the pudding in the middle of the preheated oven until it is just set and the bread is golden brown, about 1 hour. Let cool.

5. In a medium bowl set over a saucepan of simmering water, melt the butter. Whisk in the confectioners' sugar, ¼ cup at a time. Continue whisking until the mixture is creamy, about 30 seconds. Add the amaretto and then the egg yolks, one at a time, whisking constantly. Cook, whisking constantly, until the sauce is the consistency of honey, about 4 minutes. A candy thermometer should register 160°. Let cool.

6. Heat the broiler. Shortly before serving, spoon the amaretto sauce over the pudding and broil until bubbling and lightly browned, about 2 minutes. Serve warm.

—SHEILA LUKINS

CHRISTMAS PUDDING

There's nothing like the drama of a flaming Christmas pudding. Because the flavor of this dessert improves with age, you can get a good head start: Make it at least a week and up to a year ahead. Serve it with traditional warm Brandy Sauce or cold Hard Sauce, or with whipped cream. If you don't want to use suet, you can substitute one-half cup plus two tablespoons vegetable shortening.

SERVES 16

1   cup flour

1   teaspoon cinnamon

1   teaspoon grated nutmeg

½   teaspoon ground ginger

¼   teaspoon ground cloves

2   cups dark raisins

2   cups golden raisins

2   cups currants

½   cup blanched almonds, chopped fine

5   ounces cold grated suet (about 1½ cups loosely packed)

2   cups fresh bread crumbs

2   teaspoons grated orange zest

1   teaspoon grated lemon zest

½   cup brown sugar

2   carrots, grated

4   large eggs, beaten to mix

½   cup dark ale or milk

⅓   cup cognac or other brandy

    Brandy Sauce or Hard Sauce, opposite page

1.   Butter a 1½- to 2-quart Pyrex or stainless-steel bowl. Line the bottom of the bowl with a small circle of buttered waxed paper. Bring water to a simmer for steaming the pudding. In a medium bowl, whisk together the flour, cinnamon, nutmeg, ginger, and cloves.

2.   In a large bowl, combine the raisins, currants, almonds, suet, bread crumbs, the orange and lemon zests, the brown sugar, and the carrots. Stir in the dry ingredients. Add the eggs and the ale and stir until thoroughly combined.

3.   Spoon the batter into the prepared bowl. Cover the bowl with buttered waxed paper and aluminum foil, both pleated in the middle to allow for expansion. Crimp the edges tightly around the rim of the bowl or tie securely with string. Put the bowl in the center of a kitchen towel and tie the diagonal corners together over the bowl to make a sling. Holding the towel, lower the bowl into a pot that's larger than the bowl. Pour enough of the simmering water into the pot to reach about halfway up the sides of the bowl.

4.   Cover the pot and steam the pudding over moderate heat, replenishing with simmering water every half hour or so, for 7 hours. The pudding will get darker as it

cooks. Remove the pudding from the pot and let cool. Refrigerate the pudding in the bowl, well covered, for at least 1 week.

5. Several hours before serving, steam the pudding in the same way until hot through, about 1 hour. Just before serving, unmold it onto a plate. In a small pot, bring the brandy almost to a simmer. Hold a lighted match close to the surface to ignite the brandy, pour the flaming brandy over the pudding, and carry it to the table. When the flames die out, cut the pudding into wedges and serve with one of the sauces.

MAKE IT AHEAD
Here's a dessert that you *should* make ahead, even up to a year in advance. Refrigerate the pudding in the bowl, tightly covered. Uncover and sprinkle with 1 or 2 tablespoons of brandy every month or so.

BRANDY SAUCE

MAKES ABOUT 1¹⁄₃ CUPS

1   tablespoon cornstarch
1¼ cups milk
2   tablespoons sugar
1   tablespoon unsalted butter
3   tablespoons brandy

1. Put the cornstarch in a small pot. Stir in ¼ cup of the milk until smooth. Stir in the remaining milk and then the sugar and butter.

2. Bring the mixture to a boil over moderate heat, stirring constantly. Reduce the heat and simmer, stirring for 4 minutes. Remove from the heat and stir in the brandy. Serve warm.

HARD SAUCE

MAKES ABOUT 1 CUP

¼   pound unsalted butter, at room temperature
½   cup brown sugar
3   tablespoons brandy

Using an electric mixer, cream the butter and sugar until fluffy, about 5 minutes. Gradually beat in the brandy. Chill for at least 1 hour.

Marbled Pudding
with Chocolate Amaretto Sauce

Steaming keeps this cake-like chocolate and vanilla pudding exceedingly moist. Dotted with chocolate chips and topped with creamy chocolate sauce, the dessert is both pretty and delicious.

SERVES 6

1   cup plus 2 tablespoons flour

1   teaspoon baking powder

¼   pound unsalted butter, at room temperature

½   cup sugar

3   large eggs, beaten to mix

½   teaspoon almond extract

⅓   cup semisweet chocolate chips

3   tablespoons milk

¼   cup unsweetened cocoa powder

½   teaspoon vanilla extract

Chocolate Amaretto Sauce, opposite page

1. Butter a 1-quart Pyrex or stainless-steel bowl. Bring water to a simmer for steaming the pudding. In a medium bowl, whisk together the flour and baking powder.

2. In a large bowl, using an electric mixer, cream the butter and sugar until fluffy, about 5 minutes. Beat in half of the eggs. Stir half the flour mixture into the butter mixture. Stir in the remaining eggs, and then the remaining flour mixture. Transfer half of the batter to another bowl. Add the almond extract and half of the chocolate chips to one bowl of batter and stir until combined.

3. In a small bowl, stir together the milk, cocoa, and vanilla extract until combined. Add this cocoa mixture and the remaining chocolate chips to the second bowl of batter. Stir until thoroughly combined. Drop alternating heaping tablespoons of batter from each bowl into the prepared bowl.

4. Cover the pudding bowl with buttered waxed paper and aluminum foil, both pleated in the middle to allow for expansion. Crimp the edges tightly around the rim of the bowl or tie securely with string. Put the bowl in the center of a kitchen towel and tie the diagonal corners together over the bowl to make a sling. Holding the towel, lower the bowl into a pot that's larger than the bowl. Pour enough of the simmering water into the pot to reach about halfway up the sides of the bowl.

5. Cover the pot and steam the pudding over moderate heat, replenishing with simmering water every half hour or so, until a toothpick stuck in the center comes out almost clean, about 1½ hours. If there is

wet batter clinging to the toothpick, steam the pudding 5 to 10 minutes longer. Unmold the pudding onto a plate and serve hot with the warm Chocolate Amaretto Sauce.

MAKE IT AHEAD
You can make the pudding several days ahead and keep it, well-covered, in the refrigerator. To reheat, steam the pudding in the same way until warmed through, about ½ hour.

CHOCOLATE AMARETTO SAUCE

MAKES ABOUT 1 1/2 CUPS

4 ounces semisweet chocolate
2 tablespoons sugar
1 cup heavy cream
2 tablespoons unsalted butter
6 tablespoons amaretto liqueur

In a small pot, melt the chocolate with the sugar and cream over low heat, stirring. Whisk until the mixture is smooth. Do not let the sauce boil. Remove from the heat. Add the butter and stir until it melts. Stir in the amaretto.

MAKE IT AHEAD
You can make the sauce several days in advance. Reheat gently when ready to serve.

PRUNES IN RED WINE

Wine-poached prunes with lemon and orange slices make a simple French bistro dessert that's reminiscent of mulled wine. You'll need to start preparing the prunes the day before you plan to serve them.

SERVES 6

1½ pounds pitted prunes (about 1 quart)

1 quart water

2 cups full-bodied red wine

½ cup sugar

4 thin slices lemon, seeds removed

8 thin slices orange, seeds removed

1. In a large bowl, combine the prunes and the water. Cover and let sit at room temperature for 24 hours.

2. Drain the prunes and discard the soaking liquid. In a large stainless-steel saucepan, combine the prunes, wine, sugar, and the lemon and orange slices. Bring to a boil over high heat, remove from the heat, and let cool. Serve the prunes at room temperature or cold.

—PATRICIA WELLS

MAKE IT AHEAD
You can poach the prunes a few days ahead; they taste even better after the flavors have had time to meld.

VARIATIONS

■ You can spice up the dessert by adding a cinnamon stick and about six cloves to the wine mixture when poaching the prunes.

■ Instead of the traditional spices suggested above, try ten peppercorns and a bay leaf for an elusive, intriguing flavor.

■ Use a combination of dried fruits, such as apricots, apples, pears, and cherries, in place of half the prunes.

WARM WINTER-FRUIT COMPOTE

Fresh pears, prunes, dried apples, and dried apricots, all poached in a light citrus syrup, make an enticing, quick dessert. For an elegant sundae, add a little Grand Marnier to the compote and serve it over vanilla ice cream.

SERVES 6

¾ cup pitted prunes, quartered

¾ cup dried apricots, quartered

¾ cup dried apple slices, cut into ½-inch pieces

3 pears, peeled, cored, and cut into ½-inch dice

1 cup plus 2 tablespoons orange juice

6 tablespoons water

1½ tablespoons brown sugar

1½ teaspoons grated orange zest, plus four 3-inch strips orange zest, cut into matchstick pieces, for garnish

In a large stainless-steel saucepan, combine all the ingredients except the strips of orange zest, and bring to a boil over moderately high heat. Reduce the heat to low and simmer, covered, until all of the fruits are tender, about 7 minutes. Serve the compote warm, topped with the strips of zest.

—MARION CUNNINGHAM

CRANBERRY FOOL

You're missing out if you limit cranberries to sauce. Here, the tart berries are cooked with sweetened orange juice and then folded into whipped cream.

SERVES 6

¾ cup sugar

¾ cup orange juice

1 12-ounce package cranberries (about 3 cups)

1½ cups heavy cream

1. In a medium stainless-steel saucepan, combine the sugar, orange juice, and 2¾ cups of the cranberries. Bring to a boil over moderately high heat and cook until the berries pop, about 4 minutes. Remove from the heat and let cool to room temperature, about 30 minutes.

2. In a large bowl, whip the cream until it forms soft peaks when the beaters are lifted. Fold the cooled cranberry mixture into the whipped cream. Spoon the fool into stemmed glasses. Garnish with the remaining cranberries.

—THE SHOALWATER, SEAVIEW, WASHINGTON

WINTRY FRUIT SALAD

Here's a colorful blend of fruit—kiwi, apple, pear, melon, papaya, and berries—that's good to include when you're offering several desserts to a crowd. It also makes a delicious accompaniment to plain cakes, such as Ginger Angel Food Cake, page 203.

SERVES 16

1   cantaloupe, seeded

1   honeydew melon, seeded

3   kiwis, peeled, quartered, and cut into $\frac{1}{4}$-inch slices

2   apples, peeled, quartered, cored, and cut into $\frac{1}{4}$-inch slices

1   pear, peeled, quartered, cored, and cut into $\frac{1}{4}$-inch slices

1   papaya, peeled, halved, seeded, and cut into 2 by $\frac{1}{4}$-inch strips

1   pint raspberries or hulled strawberries

$\frac{1}{4}$ cup sugar

3   tablespoons lemon juice

1. Using a melon baller, scoop out rounds of cantaloupe and honeydew.

2. In a large glass or stainless-steel bowl, combine the cantaloupe and honeydew rounds with the other fruit. Add the sugar and the lemon juice and toss gently. Cover and refrigerate for 2 hours.

MAKE IT AHEAD
You can make the fruit salad a day before you plan to serve it. Keep it, covered, in the refrigerator.

VARIATIONS

■ You can add two to three tablespoons liqueur, such as Grand Marnier or Cointreau, to the fruit salad.

■ Add several tablespoons of chopped fresh mint to the fruit.

■ Use honey in place of the sugar.

chapter 14

GIFTS FROM THE KITCHEN

Strawberry Vinegar, page 279

STRAWBERRY VINEGAR

Ripe, juicy berries are crucial to making a good fruit vinegar. This vinegar makes a nice change in salad dressings or on grilled vegetables. Present it in an empty relabeled vinegar bottle, a pretty jar, or a small carafe with a cork.

MAKES ABOUT 1 1/2 CUPS

1 cup small ripe strawberries, hulled

1 12- to 14-ounce bottle white-wine vinegar

1. Combine the hulled strawberries and the bottle of white-wine vinegar in a glass jar or bowl. Cover tightly and let the strawberry-vinegar mixture stand at room temperature for 3 days.

2. Strain the mixture through a fine sieve and then pour the strawberry vinegar into a clean container. Cover tightly and store in a cool, dark place.

BASIL OIL

You'll find a million uses for this infused oil. Mix it into vinaigrettes, toss it with pasta or rice, or drizzle it over vegetables, fish, or poultry.

MAKES ABOUT 1 1/3 CUPS

1 packed cup fresh basil leaves

2 cups olive oil

1. In a medium pot of boiling, salted water, blanch the basil leaves for 5 seconds. Drain and rinse with cold water.

2. Transfer the basil leaves to a food processor or blender and puree with 1/4 cup of the oil. With the machine running, add the remaining 1¾ cups oil and process until smooth. Transfer to a glass jar, cover, and let stand at room temperature for at least 24 hours.

3. Carefully pour the clear green oil into a clean jar or bottle, leaving the thick basil puree behind. The oil will keep for at least a month in the refrigerator.

—JEAN-GEORGES VONGERICHTEN

CURRIED PUMPKIN SEEDS AND CORNNUTS

Pumpkin seeds have a subtle flavor that can be enhanced by a number of different spices. Here, curry powder adds an Indian accent.

MAKES ABOUT 4 CUPS

- 1 pound hulled pumpkin seeds (pepitas)*
- 2 tablespoons olive oil
- 1 tablespoon curry powder
- 1 teaspoon salt
- 2 3-ounce bags Cornnuts

*Available at health-food stores

1. Heat the oven to 350°. Put the pumpkin seeds in a medium bowl. In a small frying pan, combine the oil with the curry powder. Cook over moderately high heat, stirring, until the oil is very hot, about 3 minutes. Immediately pour the oil over the pumpkin seeds. Sprinkle with the salt and toss.

2. Spread the pumpkin seeds on a baking sheet and bake in the middle of the oven, stirring occasionally, until light brown, about 15 minutes.

3. Return the pumpkin seeds to the bowl, add the Cornnuts, and toss to combine. Stir the mixture occasionally as it cools. Store in airtight containers.

—BOB CHAMBERS

MIXED-NUT VARIATION

You can use a combination of nuts such as almonds, cashews, and walnuts in place of the pumpkin seeds. Bake the nuts for a shorter period of time, about ten minutes. Omit the Cornnuts.

ICED CRANBERRY AQUAVIT

Aquavit infused with cranberries and peppercorns makes a bracing aperitif. After straining the aquavit, you can use the cranberries to make a tasty sauce or relish; one containing caraway would complement the flavor of the aquavit.

MAKES 1 BOTTLE

- 1 12-ounce package cranberries (about 3 cups)
- 1 750-ml bottle aquavit
- 1 tablespoon black peppercorns

1. Divide the cranberries between two 1-quart jars. Cover the cranberries with the aquavit; reserve the aquavit bottle and cap. Add the peppercorns, dividing them equally between the jars. Cover and let stand at room temperature for at least 3 days.

2. Strain the aquavit through a fine sieve. Pour the aquavit back into the original bottle and store in the freezer.

—ANNE DISRUDE

MAKE IT AHEAD
This is a great gift to start as soon as cranberries come on the market. It keeps virtually forever.

VARIATIONS

Use either vodka or white rum in place of the aquavit. A clear alcohol such as these is best so that the pretty pink tint from the cranberries will show.

RASPBERRY KETCHUP

When you give this ketchup, you may want to attach a card with serving suggestions such as those listed below. The condiment is like a smooth chutney.

MAKES ABOUT 2 CUPS

2 pints raspberries (about 4 cups)

2 tablespoons water

½ cup sugar

1½ cups minced onions (about 2 large)

½ cup wine vinegar

2 cloves garlic, minced

1½ teaspoons ground allspice

1. In a medium saucepan, combine the raspberries, water, and 1 tablespoon of the sugar. Mash the berries with a wooden spoon while bringing the mixture to a boil over moderate heat. Reduce the heat, cover, and simmer for 5 minutes. Strain and press the fruit firmly to get all the juice and fruit puree. Discard the seeds.

2. Return the puree to the saucepan. Add the onions, vinegar, garlic, allspice, and the remaining 7 tablespoons sugar. Bring to a boil, reduce the heat, and simmer, stirring occasionally, until reduced to 2 cups, about 15 minutes. Puree in a blender or food processor until smooth. Let cool. The condiment will keep in the refrigerator, in a sealed jar or bottle, for at least a month.

SERVING SUGGESTIONS

- Thin the ketchup and use it as a basting sauce for grilled chicken.

- Heat the ketchup and serve it as a sauce for spareribs.

- Serve the raspberry ketchup instead of cranberry sauce with turkey.

- Spread the ketchup over cream cheese on bagels.

- The ketchup makes a special sandwich with leftover duck, goose, or roast pork.

- Hash-brown potatoes taste great with this condiment.

CHOCOLATE ORANGE TRUFFLES

Cocoa-dusted truffles make a rich and delicious petit four, nightcap, or late-afternoon snack. Bet you can't eat just one.

MAKES ABOUT 7 DOZEN

¼ cup unsweetened cocoa powder, sifted, more if needed

1 cup heavy cream

10½ ounces bittersweet chocolate, chopped

3 tablespoons unsalted butter

1 tablespoon grated orange zest

⅓ cup confectioners' sugar

2 tablespoons orange liqueur, such as Grand Marnier

1. Line a large baking sheet with waxed paper and sprinkle with the cocoa powder. In a medium saucepan, bring the cream to a boil. Cook at a gentle boil, stirring occasionally, until reduced to ½ cup, about 10 minutes. Remove from the heat.

2. Add the chocolate to the hot cream and stir until melted. Stir in the butter, orange zest, confectioners' sugar, and liqueur. Transfer to a bowl, cover, and refrigerate until the mixture is firm enough to handle.

3. Shape the truffle mixture into 1-inch balls and put them on the prepared baking sheet. Roll the truffles in the cocoa powder. Chill for at least 20 minutes before serving. Keep the truffles, well covered, in the refrigerator. Serve at room temperature.

VANILLA SUGAR

A vanilla bean infuses sugar with aroma and flavor, both of which grow more prominent the longer the bean sits in the sugar. Plan on at least a week. Many people keep a batch going, adding more sugar as it's used and replacing the vanilla bean when it eventually dries out.

MAKES 2 CUPS

1 vanilla bean

2 cups sugar

Put the vanilla bean into a jar and cover it with the sugar. Cover the jar with plastic wrap and then the lid. Let the sugar sit for a week to develop the flavor.

CANDIED ORANGE PEEL

Candied citrus peel makes a tasty and attractive garnish for desserts. This one would be a wonderful addition to chocolate or fruit cakes, and a fine accompaniment to an after-dinner espresso.

MAKES ABOUT ³/₄ CUP

1 large navel orange
¼ cup plus 2 tablespoons granulated sugar
¼ cup water
2 tablespoons crystal sugar (optional)

1. Using a sharp knife, cut the skin of the orange into quarters from top to bottom and peel the orange. Cut the peel into matchstick strips.

2. Blanch the peel in boiling water for 3 minutes. Drain, rinse with cold water, and repeat.

3. Return the peel to the saucepan and add the granulated sugar and water. Bring to a boil over moderate heat. Reduce the heat and simmer until the peel is translucent, about 30 minutes. Strain and let cool.

4. Heat the oven to 250°. Separate the orange-peel strips and put them on a rack set on a baking sheet. Bake until almost dry, about 20 minutes. Roll in the crystal sugar.

—LYDIE MARSHALL

MAKE IT AHEAD
You can make the candied peel up to 3 months in advance. Keep it in an airtight container.

GIFT-WRAP IDEAS

Use your imagination when wrapping your handmade gifts—anything goes. Candied Orange Peel might be presented in:

■ **A small basket** lined with colorful tissue paper.

■ **An inexpensive candy dish.** Wrap it in clear cellophane drawn together with raffia.

■ **A jelly jar.** Tie a square of paper over the lid with twine.

■ **A small white paper bag.** Fold over the top, punch holes, thread with pretty yarn, and tie to close.

■ **A small tin** in a solid color. Decorate with stick-on stars.

■ **A white cardboard cube-shaped box.** Decorate with a holiday-themed stamp and a red or green ink pad.

THREE-CITRUS MARMALADE

Nothing quite matches the flavor of homemade marmalade. You will be rewarded for your efforts with a crisp, citrusy taste.

MAKES 6 TO 7 PINTS

- 2 lemons
- 2 oranges
- 2 grapefruits
- About 4 quarts water
- 10 cups sugar, more if needed

1. Cut the lemons, oranges, and grapefruits into slices as thin as possible. Remove the seeds, wrap them in a piece of cheesecloth, and tie securely with string. Measure the volume of the fruit slices (there should be about 2 quarts) and transfer them to a large bowl.

2. Measure out twice as much cold water as there is fruit and add it to the bowl. Cover the bowl with plastic wrap and refrigerate overnight to soften the citrus peels.

3. Pour the citrus-fruit mixture into a large pot. Add the bag of seeds, which will help the marmalade set. Bring the mixture to a boil, reduce the heat, and simmer for 1½ hours.

4. Measure the citrus-fruit mixture. There should be approximately 10 cups. Return the mixture to the pot and add an equal volume of sugar. Bring the mixture to a boil, stirring to dissolve the sugar. Boil fairly rapidly, stirring frequently, for about 30 minutes.

5. Remove the pot from the heat and test to see if the marmalade sets: Put a teaspoon of the mixture on a cold plate and let it cool. The marmalade should wrinkle when pushed with your finger. If it doesn't, reboil and retest the marmalade at 5-minute intervals until it sets.

6. Remove and discard the bag of seeds and skim off any foam. Let the peel settle for about 5 minutes and then ladle the marmalade into hot, sterile jelly glasses or straight-sided canning jars to within ¼-inch of their tops. Seal with melted paraffin or sterile two-piece lids.

CRANBERRY TEA BREAD

Flavored with orange zest, cranberries, and walnuts, this moist quick bread is not overly sweet. It's best to let it sit for a day to allow the flavors to blend and then slice the loaf thin and eat it either plain or with butter.

MAKES ONE 9-INCH LOAF

- 2 cups flour
- 2 teaspoons baking powder
- ¼ teaspoon salt
- 4 tablespoons unsalted butter, cut into pieces
- ¾ cup plus 1 tablespoon sugar
- 1 cup chopped walnuts
- 1 tablespoon grated orange zest
- 1 large egg
- ⅔ cup orange juice
- 2 cups fresh or frozen cranberries (about 8 ounces)
- 1 tablespoon milk

1. Heat the oven to 350°. Butter a 9 by 5-inch loaf pan and line the bottom with buttered waxed paper.

2. In a large bowl, whisk together the flour, baking powder, and salt. Cut in the butter until the mixture resembles fine meal. Add ¾ cup of the sugar, the chopped walnuts, and the grated orange zest, and stir to blend.

3. In a small bowl, beat the egg until frothy. Stir in the orange juice and pour the mixture over the dry ingredients. Stir until just combined. Before all of the flour is incorporated, add the cranberries and stir them into the batter.

4. Pour the batter into the prepared pan. Brush the top with the milk and sprinkle with the remaining 1 tablespoon sugar.

5. Bake the bread in the middle of the oven until golden brown and a toothpick stuck in the center comes out clean, about 1 hour and 15 minutes. Cool for 20 minutes in the pan. Remove the bread from the pan and let cool completely on a rack. Wrap the loaf well and let it sit overnight.

OTHER BAKED GIFTS

Cookies and fruitcakes also make great gifts. Wrap up one or a mixture of the following with cellophane and ribbon:

- Linzer Wreaths, page 166
- Cranberry Pistachio Biscotti, page 170
- Fruitcake Cookies, page 168
- Dark Applesauce Fruitcakes, page 223

chapter 15
DRINKS

COLONEL TALBOTT'S BOURBON PUNCH

Bourbon punch always fares well at holiday parties. This one is pleasantly fruity but lives up to the name: It has plenty of punch.

SERVES 36

1 cup sugar

1 cup water

10 whole cloves

2 cinnamon sticks

2 liters bourbon

2 cups applejack or other apple brandy

2 cups orange liqueur, such as Grand Marnier

2 tablespoons aromatic bitters, such as angostura

3 seedless oranges, halved and cut into thin slices

1 lime, cut into thin slices

2 apples, cored, seeded, and cut into 1-inch cubes

1 cup strong, fresh-brewed tea

1 quart club soda

1. In a small saucepan, combine the sugar and water. Bring to a boil over moderately low heat. Cook, stirring to dissolve the sugar, for 5 minutes. Add the cloves and cinnamon sticks, remove from the heat, and let cool.

2. In a large punch bowl, combine the bourbon, applejack, orange liqueur, aromatic bitters, the orange and lime slices, the apple cubes, and the tea. Add the syrup and let stand, covered, at least 30 minutes. Just before serving, uncover the punch, add ice, and pour in the club soda.

MAKE IT AHEAD
You can combine all the ingredients except the apples and soda and keep the mixture in the refrigerator for several days. Add the apples and club soda and let sit for half an hour before serving.

CHRISTMAS MELON BALL

The Inn on the Park in Houston stirs up pleasant memories of childhood with this Christmas concoction. Consider it a grown-up snow cone! If making crushed ice is a problem, the drink is also excellent on the rocks.

SERVES 1

1½ ounces Midori or other melon liqueur

1½ ounces vodka

6 ounces orange juice

Grenadine, for serving

Maraschino cherries, for garnish

Combine the Midori, vodka, and orange juice in a small bowl or measuring cup. Pour the mixture over crushed ice (or cubes) in a tall glass. Sprinkle with grenadine and garnish with a cherry.

NORTH WOODS APPLE SOUR

A twist on the classic whiskey sour, this drink gets its sweetness from apple juice and maple syrup. With the juice, and the club soda as well, it's not so strong as the traditional version.

SERVES 4

½ cup whiskey

2 cups apple juice

¼ cup lime juice (from about 2 limes), more if needed

2 tablespoons pure maple syrup

⅛ teaspoon cinnamon

⅛ teaspoon ground cloves

Club soda

Combine the whiskey, apple juice, lime juice, maple syrup, cinnamon, and cloves. Taste and add more lime juice if too sweet. Pour into four 8-ounce glasses filled with ice, and top with club soda.

COGNAC EGGNOG

This heady potion will ensure good spirits and holiday cheer. Serve it chilled in a punch bowl or glass pitcher and let your guests indulge themselves.

SERVES 18

  8 eggs

¾ cup sugar

  3 cups milk

  2 cups heavy cream

1¼ cups cognac or other brandy

  1 teaspoon vanilla extract

¾ teaspoon grated nutmeg

1. In a large glass or stainless-steel bowl, whisk the eggs and ¼ cup of the sugar until the mixture forms a ribbon when the whisk is lifted, about 2 minutes. Put the milk, the cream, and the remaining ½ cup sugar in a medium saucepan. Bring to a boil, stirring to dissolve the sugar. Whisk the hot liquid into the egg mixture.

2. Let the mixture cool for 5 minutes. Stir in the cognac, vanilla, and nutmeg. Pour the eggnog into a 2-quart container, cover, and refrigerate.

MAKE IT AHEAD
Eggnog will keep in the refrigerator for 3 days.

U.N. PLAZA EGGNOG

For many, eggnog is the quintessential holiday-season beverage. This rich, coffee-almond-flavored version from the U.N. Plaza Park Hyatt Hotel can easily be multiplied to fill your holiday punch bowl.

SERVES 1

  3 ounces eggnog, chilled

  1 ounce amaretto

½ ounce coffee liqueur, such as Kahlúa

     Bittersweet chocolate, shaved, for garnish

In an old-fashioned glass, combine the eggnog and liqueurs and stir. Garnish with shaved chocolate.

MULLED WINE

The trick to successful mulled wine lies in the heating. The wine should be warmed, not boiled.

SERVES 4

- 3 allspice berries
- 6 whole cloves
- 5 cinnamon sticks
- ¼ teaspoon caraway seeds, crushed (optional)
- ½ cup sugar
- 2 cups water
- 2 lemons, cut into thin slices
- 1 bottle red wine

1. Tie the spices in a square of cheesecloth. In a large stainless-steel saucepan, combine the sugar with the water, add the spice bag, and bring to a boil over high heat. Reduce the heat to moderately low. Simmer for 10 minutes, stirring occasionally. Remove from the heat. Add the lemons and let stand, covered, for 20 minutes.

2. Add the wine and warm until hot but not boiling. Remove and discard the spice bag. Ladle the wine into mugs or glasses.

FRAUNCES TAVERN'S SYLLABUB

Though lighter than eggnog, syllabub still satisfies. With a thick, frothy topping of flavored cream, it can make an interesting alternative to dessert.

SERVES 6

- 1¼ cups sugar
- 6 cups red wine
- ½ cup sweet sherry
- Grated zest and juice of 1 lemon
- 2 cups chilled heavy cream
- Grated nutmeg, for garnish (optional)

1. In a medium glass or stainless-steel bowl, stir ¾ cup of the sugar into the wine and stir to dissolve. Divide the sweetened wine among six glasses.

2. In another medium glass or stainless-steel bowl, combine the sherry, the lemon zest, the lemon juice, and the remaining ½ cup sugar. Stir until the sugar dissolves.

3. Add the cream and slowly whisk until it froths. Spoon into the glasses. Sprinkle lightly with nutmeg, if desired.

—FRAUNCES TAVERN, NEW YORK CITY

GLUHWEIN

The German *glühwein* is just one of many ways to say spiced, heated wine. This recipe can easily be increased to serve at parties.

SERVES 2

1 cup water

1 thick slice of lemon

4 whole cloves

2 cinnamon sticks

2 cups red wine

Sugar

In a medium stainless-steel saucepan, combine the water, lemon, cloves, and cinnamon sticks, and bring to a boil. Boil for 5 minutes, then remove from the heat. Add the wine and reheat without allowing to boil. Add sugar to taste. Serve in mugs or glasses.

BISCHOP WYN

For a special effect, float some brandy on top of each serving and ignite the alcohol with a match.

SERVES 16

1 gallon full-bodied red wine

2 quarts water

1 teaspoon whole cloves

2 teaspoons cinnamon

½ cup raisins

1 orange, sliced

Sugar

KITCHEN TIP

When pouring hot liquid into a glass, put a spoon in the glass and pour the hot liquid down the back of the spoon. This will keep the glass from cracking.

In a large enameled or stainless-steel pot, combine the wine, water, cloves, cinnamon, raisins, and orange. Add sugar to taste. Heat, but do not boil. Serve in mugs or glasses.

CIDER WASSAIL BOWL

Apples appear in three forms in this holiday punch: slices, cider, and brandy.

SERVES 12

1 tart apple, cut into ½-inch slices

1 teaspoon lemon juice

¼ cup plus 1 tablespoon brown sugar

1 tablespoon butter

1 quart apple cider

1 tablespoon grated lemon zest

1 tablespoon grated orange zest

5 cardamom pods

6 allspice berries

1 cinnamon stick, broken in half

6 whole cloves

½ cup rum, preferably dark

½ cup Calvados or other apple brandy

12 ounces light ale

Grated nutmeg, for garnish

Heat the oven to 300°. Toss the apple slices in the lemon juice. Arrange in a shallow baking pan in a single layer. Sprinkle with 1 tablespoon of the brown sugar. Dot with the butter. Bake until tender, about 20 minutes. In a large saucepan, bring the cider, zests, and remaining ¼ cup brown sugar to a boil over high heat, stirring to dissolve the sugar. Tie the cardamom, allspice, cinnamon, and cloves in cheesecloth; add to the cider. Cover and simmer 20 minutes. Add the rum, Calvados, and ale. Return to a simmer. Remove from the heat. Discard the spice bag. Pour into a punch bowl. Garnish with the apples. Sprinkle with nutmeg. Serve warm.

—MELANIE BARNARD

MULLED CIDER

The assortment of sweet spices in this cider makes it especially flavorful.

SERVES 2

2½ cups apple cider

1 teaspoon grated lemon zest

1 cardamom pod, slightly crushed, or a pinch of ground cardamom (optional)

1 cinnamon stick, broken in half

3 whole cloves, lightly crushed

2 allspice berries, lightly crushed

1 slice of orange, halved

Ground cinnamon, for garnish

In a small saucepan, combine the first six ingredients. Bring to a boil over high heat. Reduce the heat; simmer for 10 minutes. Strain into mugs. Float half an orange slice sprinkled with cinnamon in each mug.

—LINDA MERINOFF

SPIRITED CITRUS CUP

Heated orange and lemon juice, sweetened with honey and enlivened with cognac and Triple Sec, provides a warm glow on the coldest winter nights.

SERVES 12

¼ cup honey

½ teaspoon grated orange zest

2½ cups water

2 cups orange juice

3 tablespoons lemon juice

6 whole cloves

1¼ cups cognac or other brandy

2 tablespoons orange liqueur, such as Triple Sec

1. In a medium saucepan, combine the honey, orange zest, and water. Bring to a boil, stirring occasionally, and cook until the honey dissolves completely.

2. Add the orange juice, lemon juice, and cloves. Return to a boil. Remove from the heat and stir in the cognac and orange liqueur. Serve in punch cups or mugs.

NORMAN HOT TODDY

You've always heard about hot toddies, but have you ever actually tasted one? This drink is delicious and quick. Now's your chance.

SERVES 4

1 cup milk

⅓ cup heavy cream

5 cinnamon sticks

¾ cup Calvados or other apple brandy

⅓ cup apricot brandy

Sugar

Grated nutmeg, for garnish

1. In a medium saucepan, combine the milk, cream, and one of the cinnamon sticks. Bring to a simmer over moderate heat. Reduce the heat to low and stir in the Calvados and the apricot brandy. Heat until just warmed through; don't allow to boil.

2. Meanwhile, put a large pinch of sugar into each of four mugs and pour in the hot toddy. Sprinkle with nutmeg and add a cinnamon swizzle.

Hot Rum Milk with Cardamom

Neither too strong nor too sweet, this is a comforting warm drink. Use whole cardamom pods, not the seeds, or the flavor will be too intense.

SERVES 4

- 1 quart milk
- 2 heaping tablespoons cardamom pods (about 40)
- 3 tablespoons sugar
- ½ cup dark rum

1. In a medium saucepan, combine the milk, cardamom, and sugar. Heat, stirring to dissolve the sugar, until the milk begins to foam.

2. Put 2 tablespoons of rum in each of four mugs or glasses. Strain the hot milk into the mugs.

—ANNE DISRUDE

Hot Scot

If you are serving this as an after-dinner drink, the butter adds a truly comforting effect. As a nightcap, the butter can be omitted.

SERVES 4

- 1 quart milk
- ½ cup Scotch whiskey
- ¼ cup Drambuie
- 4 teaspoons butter (optional)
- 4 dashes aromatic bitters, such as angostura

1. In a medium saucepan, heat the milk until warmed through. Do not boil.

2. Meanwhile, into each of four large mugs, put 2 tablespoons of the Scotch whiskey, 1 tablespoon of the Drambuie, 1 teaspoon of the butter, if using, and a dash of the aromatic bitters. Strain the hot milk into the mugs and stir the mixture until the butter melts.

HOT BUTTERED RUM

For this tree-decorating favorite, a "batter" of brown sugar, honey, butter, and spices is mixed up ahead of time and then spooned into the individual servings of hot rum.

SERVES 12

½ pound butter, softened

1⅓ cups brown sugar

1 teaspoon grated nutmeg

1 teaspoon cinnamon

Pinch ground cloves

1 cup honey

12 ounces rum, preferably dark, more if needed

Boiling water

1. In a large bowl, cream the butter with the brown sugar, nutmeg, cinnamon, cloves, and honey. Beat until the mixture is completely blended and somewhat fluffy.

2. Pour 1 to 1¼ ounces of rum, according to your taste, into each of twelve 8-ounce mugs. Fill each mug with boiling water to within an inch of the rim. Top with a large spoonful of the "batter" and serve.

MAKE IT AHEAD
The "batter" will keep several days if refrigerated. Allow it to return to room temperature before using.

VARIATIONS

■ In place of the boiling water, use hot brewed tea. The rum, honey, spices, and tea make a marvelous combination. It's particularly good with a strong-flavored tea such as Lapsang Souchong or Earl Grey. Add a squeeze of lemon at the end, if you like.

■ For Hot Maple Buttered Rum, use pure maple syrup in place of the honey.

ORANGE VANILLA COFFEE

The choice of orange liqueur used in this recipe will have a distinct effect on the flavor of the drink. Grand Marnier, for instance, gives a strong, rich taste, while Cointreau provides a pleasantly flowery nuance.

SERVES 4

3 cups fresh-brewed coffee

¼ cup heavy cream

4 teaspoons sugar

¼ teaspoon vanilla extract

2 tablespoons plus 2 teaspoons orange liqueur, such as Grand Marnier or Cointreau

Grated orange zest, for garnish

1. In a medium saucepan, combine the coffee, cream, sugar, and vanilla. Heat until simmering.

2. Meanwhile, pour 2 teaspoons of the orange liqueur into each of four large mugs. Pour the hot coffee mixture over the liqueur. Sprinkle with orange zest.

VARIATIONS

■ Instead of adding the cream to the coffee, increase the cream to ½ cup and whip it with 1 tablespoon sugar until it holds soft peaks. Top the hot coffee with dollops of the whipped cream and sprinkle with the orange zest.

■ For added sparkle, turn the orange zest into orange sugar. Before making the coffee, mix the orange zest with an equal quantity of sugar. Spread the mixture out on a plate and let dry for at least 20 minutes. You can keep the orange sugar for a week or two.

■ ■ ■

Christmas Cocktail Party

Salmon-Caviar Toasts, page 13

Pumpkin-Seed Puree, page 15,
with a raw vegetable platter

Mushroom Leek Turnovers, page 18

Parmesan Christmas Trees, page 23

Granny's Molasses Spice Cookies, page 165

Cider Wassail Bowl, page 295

■ ■ ■

Easy Buffet Dinner

Assorted cheeses

Toasts and breadsticks

Black and green olives

—

Baked Ham with Mustard and
Apple-Jelly Glaze, page 97

Southwest Corn Dressing, page 105

Sweet Potatoes with Cider and
Brown Sugar, page 139

Field Salad with Mushrooms
and Walnuts, page 156

Assorted rolls

—

Orange-and-Honey
Bread Pudding, page 245

Granny's Molasses Spice Cookies, page 165

■ ■ ■

Quick Cocktail Party

Confetti Shrimp, page 14

Prosciutto-Wrapped Hearts of Palm, page 17

Sausage-Stuffed Mushrooms, page 17

Pistachios

Colonel Talbott's Bourbon Punch, page 290

■ ■ ■

Holiday Buffet for a Crowd

Fennel Tart with Rosemary, page 38

Potted Shrimp, page 41

—

Roast Wild Turkey with Blue-Corn-Bread
and Chorizo Stuffing, page 64

Orange and Bourbon Glazed
Country Ham, page 99

Sweet-Potato Sham, page 138

Baked Wild Rice with Carrots
and Mushrooms, page 148

Braised Red Cabbage with
Maple-Glazed Chestnuts, page 153

Mixed Salad with Kumquats
and Pecans, page 157

Cranberry Walnut Relish, page 160

—

Bûche de Noël, page 211

Gingerbread Cookies, page 174

Warm Winter-Fruit Compote, page 274

■ ■ ■

Christmas-Caroling Party

Mushrooms with Dilled Sour Cream
on Toast, page 40

———

Crusty Baked Ham, page 96

Braised Red Cabbage with
Maple-Glazed Chestnuts, page 153

Baked sweet potatoes

Hard rolls

———

Cranberry Jelly Roll, page 216

Gilded Chocolate Shortbread, page 173

Mulled Cider, page 295

■ ■ ■

Tree-Trimming Party

Salt and Pepper Pretzels, page 22

Chicken-Liver and
Apple Crescents, page 20

Potted Shrimp, page 41

Orange and Chocolate Mousse, page 249

Fruitcake Cookies, page 168

Heavenly Puff Angels, page 179

■ ■ ■

Christmas Dinner 1

Chesapeake Scalloped Oysters, page 44

———

Traditional Roast Stuffed Turkey
with Pan Gravy, page 49

Potato Puree with Scallions, page 147

Parslied Carrots, page 151

Steamed Brussels Sprouts and
Red Grapes, page 151

Jellied Cranberry Sauce, page 160

———

Christmas Pudding, page 268

■ ■ ■

Christmas Dinner 2

Oyster and Spinach Soup, page 32

———

Roast East Hampton Golden Goose,
page 76

Baked Wild Rice with Carrots
and Mushrooms, page 148

Sweet-Potato and
Butternut-Squash Puree, page 134

Braised Red Cabbage with
Maple-Glazed Chestnuts, page 153

———

Cranberry Pie, page 185

■■■

Christmas Dinner 3

Butternut-Squash and Leek Soup, page 33

Mediterranean Animal Crackers, page 26

—

Roasted Goose with Chestnut
and Apple Stuffing, page 74

Potato Puree with Scallions, page 147

Steamed Brussels Sprouts and
Red Grapes, page 151

Jellied Cranberry Sauce, page 160

—

Maple Pecan Pie, page 194

Fruitcake Cookies, page 168

■■■

Christmas Dinner 4

Broiled Crumbed Oysters
and Shallots, page 45

—

Roast Cranberry-Glazed Ducks with
Cranberry Gravy, page 86

Fragrant Barley, page 149

Spiced Butternut Squash, page 131

Field Salad with Mushrooms
and Walnuts, page 156

—

Frosty Lime Pie, page 230

Pfeffernüsse, page 181

■■■

Christmas Dinner 5

Bacalao Gloria, page 43

—

Quick-Roasted Turkey with
Lemon Corn-Bread Stuffing, page 51

Carrot and Squash Puree, page 133

Steamed green beans

Mixed green salad

—

Christmas Bread Pudding with
Amaretto Sauce, page 267

■■■

Christmas Dinner 6

Mushroom Consommé, page 37

—

Ken Hom's Boned Stuffed Turkey, page 66

Sweet-Potato and Turnip Puree, page 141

Glazed Roasted Shallots and
Garlic, page 152

Steamed snow peas

Candied Quinces, page 161

—

Christmas Orange-and-
Currant Shortcakes, page 247

Linzer Wreaths, page 166

■ ■ ■

New Year's Eve Dinner 1

Sausage-Stuffed Mushrooms, page 17

Salmon-Caviar Toasts, page 13

———

Jerusalem-Artichoke Soup, page 36

———

Roast Beef with Pan Gravy, page 100

Individual Yorkshire Puddings, page 101

Parslied Carrots, page 151

Steamed green beans

———

Peach and Ginger Trifle, page 241

Chocolate Orange Truffles, page 284

■ ■ ■

New Year's Eve Dinner 2

Salmon-Caviar Toasts, page 13

———

Oyster and Spinach Soup, page 32

———

Roasted Goose with Chicken-Liver
Stuffing, page 71

Baked Wild Rice with Carrots and
Mushrooms, page 148

Mixed Salad with Kumquats
and Pecans, page 157

———

Frozen Praline Meringue, page 227

Chocolate-Dipped Snowballs, page 171

■ ■ ■

New Year's Eve Dinner 3

Confetti Shrimp, page 14

Pumpkin-Seed Puree, page 15,
with a raw vegetable platter

Blue-Corn Pizzelle, page 27

———

Cauliflower Oyster Stew, page 31

———

Roast Duck with
Port-Soaked Prunes, page 84

Steamed kasha

Field Salad with Mushrooms
and Walnuts, page 156

———

Fudge Pie, page 193

Spicy Nut Meringues, page 180

■ ■ ■

New Year's Eve Dinner 4

Parsnip Vichyssoise, page 35

———

Pork Loin with Wild-Mushroom
Sage Stuffing, page 91

Baked Squash with Butter and
Maple Syrup, page 132

Steamed kale

———

Fig and Hazelnut Shortcakes with
Ruby-Port Sauce, page 251

Lacy Ginger Snowflakes, page 177

■ ■ ■

New Year's Day Brunch

Fennel Tart with Rosemary, page 38

Cider-Glazed Ham with Sweet-and-Sour
Grape Sauce, page 98

Baked Squash with Butter and
Maple Syrup, page 132

Brioche and Oyster Pudding, page 145

Field Salad with Mushrooms and
Walnuts, page 156

Pineapple Crumbcake, page 222

Orange Vanilla Coffee, page 299

■ ■ ■

Holiday Tea Party

Prosciutto-Wrapped
Hearts of Palm, page 17

Romano Leaf Wafers, page 25

Double-Vanilla Pound Cake with
Walnut Butter, page 220

Dark Applesauce Fruitcakes, page 223

Cranberry Pistachio Biscotti, page 170

Lebkuchen, page 176

Heavenly Puff Angels, page 179

Mulled Wine, page 293

Tea

■ ■ ■

Dessert and Coffee Party 1

Linzer Wreaths, page 166

Gilded Chocolate Shortbread, page 173

Spicy Nut Meringues, page 180

Cranberry Orange Cream Tart, page 186

Bûche de Noël, page 211

Apple Quince Crumble with Eggnog
Custard Sauce, page 262

Wintery Fruit Salad, page 275

Hot Buttered Rum, page 298

Orange Vanilla Coffee, page 299

■ ■ ■

Dessert and Coffee Party 2

Chocolate-Dipped Snowballs, page 171

Heavenly Puff Angels, page 179

Pecan Bourbon Torte with Bourbon
Buttercream Frosting, page 204

Cranberry Fool, page 274

Glühwein, page 294

Coffee

Index

Page numbers in **boldface** indicate photographs.

Contributors

Jean Anderson is a food writer and author of numerous cookbooks, including most recently *The Nutrition Bible* (Morrow), which she co-authored with Barbara Deskins, Ph.D., and the upcoming *The Century Cookbook* (Clarckson Potter).

Lee Bailey is the author of a number of cookbooks, including *Lee Bailey's Corn*, *Lee Bailey's Onions*, and *Lee Bailey's Portable Food* (all three from Clarckson Potter).

Melanie Barnard is a columnist and a cookbook author. Her books include *Low-Fat Grilling* and, most recently, *365 More Ways to Cook Chicken* (both from HarperCollins).

Bob Chambers is the executive chef at Lâncome-L'Oréal in New York City.

Julia Child is the country's foremost television cooking teacher and the doyenne of French cooking in America. Her books include *Mastering the Art of French Cooking*, *The Way to Cook*, and *In Julia's Kitchen with Master Chefs* (all from Knopf).

Peggy Cullen is a food writer, baker, and candymaker living in New York City.

Marion Cunningham is a columnist, cooking teacher, and cookbook author. Her books include *The Fanny Farmer Cookbook* and, most recently, *Cooking with Children* (both from Knopf).

Anne Disrude is a New York City-based food stylist.

Jim Fobel is the author of eight books, most recently *Big Flavors* (Clarckson Potter), which was chosen as the Best Cookbook of the Year by the James Beard Foundation.

Camille Glenn is a columnist, food writer, and teacher. She is the author of *The Heritage of Southern Cooking* (Workman).

Joyce Goldstein, chef/owner of the former Square One in San Francisco, is now a restaurant consultant. She is the author of *Back to Square One* (Morrow), *The Mediterranean Kitchen* (Morrow), *Mediterranean the Beautiful* (Collins), and, most recently, *Kitchen Conversations* (Morrow).

Dorie Greenspan is the author of *Sweet Times*, *Waffles from Morning to Midnight*, and *Baking with Julia*, the cookbook that accompanies Julia Child's PBS series of the same name (all three books from Morrow). She is currently working on a book, tentatively titled *Delicious Liaisons* (Little, Brown and Co.), with Pierre Hermé, the pastry chef of Fauchon.

Rosalee Harris is the co-author of *Cookies* (Harmony Books).

Ken Hom is a cooking teacher and author of many books, most recently *Ken Hom's Chinese Kitchen* (Hyperion).

Michael James was a chef who started the Great Chefs program at The Mondavi Winery. He authored *Slow Food* (Little, Brown and Co.) and collaborated with Simone Beck on *New Menus from Simca's Cuisine* (Harcourt Brace).

Nancy Harmon Jenkins is a food historian and the author of *The Mediterranean Diet Cookbook* (Bantam) and two forthcoming books on traditional foods of Puglia and Tuscany (Broadway Books).

Susan Herrmann Loomis is a journalist and the author of *The Great American Seafood Cookbook*, *The Farmhouse Cookbook*, *Seafood Celebrations*, and *The French Farmhouse Cookbook* (all from Workman). She is working on *The Italian Farmhouse Cookbook* (Workman).

Sheila Lukins is the food editor of *Parade* magazine and the author of *Sheila Lukins All Around the World* and co-author of *The New Basics* and *The Silver Palate Good Times Cookbook* (all from Workman).

Deborah Madison is a cooking teacher as well as a former chef and restaurateur. She is the author of *The Greens Cookbook* and *The Savory Way* (both from Bantam) and *The Vegetarian Taste* (Chronicle Books). She is at work on another vegetarian cookbook to be released in 1997.

Nicholas Malgieri is the director of baking programs at Peter Kump's School of Culinary Arts in New York City and the author of several books, including *How to Bake* (HarperCollins).

Richard Marmet is the founder of Best Cellars, a retail business specializing in reasonably priced wines for every day.

Lydie Marshall is a cooking teacher and the owner of A la Bonne Cocotte cooking school in New York City. She is the author of *Chez Nous* and *A Passion for Potatoes* (both from HarperCollins).

Michael McLaughlin is a food writer and author of many books, most recently *The Little Book of Big Sandwiches* and *Good Mornings* (both from Chronicle).

Linda Merinoff is a food writer and author whose books include *Gingerbread* (Fireside) and *Pig-Out with Peg: Secrets from the Bundy Family Kitchen* (Avon).

Joan Nathan is a columnist and food writer. She is the author of a number of cookbooks, including *Jewish Cooking in America* (Knopf) and *The Children's Jewish Holiday Kitchen* (Schocken Books). She is currently working on a cookbook about the foods of modern Isreal.

Jacques Pépin, the famed cooking teacher, is the author of numerous cookbooks, the most recent of which are *Jacques Pépin's Simple and Healthy Cooking* (Rodale) and *Jacques Pépin's Table* (KQED Books).

Maria Piccolo is a co-owner of Sweet Seasons, a catering company in Marblehead, Massachusetts.

Stephan Pyles is chef/owner of Star Canyon in Dallas. He is the author of *The New Texas Cuisine* (Doubleday) and a forthcoming book about tamales.

Richard Sax was the author of numerous books, among them *Classic Home Desserts* (Chapters) and *Get in There and Cook* (Clarckson Potter), due out in March 1997.

Martha Stewart is the editor in chief of *Martha Stewart Living*. She is the author of numerous cookbooks and entertaining books, including *Martha Stewart's Menus for Entertaining* and *The Martha Stewart Cookbook* (both from Random House).

Grace Stuck was a great Swedish cook from Minnesota. Her granddaughter, Susan Stuck, is the food editor of *Eating Well* magazine.

Jean-Georges Vongerichten is chef/owner of JoJo and Vong, both in New York City, and the author of *Simple Cuisine* (Macmillan USA).

Patricia Wells is a journalist and the author of numerous food books, including *Patricia Wells' Trattoria* (Morrow) and the forthcoming *At Home with Patricia Wells* (Scribner).

We would also like to thank the following individuals and restaurants for their contributions:

Nancy Christy; Pearl Byrd Foster; Fraunces Tavern, New York City; Gordon, Chicago; Laure Cantor Kimpton; Silvio Pinto; The Shoalwater, Seaview, Washington; and the U.N. Plaza Park Hyatt Hotel, New York City.

Photo Credits

COVER PHOTO: **Elizabeth Watt** (Heavenly Puff Angels, page 179)
BACK PHOTOS: (*top row*) **Mark Thomas** (Salmon-Caviar Toasts, page 13, and Parsnip Vichyssoise, page 35); (*middle row*) **Jerry Simpson** (Parslied Carrots, page 151), **Mark Thomas** (Pork Loin with Wild-Mushroom Sage Stuffing, page 91); (*bottom row*) **Elizabeth Watt** (Gilded Chocolate Shortbread, page 173, and Linzer Wreaths, page 166).

Karen Capucilli: 102, 104, 112, 120; **Dennis Galante:** 42, 80, 224, 226; **Dennis Gottlieb:** 46, 48, 200; **Steven Mark Needham:** 24, 276, 278, 282; **Maria Robledo:** 246, 250, 258; **Jerry Simpson:** 28, 30, 58, 142, 150, 154, 158, 182, 184, 272; **Michael Skott:** 8, 16, 128, 136, 236; **Mark Thomas:** 6, 10, 12, 34, 68, 70, 88, 90, 130, 192, 198, 208, 218, 238, 240, 266; **Elizabeth Watt:** 162, 164, 172, 178; **Mark Weiss:** 144.